MINING SOCIAL MEDIA

MINING SOCIAL MEDIA

MEDIA

Finding Stories in Internet Data

by Lam Thuy Vo

no starch press

San Francisco

Printed in USA

First printing

23 22 21 20 19   1 2 3 4 5 6 7 8 9

ISBN-10: 1-59327-916-7
ISBN-13: 978-1-59327-916-5

Publisher: William Pollock
Production Editor: Meg Sneeringer
Cover Illustration: Gina Redman
Developmental Editors: Jan Cash and Alex Freed
Technical Reviewer: Melissa Lewis
Copyeditor: Rachel Monaghan
Compositor: Danielle Foster
Proofreader: Emelie Burnette
Indexer: Beth Nauman-Montana

For information on distribution, translations, or bulk sales, please contact No Starch Press, Inc. directly:
No Starch Press, Inc.
245 8th Street, San Francisco, CA 94103
phone: 1.415.863.9900; info@nostarch.com
www.nostarch.com

Library of Congress Cataloging-in-Publication Data:

Names: Vo, Lam Thuy, author.
Title: Mining social media : finding stories in Internet data / Lam Thuy
   Vo.
Description: San Francisco : No Starch Press, Inc., 2019. | Includes
   bibliographical references and index.
Identifiers: LCCN 2019030568 (print) | LCCN 2019030569 (ebook) | ISBN
   9781593279165 (paperback) | ISBN 9781593279172 (ebook)
Subjects: LCSH: Social sciences--Research--Methodology. | Internet
   research. | Data mining. | Social media--Research. | Quantitative
   research. | Qualitative research.
Classification: LCC H61.95 .V63 2019 (print) | LCC H61.95 (ebook) | DDC
   302.23/1072--dc23
LC record available at https://lccn.loc.gov/2019030568
LC ebook record available at https://lccn.loc.gov/2019030569

To má Lua, ba Liem, and anh Luan

About the Author

Lam Thuy Vo is a senior reporter at BuzzFeed News where her area of expertise is the intersection of technology, society, and social media data, and where she covers the spread of misinformation, hatred online, and platform-related accountability. Previously, she led teams and reported for The Wall Street Journal, Al Jazeera America, and NPR's Planet Money, telling economic stories across the US and throughout Asia. She has also worked as an educator for a decade, developing newsroom-wide training programs, workshops for journalists around the world, and semester-long courses for the Craig Newmark CUNY Graduate School of Journalism. She has also spoken at Pop-Up Magazine, the Tribeca Film Festival's Interactive Day, and TEDxNYC, among other larger events.

About the Technical Reviewer

Melissa Lewis is a data reporter for Reveal from The Center for Investigative Reporting. Prior to joining Reveal, she was a data editor at *The Oregonian*, a data engineer at Simple, a data analyst at Periscopic, and a neuroscience research assistant at Oregon Health & Science University. She is an organizer for PyLadies Portland and the Portland chapter of the Asian American Journalists Association.

BRIEF CONTENTS

CONTENTS IN DETAIL

PART II: DATA ANALYSIS   99

6
INTRODUCTION TO DATA ANALYSIS   101

7
VISUALIZING YOUR DATA   123

8
ADVANCED TOOLS FOR DATA ANALYSIS   135

9
FINDING TRENDS IN REDDIT DATA

10
MEASURING THE TWITTER ACTIVITY OF POLITICAL ACTORS

11
WHERE TO GO FROM HERE

INDEX

ACKNOWLEDGMENTS

This is perhaps not a "thank you" but an acknowledgment of the people who once were part of my timeline and in one way or another broke my heart: without the pain there would not have been Quantified Breakup, a tumblr of data visualizations about emotional resiliency as captured through one's digital footprint. It was this project that essentially propelled my work into new directions—the exploration of social media data and "quantified selfies." It was also during a talk about this project that the wonderful Jan Cash, an editor at No Starch Press at the time, approached me to write this book.

More importantly, there are those who remain in my timeline and who have been exceptionally supportive of me. Thanks to má Lua and ba Liem for making me an empathetic and curious tinkerer, to my brother Luan Vo Nguyen Quang and my sister-in-law Tiffany Talsma for their steadfast and years-long support from across all continents, to Cathy Deng and Jamica El for constant encouragement during my early Python days in the Bay Area, to Julia B. Chan, Lo Benichou, Aaron Williams, Ted Han and Andrew Tran for the camaraderie in an industry full of competitors, to John Wingenter, Adrienne Lopes, Vita Ayala, Mariru Kojima and Toyin Ojih Odutola for providing family far away from family, and to my niece Elynna Quynh Vo who's the future.

INTRODUCTION

We experience the social web in brief moments that flash by, often without ever coming back to them. Liking a photo on Instagram, sharing a post that someone published on Facebook, or messaging a friend on WhatsApp—whatever the specific interaction, we do it once and likely don't think about it after.

But from swipes to clicks to status updates, our online lives are being captured by social media companies and used to fill some of the largest data servers in the world. We are producing more data than ever before. By looking at these data points as a whole, we can gain tremendous insight into human behavior. We can also investigate the harm done by these systems, from detecting false online actors (for example, automated bot accounts or fake profiles that seed misinformation) to understanding how algorithms surface questionable content to viewers over time.

If we look at these data points collectively, we can find patterns, trends, or anomalies and, hopefully, better understand the ways in which we consume and shape the human experience online. This book aims to help those who want to go from simply observing the social web one post or tweet at a time to understanding it on a larger, more meaningful scale.

What Is Data Analysis?

The main goal for any data analyst is to gain useful insights from large quantities of information. We can think of data analysis as a way to interview a vast number of records: we may ask about unusual single events, or we may be looking into long-term trends. Interviewing a data set can be a lengthy process with various twists and turns: it might take a few different approaches to find the answers to our questions, the same way it might take a few different meetings to get a good sense of an interviewee.

Even if our questions are simple and focused, getting to the answers can still require us to make several logical and philosophical decisions. What data set may be useful to examine our own behavior, and how would we get that data? If we wanted to determine the popularity of a Facebook post, would we measure that in number of reactions (likes, hahas, wows, and so forth), the number of comments it received, or a combination of both metrics? If we wanted to better understand how people discuss a specific topic on Twitter, what would be the best way to categorize tweets about it?

So while analyzing data takes a certain amount of technical know-how, it's also a creative process that requires us to use our judgment in an intentional and informed way. In other words, data analysis is both science and art.

Who Is This Book For?

This book is written for people who have little to no previous programming experience. Given the huge role of social media, the internet, and technology in all of our lives, this book aims to explore them in an accessible and straightforward way. Through practical exercises, you'll learn the foundational concepts of programming, data analysis, and the social web.

On some level, this book is targeted to someone just like my former self—a person who was fiercely curious about the world but also intimidated by jargon-filled forums, conferences, and online tutorials. We'll take a macro and micro approach, looking at the ecosystem of the social web as well as the minutiae of writing code.

Coding is more than just a way to build a bot or an app: it's a way to satisfy your curiosity in a world that is increasingly dependent on technology.

Conventions Used in This Book

To access and understand data from social media, we need to learn where that data is stored, how to access it, and how we can make sense of it. In other words, analyzing data from the web involves multiple steps: gathering the data, researching and exploring it, and analyzing it. In the final step, we'll also draw conclusions from the data and answer our questions about the human behavior and actions that produced it in the first place.

With all that in mind, it's important to note that this book is not just a compilation of code snippets, ready to be plugged in and used. While it contains scripts that may help you gather and analyze data from the social web, it was first and foremost designed to teach the fundamental concepts and tools of the data analysis process. Think of the chapters as a step-by-step guide for aspiring researchers who are eager to investigate a specific topic or question. My hope is that you'll come out with the basics you need to start learning and exploring on your own in this field. After all, the landscape of social media is in constant flux, which means that you'll need to be flexible and continually adapt your analytical approach to understanding the data it produces.

Similarly, conventions in this book were chosen and designed to prioritize your learning rather than the elegance of the code. For instance, this code uses a lot of global variables. (Don't panic! We'll cover what variables are in the coming chapters.) While this may not be the most efficient way to code, it's one that's friendly to people who might be new to Python.

As for the tools covered, I had two main criteria. I tried to choose tools that are available for free on the web, and that have a relatively low barrier to entry, allowing beginners to get started with simple projects.

What This Book Covers

The chapters of this book are structured to follow the journey of a data sleuth. We'll begin by covering how and where to find data from the social web. After all, we need data before we can go about analyzing it! Then, in the later chapters, you'll learn about the tools necessary to process, explore, and analyze the data we've mined.

Part I: Data Mining

Chapter 1: The Programming Languages You'll Need to Know Introduces frontend languages (HTML, CSS, and JavaScript) and why they're important within the context of social media data mining. You'll also learn the basics of Python through practical exercises in the interactive shell.

Chapter 2: Where to Get Your Data   Explains what APIs are and what kind of data you can access through them, and walks you through accessing data in JSON format. This chapter also covers the process of formulating a research question for data analysis.

Chapter 3: Getting Data with Code   Shows you how to gather the data returned from the YouTube API and use Python to restructure it from JSON to a spreadsheet, specifically a *.csv* file.

Chapter 4: Scraping Your Own Facebook Data   Defines scraping and describes how to inspect HTML to structure content from web pages into data. It also covers data archives that social media companies provide to users of their own data and shows you how to extract data into *.csv* files.

Chapter 5: Scraping a Live Site   Explains the ethical considerations of scraping websites and walks you through the process of writing a scraper for a Wikipedia page.

Part II: Data Analysis

Chapter 6: Introduction to Data Analysis   Covers the various processes involved in data analyses and introduces Google Sheets by analyzing data from an automated account, or *bot*.

Chapter 7: Visualizing Your Data   Explores how visualization tools—like making charts within Google Sheets and using conditional formatting to highlight data variations—can help us better understand our data.

Chapter 8: Advanced Tools for Data Analysis   Transfers concepts you learned from analyzing data in Google Sheets into the realm of programmatic analysis. You'll see how to set up virtual environments in Python 3, navigate Jupyter Notebooks (a web application that is capable of reading and running Python code), and use the Python library pandas. You'll also explore the structure and breadth of your data sets.

Chapter 9: Finding Trends in Reddit Data   Builds on the previous chapter to show you how to modify data, filter data, and run basic aggregation using functions in pandas.

Chapter 10: Measuring the Twitter Activity of Political Actors Explains how to format data as timestamps, modify it more efficiently with lambda functions, and resample it temporally in pandas.

Chapter 11: Where to Go from Here   Lists resources for becoming a better Python coder, learning more about statistical analyses, and analyzing text using natural language processing and machine learning.

Downloading and Installing Python

To work through the exercises in this book, you'll need to set up a number of tools on your computer. I'll help you with most of these—including signing up for a Google account and installing Python libraries—in the relevant chapters. But there's one setup we need to do now, before we dive into the content of this book: getting Python installed on your machine.

While there are various ways to set up Python, one of the most straightforward is to go to *http://python.org/downloads/* and download the latest version of Python for your Windows or macOS machine. There you should be able to find various installers for 64-bit and 32-bit computers (keep reading for more on the difference between these two).

WARNING *Like all programming languages, Python has undergone quite a few changes. Python 2 is an older version of the language that will not work with the exercises in this book, so make sure you download the latest version of Python 3 from the website. There may be other numbers attached to the name of the latest Python version (for example, Python 3.7.3 represents version 7.3 of Python 3), but the important thing is that the first number after the word Python is 3.*

Installing on Windows

To find out whether your Windows machine is 64-bit or 32-bit, select **Start ▸ Control Panel ▸ System** and see whether it says 64-bit or 32-bit under System Type.

Once you've done that, download the Python installer (which ends with the file extension *.exe*) and then double-click it. On the installer display screen that opens, follow these instructions:

1. Select **Install for All Users** and click **Next**.
2. Click **Next** again to install Python to *C:\Python34*.
3. You should be prompted to "Customize Python." You won't need to do that for the exercises in this book, so click **Next** again.

Installing on macOS

To find out whether your Mac is 64-bit or 32-bit, click the Apple menu and select **About This Mac**. This should open a window with some basic information about your Mac. Next to the word *Processor*, if it says Intel Core Solo or Intel Core Duo, you have a 32-bit machine. If it says something else, like Intel Core 2 Duo or Intel Core i5, you have a 64-bit machine.

Then download the appropriate installer file (which ends in *.dmg*) for your computer. Once you've downloaded the file, double-click it to start the installation. This should pop up an installation window (sometimes it may ask you to enter the admin password for your computer). Follow these instructions to complete the installation:

1. You should see a number of screens describing the software (an introduction and a *Read Me* section). Click **Continue** to go past them and agree to the software license.
2. Select your main hard drive name (for example, **HD Macintosh**) and click **Install**.

Getting Help When You're Stuck

Learning how to code is an incremental journey, one where you'll fail continually but learn from your mistakes. A missing colon, a minor spelling mistake, a misplaced comma—these are all small things that may throw off beginners and be a source of discouragement. But don't despair! Every coder goes through this process; learning how to spot and eliminate errors is just part of programming.

As mentioned, social media's ever-changing nature means we have to continuously adapt—one day we might have to analyze text-based reactions, and another day we might be looking at thousands of images. To be a good coder, in other words, means that you have to be a *resourceful* coder, one who knows how to look for and ask for help solving any problems you encounter.

First, there are certain ways to search Google for coding solutions that may yield better results. For instance, it can be helpful to construct your searches following this formula: *coding language + verb + specific keywords.* One example might be "Python open .csv file."

NOTE *For more information about optimizing your search terms, check out the article "Googling for Code Solutions Can Be Tricky—Here's How to Get Started" by Suyeon Son, available at* https://knightlab.northwestern.edu/2014/03/13/googling-for-code-solutions-can-be-tricky-heres-how-to-get-started/.

This formula is a good starting point to find related coding examples or similar questions other people have asked, many of which might be posted on Stack Overflow, a forum where coders exchange helpful solutions. As you read through the search results, you may end up seeing more keywords and can refine your query.

Then there are error messages. One of the most frustrating things for new coders to get used to is the fact that the smallest mistakes may result in broken code and cryptic error messages. When you write a line of code that contains a mistake, Python usually displays an error instead of running your code. Here's an example of an error I'd get if I tried to add two different data types—a text and a number (we'll cover data types and mathematical operations in the first chapter!):

```
>>> "R2D" + 2
Traceback (most recent call last):
  File "<stdin>", line 1, in <module>
❶ TypeError: can only concatenate str (not "int") to str
```

With Python errors, the gist of the problem is usually at the end of the error message ❶. In this case, that's `TypeError: can only concatenate str (not "int") to str`. To find a solution to this error, you can copy this error and paste it into a search engine, as shown in Figure 1.

A lot of the results for this query are links to platforms like the aforementioned Stack Overflow. It's worth reading through the answers and trying the various solutions suggested by the forum participants. Answers with more upvotes may be most useful, and it can also be helpful to review answers for any dialogue that took place between the person posting the question and the respondents. If that doesn't yield the solution to your coding issue, consider creating an account on Stack Overflow or a similar online platform and actively reaching out to the community of developers for help.

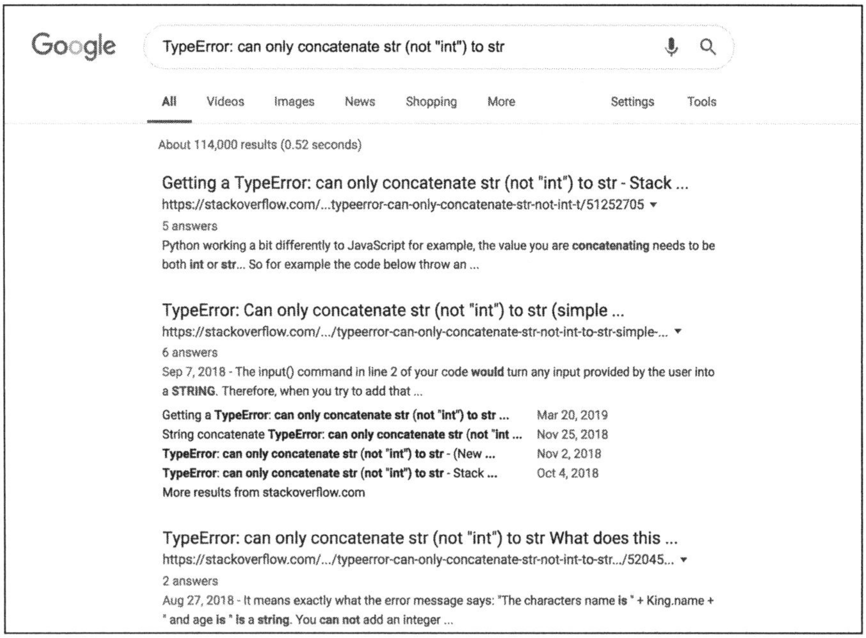

Figure 1: Google search results for the error `TypeError: can only concatenate str (not "int") to str`

The following list describes the most effective ways to get users of Stack Overflow and similar forums to help you, modeled on tips provided in another No Starch book, *Automate the Boring Stuff with Python* by Al Sweigart:

- State your objective, not just what you did. This allows developers to see whether there may be alternative methods to achieve what you're hoping to do.

- Explain what you did, what you've tried already to solve your problem, and any other information that may be relevant for developers to know to be able to help you (for instance, make sure you mention what Python version you're using and what computer you're working with).

- If you encountered errors, copy and paste the entire error message into your forum post (though be sure to protect your privacy and the privacy of others by redacting any identifying information, like your full name if it's also the name of your computer, or passwords and other login details). To embed really long snippets of code into your post in space-efficient ways, you can use helpful platforms like Paste Bin (*http://pastebin.com/*).

- Last but not least, consult Stack Overflow's handy guide for other best practices for asking questions on the forum: *https://stackoverflow.com/help/how-to-ask/*.

Asking strangers on the internet for help may seem daunting, but it can yield wonderful results if you make it a point to ask politely and with respect for people's time.

Summary

So many of our interactions and our behavior are now captured on social media platforms. While companies like Facebook or Twitter have certainly found ways to leverage this data in aggregate, I firmly believe that researchers and users themselves should be enabled and empowered to glean their own insights from some of these vast data sets. This book offers a beginner-friendly introduction to this kind of data analysis.

I've been an instructor for more than a decade and truly love seeing students and peers succeed. While the scope of this book is limited, I hope that it sparks enough curiosity in beginners to compel them to continue learning. For that purpose, feel free to explore the majority of my teaching materials on my website at *https://lamivo.com/tips.html.*

Now, without further ado, let's get started!

PART I

DATA MINING

1

THE PROGRAMMING LANGUAGES YOU'LL NEED TO KNOW

 Whether we're talking about a Facebook post, a tweet, or a Yelp review, we need to understand how online platforms are structured in order to extract information from them. To do that, we need to learn the basics of coding and web development.

This chapter gives you an overview of how the web works with respect to web languages and within the context of our data mining efforts. Understanding how databases and web pages interact will help us investigate what kind of social media data is available online and how we can harvest it.

So where should we start? For beginners, the coding landscape can certainly be a little daunting (it definitely was to me!). It's a world chock-full of acronyms, technical jargon, and multiple programming languages. Navigating all these languages can be overwhelming, so first let's zoom out and look at the role they play.

Frontend Languages

Web languages can be broadly categorized into two groups: *frontend languages* and *backend languages*. We'll begin this chapter by talking about the three frontend languages a web browser uses to read, interpret, and render the visual elements that we see in the browser window and on website tabs: HTML, CSS, and JavaScript. These languages are important for us to know because they contain the content we want to mine from social media websites.

Backend languages, which we'll cover in the second half of the chapter, communicate with servers, databases, and data streams. They come into play when we want to harvest social media data by connecting directly to the computers that store that data.

How HTML Works

Much of the social media content we want to collect lives on websites, and websites are made up of *HyperText Markup Language (HTML)*. HTML structures the text and images that make up a website's content so that a browser can *render*, or display, that content for a user to view. The HTML code itself is just a text file, but when an HTML file is opened in a browser, it tells the browser to format and display content as a web page.

Web pages consist of files that end in a *.html* extension. The home page of most websites is *index.html*, so this is the file our browser usually looks for when we visit a website. These files usually live on a *server*, which is like a hard drive on a computer that is always switched on and is accessible by other computers through the internet. A *uniform resource locator (URL)* is a bit like an address to a folder on a server.

When our browsers go to a URL, they download lines of code that they then interpret and render in a visual form. A simple website could consist of only one line of code, like the one shown in Figure 1-1.

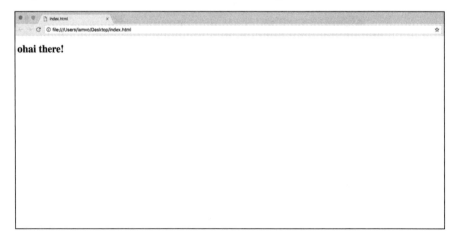

Figure 1-1: A very basic website

The code underlying that website looks like this:

```
<p> ohai there! </p>
```

In this context, the content is the sentence ohai there!. The two pieces of text surrounding the content are known as *HTML tags*.

The tags are a combination of text and angle brackets (<>) that tell a browser how each type of content should be organized. For example, the <p> and </p> tags in the code example tell the browser the sentence is a paragraph. Tags can also tell the browser whether content is a headline, an image, or another type of content. The tags and contents of the tags together are called *elements*. Each element typically starts with an *opening* or start tag, such as <p>, and ends with a *closing* or end tag, which is the same as the opening tag but with a backslash after the first bracket, such as </p>. The opening and closing tags hold content between them that will be rendered on the website. Some elements, like <img>, are called *void* elements and do not require a closing tag.

Figure 1-2 labels a basic HTML paragraph element.

Figure 1-2: An HTML paragraph element

When the element in Figure 1-2 is rendered in a browser, it will look like Figure 1-3.

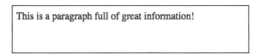

Figure 1-3: How the paragraph element from Figure 1-2 looks when opened in a browser

To summarize, HTML tags are a way to tell browsers *how* to structure content, while the information between the tags tells browsers *what* content should be rendered on the website.

HTML elements can also be *nested*, meaning a tag contains one or multiple other tags and their content. This feature is often used to cluster related elements. A header and a paragraph, for instance, may be nested inside a *div element*, which defines a division. Nesting the elements indicates that the header and paragraph inside the div element belong together. To show nesting, you usually use *indentation*—that is, add spaces or tabs in front of a line of code—which is optional but makes code more legible.

For example, we can place the paragraph element from Figure 1-1 into a <div> tag like so:

```
<div>
    <p>This is a paragraph full of great information!</p>
</div>
```

The entire paragraph element is now contained within the opening and closing <div> tags. To show that the paragraph element is nested, we've also put it on a line separate from the <div> tags and indented that line by four spaces. When rendered in a browser, the nested paragraph element should look like Figure 1-4.

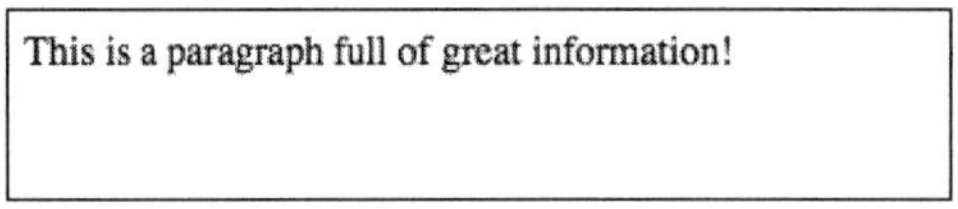

```
This is a paragraph full of great information!
```

Figure 1-4: The div and nested paragraph elements rendered in a browser

HTML ignores the indentation, and a div element is invisible when rendered. This means that the browser renders only the content inside the paragraph tags, and the element looks the same as it did in Figure 1-3.

Although you can't actually see div elements and other invisible HTML structures in the browser, they're useful because they organize a website into chunks. Think of the many parts that make up a tweet, for instance. Each tweet contains Twitter information on the person who posted it (their username, Twitter handle, and Twitter profile photo), a timestamp, the tweet text, the number of retweets for the tweet, and the number of favorites. Those parts are all clustered together in nested HTML tags. Nesting can become quite intricate, depending on how complicated a website is and how many elements are related to one another. Some nested elements may even be further nested inside other elements!

When you're mining information from a website, it helps to know how content is structured within HTML elements and where the particular information you're trying to find is located. We'll revisit how to navigate nested elements to examine the HTML structure of a tweet a little later. First, though, we need to talk about CSS, which is deeply tied to HTML.

How CSS Works

All of our examples so far have been nothing but plain text, but websites are usually made up of more than that. For example, the text of a tweet may be a different font, color, and size than the text that displays the date and time when a tweet was published. You may be wondering how a browser knows to render HTML in different colors, fonts, and sizes. This is where *Cascading Style Sheets (CSS)* comes in.

CSS is what gives HTML files their colors, features, and (some may even say) character! CSS is the language that allows us to assign different types of HTML content a specific look and feel. You can think of CSS as a set of visual guidelines that tell the browser how each HTML element needs to look on a web page.

For example, it's only through CSS that your page goes from looking like Figure 1-4 to looking like Figure 1-5.

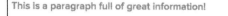

Figure 1-5: The div and paragraph elements rendered in a browser with CSS formatting

In the universe of social media data, CSS is often used to make sure that types of elements are rendered in a consistent way. On a timeline of tweets, for instance, every tweet timestamp needs to be rendered in the same font, color, and size.

There are various ways to assign CSS styles to an HTML tag. One method is through *inline CSS*, which assigns CSS in the same line where the HTML tag is created. You can see an example of this in Listing 1-1.

```
<div ❶style="❷color: #272727;">
    <p>This is a paragraph full of great information!</p>
</div>
```

Listing 1-1: Formatting an HTML <div> tag using inline CSS

In this example, an *attribute* is added to the opening tag of the div element. An attribute is additional information that is associated with each HTML tag. The attribute name goes after the opening angle bracket < and the tag name (in this case, div) and before the closing angle bracket >. The name is followed by an equal sign (=), and then by the attribute's content, which is contained between double quotes (though HTML also accepts single quotes). Attributes generally are characteristics that are *attributed* to the tag in which they are located. Attributes are passed down to nested HTML elements. In this case, the div element has a style attribute ❶ in which we add inline CSS, meaning that now any content inside that <div> tag has to follow the CSS style rule defined in the style attribute. Since the paragraph element is nested inside the div element, the paragraph element and its contents *inherit* any styles that are assigned to the div.

CSS uses *properties* to change the colors, fonts, and other formatting options we can use on a website. Properties are similar to HTML attributes, but are formatted with a colon (:) separating the property name from the property's value. For example, within the style attribute is the color property ❷, which determines the color of our font. Websites use *hexadecimal* colors (for a tutorial, see *https://www.w3schools.com/colors/*), which represent colors as a combination of six numbers and letters. In this case, #272727 represents a dark gray.

Another way you can add CSS to HTML is by writing style rules in an *internal style sheet*. The style sheet is internal because the CSS is inserted directly into the HTML code between style tags, `<style></style>`, but isn't inline with the tags it's formatting.

When you look at a website using an internal style sheet, you'll find classes and IDs within those `<style>` tags. A *class* is a style rule that is defined in the `<style>` tag and can be applied to multiple HTML elements. By using a class, you can define the style rule once and apply it to each element individually. Each HTML element can have multiple classes. An *ID* is like a class in that you define the style rules in the `<style>` tag, but an ID shouldn't be used for more than one HTML element.

Listing 1-2 shows an example of an internal style sheet that defines how to style a class and ID.

```
<style>
.my_styles❶{
    color: #272727;
    font-size: 16px;
    font-weight: 600;
    text-shadow: 2px 2px #d8d8d8;
}
#my_div❷{
    font-family: "Proxima Nova", Helvetica, sans-serif;
}
</style>

<div class="my_styles" id="my_div">❸
    <p>This is a paragraph full of great information!</p>
</div>
```

Listing 1-2: Assigning CSS styling to HTML using an internal style sheet

Each style rule is located between the `<style>` tags. The first set of style rules is inside a class, which is started with a period (.) ❶ and the name of the class. In this case, the class is my_styles (note that there are no spaces in the name). The class name is followed by two braces ({ }), which contain the style rules for the class. In this case, you can see that our CSS specifies the color, font-size, font-weight, and text-shadow for any element the my_styles class is applied to. The next rule shown in the example creates an ID, which we call my_div ❷. IDs are denoted by a hashtag followed by the ID name. The style rules for IDs are also contained between braces. The internal style sheet ends with a closing `</style>` tag.

Even though the CSS style rules are defined in this HTML, that doesn't mean they're applied to any HTML elements yet. In order to format HTML elements, you need to assign either the class or the ID to a tag.

To do this, we assign the "my_styles" class and the "my_div" ID to the `<div>` tag's class and id attributes ❸. This means that anything that is inside the div element is now styled according to both the my_styles class and my_div ID rules.

Figure 1-6 shows the look and feel that this CSS and HTML creates.

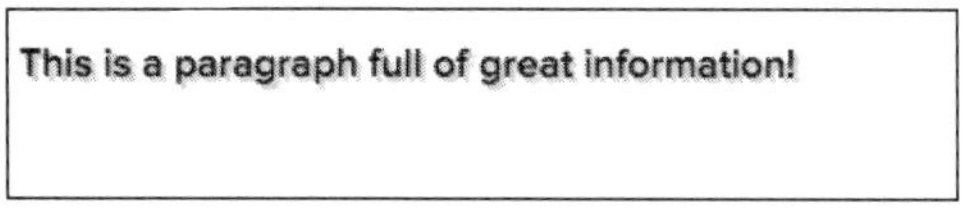

Figure 1-6: An inline CSS style sheet applied to the
nested div element from Listing 1-2

Often, developers will write hundreds (if not thousands) of lines of
CSS when designing a website. When style rules become complicated and
plentiful, developers will often put them into a separate document called
a *style sheet*, which they load inside their HTML pages through an external
link tag like the following:

```
<link rel="stylesheet" type="text/css" href="css/mystyle.css">
```

CSS style sheets are saved using the *.css* extension and stored on a server.
External style sheets are formatted in the same way as internal style sheets,
except that you don't need the HTML <style> tag since the external sheet
isn't an HTML file.

This is a lot of information about making a website look beautiful. It
may not seem relevant to our purposes now, but CSS is important because it
helps us understand how a web designer might structure repetitive elements
on a website. For example, if a designer uses a class to style all the headlines
of Facebook posts in a particular way, it'll be much easier for us to find each
HTML element that contains headlines.

Now that you've seen the basics of how a website is designed and structured, let's look at an example from Twitter that shows HTML and CSS
in action.

How Tweets Are Structured in HTML and CSS

Let's start by looking at a tweet from a Twitter timeline, shown in Figure 1-7.

Figure 1-7: An example of a tweet displayed on a Twitter timeline

Each item on the timeline represents a tweet, and each tweet has a subset of information attached to it. And, as you've probably gleaned by now, each tweet is rendered and organized using HTML and CSS.

While the browser renders neat visuals for users to see, there's a lot more at play in this website than we may initially suspect. Let's look under the hood to see what a tweet looks like as lines of code. To do this, we need to open up a nifty little browser feature called *developer tools*. These are tools that are built into some browsers, like Chrome, and are available as plug-ins for other browsers, like Firefox. We'll go through this book's examples using Chrome, a free browser you can download from *https://www.google.com/chrome/*.

Using Google Chrome, go to a Twitter timeline and click a single tweet. To access the HTML of the tweet in Chrome, select **View ▸ Developer ▸ Developer Tools** from Chrome's menu or press CTRL-SHIFT-I in Windows or COMMAND-OPTION-I on a Mac.

This should open a second view in your browser called the *Web Inspector*. The Web Inspector allows you to look at the code underlying the website, as shown in Figure 1-8.

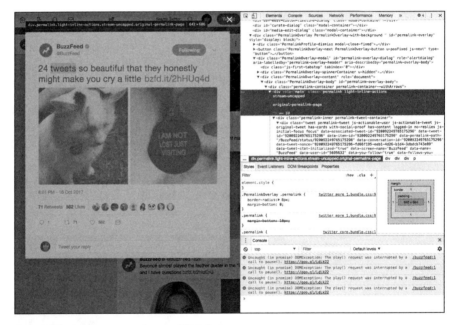

Figure 1-8: A tweet opened in the Web Inspector

Mouse over the code line by line. As you do so, Chrome should highlight the parts of the web page that correspond with the code you are mousing over. You can expand or collapse nested HTML by clicking the small triangles to the left of the HTML tags. The first few tags you mouse over will probably highlight the whole website, but for our purposes we only want to see the code that makes up a single tweet. When you do this on your own, you'll need to drill down into each nested tag until Chrome highlights only the section of the website you're looking for. For large and complex websites, this process might take a while.

For this example, we're going to skip right to what we're looking for. Click inside the Web Inspector (not on the web page!) and press CTRL-F on Windows, or COMMAND-F on Mac. A search bar should appear in the inspector window. Enter `permalink-container` into the search bar and press ENTER. You should be taken to a div class that highlights just the single tweet.

Now you can see that the tweet consists of a bunch of code nested inside a <div> tag that's been assigned the class `permalink-container`. Notice that this code is made up of tags and classes like the simple HTML examples we've covered so far. Although real website data looks complex, the information is embedded in tags just as it is in simpler HTML code.

Let's look at the tweet code more carefully. There's a lot of information, but don't worry! We'll break it down and look at it one part at a time. Listing 1-3 shows a condensed (since there can be over 600 lines of code per tweet!) version of the tweet from Figure 1-8.

```
❶<div class="permalink-container permalink-container--withArrows">
    <div role="main" class="permalink light-inline-actions  stream-uncapped
original-permalink-page">

        <div class="permalink-inner permalink-tweet-container">

            ❷<div class="tweet permalink-tweet js-actionable-user
js-actionable-tweet js-original-tweet has-cards with-social-proof
has-content logged-in no-replies js-initial-focus focus" data-associated-
tweet-id="920092249765175296" data-tweet-id="920092249765175296"
data-item-id="920092249765175296" ❸data-permalink-path="/BuzzFeed/
status/920092249765175296" data-conversation-id="920092249765175296" data-
tweet-nonce="920092249765175296-f30dd53d-6fe8-4553-9224-69186d43d82c"
data-tweet-stat-initialized="true" data-screen-name="BuzzFeed" data-
name="BuzzFeed" data-user-id="5695632" data-you-follow="true"
data-follows-you="false" data-you-block="false" data-reply-to-users-
json="[{&quot;id_str&quot;:&quot;5695632&quot;,&quot;screen_name&quot;:&quot
;BuzzFeed&quot;,&quot;name&quot;:&quot;BuzzFeed&quot;,&quot;emojified_name&
quot;:{&quot;text&quot;:&quot;BuzzFeed&quot;,&quot;emojified_text_as_html&q
uot;:&quot;BuzzFeed&quot;}}]" data-disclosure-type="" data-has-cards="true"
tabindex="0">

                <div class="content clearfix">
                    <div class="permalink-header">
                        <a class="account-group js-account-group js-action-
profile js-user-profile-link js-nav" href="/BuzzFeed" data-user-id="5695632">
                            <img class="avatar js-action-profile-avatar"
src="https://pbs.twimg.com/profile_images/687767655214891008/n9pHVYUl_bigger.
png" alt="">
                            <span class="FullNameGroup">
    ❹<strong class="fullname show-popup-with-id " data-aria-label-
part="">BuzzFeed</strong><span>&rlm;</span>
--snip--
</div>
```

Listing 1-3: The HTML making up a single tweet

Each tweet lives in a structure like this on Twitter, and by the end of this book, you'll be able to use code to automatically pull out the information you need from hundreds or thousands of these structures. The HTML in this example is complicated and confusing at first glance, but you can make sense of it by looking at it piece by piece.

For example, the ⟨div⟩ tag with the class permalink-container is the HTML tag that encases the entire tweet ❶. Nested within that tag is a ⟨div⟩ with the class tweet ❷ and some information that is related to the tweet but not displayed. Some of that information is labeled with an easy-to-understand name like data-follows-you, which tells the browser whether the owner of the tweet is following your Twitter account. Other information, like the data-permalink-path ❸, has an opaque name you'll need to figure out through some detective work. In this case, the data-permalink -path is the link that goes at the end of the tweet's *https://twitter.com/* URL. At the end of this code snippet is a ⟨strong⟩ tag, which makes text bold, that is assigned the class fullname ❹. The content of the ⟨strong⟩ tag is the Twitter account name, BuzzFeed.

While the code initially looked overwhelming, by combing through it carefully we have found important information that is connected to the tweet. The same is true of much of the data we'll mine from social media.

How JavaScript Works

HTML and CSS are directly relevant to our data gathering because they are closely related to the social media content we're interested in grabbing, but there are a few other moving parts involved in a website, such as JavaScript.

JavaScript is the programming language that brings interactivity to a website and can manipulate the elements rendered on a page. It allows us to dynamically change a website before or even after it has been rendered. In other words, with JavaScript we can change attributes or properties of HTML and CSS, or even create HTML elements on a page.

Let's see how this works by using JavaScript to change the color of the paragraph in Listing 1-4.

```
<div class="my_styles" id="my_box">
    <p>This is a paragraph full of great information!</p>
</div>
```

Listing 1-4: A paragraph nested in a div

In a browser, this code would render as Figure 1-9.

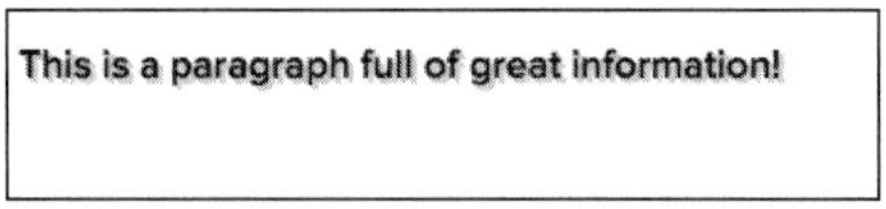

This is a paragraph full of great information!

Figure 1-9: A paragraph with some styles applied

The code in Listing 1-4 contains a <div> tag that's been assigned a class called my_styles and an ID called my_box. Using JavaScript, we can select the paragraph's HTML tag using either its class or its ID. Once we have the tag's class or ID, we can assign the tag a new class or a new style using JavaScript.

Let's add some JavaScript to the code from Listing 1-4 that selects our HTML element using the ID my_box, as in Listing 1-5.

```
❶ <div class="my_styles" id="my_box">
       <p>This is a paragraph full of great information!</p>
   </div>
❷ <script type="text/javascript">
          ❸document.getElementById("my_box").style.color = "red"
   </script>
```

Listing 1-5: Using JavaScript to select an element by ID and modify its color

JavaScript must go between <script> tags, which tell the browser that the contents of the tag are code written in a language other than HTML. The browser needs to know what language we're using, so we assign the type attribute of the <style> tag to text/javascript ❷.

While you may not know how to read JavaScript, you can often decipher quite a bit simply by reading it. Let's try walking through the JavaScript at ❸ one piece at a time. First we're looking through the document. Then we're using a part of JavaScript called getElementById(), which tells you exactly what it does—it gets an element according to its ID! In many programming languages, when code appears with parentheses, the part outside the parentheses acts on the content inside the parentheses. In this case, my_box is inside the parentheses, so we're telling getElementById() to act on my_box. This grabs the div element with the my_box ID at ❶. Then, we give the div we just grabbed a new CSS style and color. In this case we are applying the style "red".

Through this piece of JavaScript, we have now changed the color of the text that is rendered in the browser so it looks like Figure 1-10, where the darker gray represents a red text color.

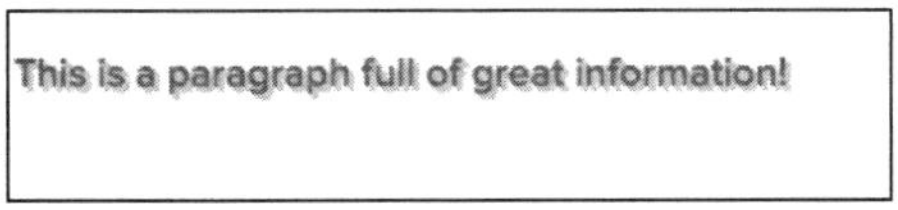

Figure 1-10: A style applied to a div using JavaScript

That is the basic way in which JavaScript works. You won't need to know how to write JavaScript for this book, but you should understand that it's a vastly important part of web pages and it's capable of changing a website's content, including the content we're looking to gather from social media websites.

Backend Languages

As you've seen, a lot of the data we're interested in is in plain sight when we inspect the code of social media websites, but there are other methods of obtaining data that are invisible to everyday users. These methods are developed for and geared toward programmers, so in order to access them, you'll need to become a programmer, too. In order to do that, you'll need to learn a backend language.

Backend languages can create, update, and communicate with databases that are stored on servers. You can think of a server as a hard drive that you access through the internet: it's a big physical drive that contains a bunch of information, including the databases full of social media data and all the HTML and CSS files that make up the websites we can view online. Backend languages also allow you to create files like a text file or a spreadsheet on your computer and write your data directly into those files.

Using Python

Throughout this book we'll use Python as our backend language to both gather and analyze data. *Python* is an open source programming language, meaning it is developed by an active community and offered to developers to use for free, even for commercial purposes. It is regularly updated and comes in several versions. We'll be using the latest version: Python 3.7.

The lessons in this book are not designed to make you an expert in Python, but rather to help you understand basic coding concepts, how the language works, how to read and comprehend existing scripts (which are text files containing code), and how to modify code for your own needs. In other words, you won't be building fancy apps and writing complicated scripts in Python after reading this book, but you'll know just enough to be "dangerous" and build scripts for your own purposes.

Whether you have Python on your machine or not, you should download and install Python 3, the latest version, through Python's official website (*https://www.python.org/downloads/*).

Getting Started with Python

In order to use Python for our purposes, we need to understand basic coding concepts, so the next few exercises are constructed to introduce you to several of these. Think of each exercise as a vocabulary or grammar lesson that will get you one step closer to writing a complete "sentence"—in this case, a functional line of Python code.

For these exercises, you'll need to enter lines of code into an *interactive shell*, which is an interface that can read and understand Python. First you'll need to open a *command line interface (CLI)*, a program on your computer that allows you to run commands. On Macs, you'll use the Terminal, which is available from the *Applications* folder. On Windows, you can use the Command Prompt, which is available through the Start menu.

Open your CLI and enter **python3** on Mac or **python** on Windows. That should open your interactive shell. You'll know your interactive shell is open if you see the *prompt*, which looks like three angle brackets (>>>), as shown in Figure 1-11.

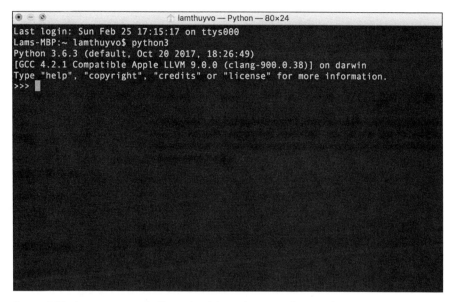

Figure 1-11: An interactive shell accessed through Terminal, Mac's built-in CLI

Now your CLI window knows how to interpret Python code. Start by entering the following simple command and hitting ENTER:

```
>>> print("hello!")
```

Congratulations! You just wrote your first line of Python. You told your interactive shell to print out the text hello!, which should now be displayed right after the command you entered, like this:

```
>>> print("hello!")
hello!
```

The command you entered, called a *print statement*, prints the quoted text you enter between the parentheses.

On top of being able to print out text, Python can also do math, so let's give that a try. Enter this equation into your interactive shell:

```
>>> 5 + 4
9
```

In Python, the mathematical equation is called an *expression*, which is a line of code that allows us to modify values using operators. Expressions are one of the most fundamental concepts in programming: they let you modify things like these numbers into something different.

In this example, we took two values—5 and 4—and modified them through a mathematical *operator*, which performs an operation on values. In this case, the plus sign (+) is the operator.

Each value has a type associated with it, referred to as a *data type*. Data types are categories of information. For example, a number could be one data type, while text would be another. Each data type is treated differently by Python, and not all operators will work with all data types, so you'll need to be able to distinguish between them.

You'll use several data types in Python, including *integers* to represent whole numbers such as 1, 2, 3, 4, 5, and so on. You'll also use *floats*, which are numbers that contain decimals like 1.2 and 3.456. When you need to use text, you'll use *strings*, characters that are "strung" together. Strings are contained between double quotes (") or single quotes ('). Strings can include alphabetical characters, numbers, spaces, and other symbols. For example, "Lam", 'Lam is a writer', and '123567' are all strings.

Working with Numbers

Python offers a number of math operators. As you've seen, there's the plus sign (+), which adds values on either side of the sign to one another, but you'll also find other math operations you've used in school.

For example, the minus sign - subtracts the value on the right side from the one on the left:

```
>>> 2 - 1
1
```

In addition to the plus and minus operators, you'll find some familiar operators that use unfamiliar symbols. For example, multiplication in math class uses the × multiplication symbol, but in Python, you'll use the asterisk (*) instead:

```
>>> 2 * 3
6
```

Similarly, division uses another unfamiliar sign, the forward slash (/), and results in a float:

```
>>> 6 / 4
1.5
```

Python has several other operators for numbers, but let's move on to modifying other data types for now.

Working with Strings

Instead of using Python to modify integers and floats, let's try to modify some strings. Go to your interactive shell and enter:

```
>>> "Hello, my name is " + "Lam"
'Hello, my name is Lam'
```

Yay! We just combined two strings into one string using the *string concatenation operator* (+). *Concatenation* is the act of combining things together.

Although the string concatenation operator uses exactly the same symbol as the addition operator for adding numbers together, they're different because they operate on different data types.

Anything that is between two double quotation marks or two single quotation marks is a string, even if it looks like another data type, like a number. For example, if we add a number between two quotation marks to another number between two quotation marks, Python will *not* perform math on them, but rather create a new string from them:

```
>>> "5" + "4"
'54'
```

The string "5" isn't the same as the integer 5, and likewise with "4", which is a string. When these two values are operated on by the plus sign, they're concatenated rather than added. Make sure you have a good grasp of the different data types, since you'll get errors if you use them improperly. For example, if you tried to use the plus sign on a string and an integer, like "5" + 4, you'd get an error, since Python wouldn't know whether you're using the addition operator or the string concatenation operator.

Note that Python accepts either single quotes or double quotes interchangeably to denote strings, but be sure you're consistent: if you start a string with a double quote, you must end it with a double quote. The same goes for single quotes. In general, it is best to pick one convention—double or single quotes—and stick with it throughout a script.

Storing Values in Variables

Now that you've seen how expressions let you modify values, we'll move on to another important concept: *variables*. Variables are a way to store values like integers, floats, or strings. Imagine a variable as a labeled box. Once you put your values inside that box, you can refer to them using the label. You can also change the values inside your box and replace them with other values. Putting a piece of data into your variable "box" is referred to as *assigning* a value to a variable.

To create a variable, give it a name. This name should be descriptive, in the same way you'd label a box full of pots and pans "kitchen utensils" instead of "stuff." You can name your variable nearly anything in Python, but the name can't have spaces and can't already be in use. For example, you can't have two variables with the same exact name, and you can't use names that could be confused with other Python code, like a plain number that could be mistaken for an integer.

Once you've settled on a name for your variable, you use the *assignment operator*, which is an equal sign (=), to store a value in it.

For instance, to assign the string "Lam" to a variable called name, you enter name, the assignment operator, and then the value you want to assign, "Lam", in your interactive shell like so:

```
>>> name = "Lam"
```

You have now told the interactive shell that the variable name stores the value "Lam". Unlike in our earlier examples, you shouldn't get any output here.

To print out the value stored within the variable name, you enter the variable name in the print() command instead of the string value:

```
>>> print(name)
Lam
```

The variable name stores "Lam", so the print() command simply outputs the string value.

We can use variables in the place of the string value in expressions, too, as in the following code:

```
>>> "My name is " + name
'My name is Lam'
```

Python takes the string "My name is " and concatenates the value stored in the name variable to it.

We can also change what we store in a variable by assigning it a different value. Let's see how this works one step at a time:

```
>>> name = "Lam"
>>> "My name is " + name
'My name is Lam'
>>> name = "Rosa"
>>> "My name is " + name
'My name is Rosa'
```

In the first line, we assign the string "Lam" to name. Then we print it out in an expression, which results in the string "My name is Lam". Next, we assign name the value "Rosa" so that Python will store the new value in our variable. If we use the same print() command we used earlier, Python will use the currently stored value and print "My name is Rosa".

What's also great is that we can store numbers in variables and perform math in them:

```
>>> initial_age = 10
>>> time_passed = 20.5
>>> initial_age + time_passed
30.5
```

First we assign the integer 10 to the initial_age variable. Then we assign the float 20.5 to the time_passed variable. In the third line, we add the value assigned to initial_age to the value assigned to time_passed by using the plus sign. Since we're adding two numerical values that are stored in the variables initial_age and time_passed, the result is 30.5.

As you can see in these examples, we can assign different kinds of data types to a variable—a variable can hold strings, floats, and integers. Variables play a big role in gathering data points or values from the social web. For example, we can gather each data point from a website, temporarily store it in the appropriate variable, and then write each data point into a spreadsheet.

Storing Multiple Values in Lists

In addition to storing one value, a variable can also hold multiple values in the form of a *list*. A list is a Python data type that can hold multiple other data types. To create a list in Python, you enter the values you want to store in the list, separated by commas (,) and in between two brackets ([ ]). Try making a list in the interactive shell as shown here:

```
>>> ["Lam", "Rosa"]
['Lam', 'Rosa']
```

You can also store a list in a variable by assigning the variable a list value just as you would assign it a string value. In the interactive shell, create a list as follows:

```
>>> names = ["Lam", "Rosa"]
```

To print the list, use the print() command:

```
>>> print(names)
['Lam', 'Rosa']
```

Lists can also be a great way to handle different data types, like a mix of integers and strings:

```
>>> numbers = [0, 2.6, 7]
>>> tweet_statistics = [536, 301, "New York"]
```

As you can see, the first variable numbers stores a list of integers and floats (0, 2.6, and 7), while the second variable tweet_statistics stores a list of integers (536 and 301) and a string ("New York").

Lists of different data types can be very useful when we're harvesting different kinds of data from the social web. For example, we may want to store Twitter handles of people who have favorited a tweet as a list. We could also store statistics related to a tweet in a list. The list of values stored in the variable tweet_statistics, for instance, could represent the number of favorites (536), the number of retweets (301), and the location ("New York") associated with a tweet.

Whichever type of data we're looking at, lists are likely one way we'll use to store it. Being familiar with lists can help us tremendously when we start gathering data.

Working with Functions

In the previous exercises, we learned that Python has transformative powers. Through expressions we can access and modify data. That, in itself, is hugely powerful, but what's even more powerful is Python's ability to repeat actions more quickly than a human ever could.

Imagine trying to count the number of posts that a Facebook page has published. It's one thing to manually count every post for a single page, but imagine having to count the total number of posts published by 10, 100, or maybe even 1,000 Facebook pages—that could take you hours, days, or even weeks! If you were to write a Python script once that counts the posts of a page, you could reuse that same script to count the posts of any number of pages and, better yet, Python would be able to count the posts nearly instantaneously compared to what you could do manually.

To take advantage of this ability, we need *functions*. Functions are like a set of instructions that can be executed over and over again, like a recipe.

For example, imagine making an apple pie. You might not need directions to make an apple pie if you were making just one by yourself, but if you had to make a dozen apple pies and needed help from other people, you'd probably want to write the instructions down. That way, no matter how many helpers you have, they could follow the instructions and you wouldn't have to explain the recipe to each person individually.

Functions are like the set of directions you've written down. Once you have that set of instructions, you can execute the function however many times you want and you can have other programs follow the directions, too.

To execute a function, you write out the name of the function followed by opening and closing parentheses. Within the parentheses, you specify which value or variable should be modified by the function. The data you put inside the function's parentheses is referred to as an *argument*. For example, the print() command we've been using is a function whose name is print, which takes strings as arguments between its parentheses.

We'll start by discussing Python's built-in functions. When we install Python on our computer, there's a set of functions that have been developed and baked into Python by the many people who create and maintain it. Those are functions we can use right away, like the print() command.

Another one of these built-in functions is len(), which measures the length of a value. For example, we can use len() to measure the length of a string like this:

```
>>> len("apple pie")
9
```

This code counts the number of characters, including spaces, in the string. When we execute the function, which is also referred to as *calling* the function, it returns the integer 9, meaning there are nine characters in the string.

We can measure the length of a list of values, too. Let's make a list called apples and use the len() function to count how many items are in the list:

```
>>> apples = ["honeycrisp", "royal gala"]
>>> len(apples)
2
```

In this case we have two items in our list that are both strings: "honeycrisp" and "royal gala". When we call the len() function on apples, then, it returns the integer 2.

Built-in functions cover a lot of the basic tasks in Python. For a longer list of built-in functions, the Python community has put together a useful page at *https://docs.python.org/3/library/functions.html*.

Creating Your Own Functions

To create our own function, which is referred to as *declaring* a function, we enter the following in our interactive shell:

```
>>> def write_sentence(word):
        new_sentence = word + " is my favorite kind of apple."
        print(new_sentence)
```

To define our function, we use the keyword def, which signals to Python that we're about to write a function. Then we define a name for the function—in this case, write_sentence—and add parentheses directly after it. If we want the function to modify an argument, we enter an argument name inside the parentheses. We'll use the argument name to refer back to the object we want to modify within our function.

The colon (:) signifies that everything in the following indented lines is part of the function. In web languages like HTML, indentation is optional, but in Python, indentation is meaningful and required. Indentation, which we implement by using either the TAB key or four spaces at the beginning of a line, tells Python which parts of the code are grouped together.

Python will associate everything that is indented with the function's instructions until it encounters a line of code that is unindented. Once Python encounters an unindented line, it knows it's reached the end of the function and moves on to the next part of the code.

Within the indented code, we define a variable named new_sentence and then put together a new string using the plus sign and the string " is my favorite kind of apple.". We store the result of this expression in the variable new_sentence, then print new_sentence.

Defining a function isn't the same as calling a function. Remember a function is like a recipe, so defining a function is like writing the recipe down. But without executing the steps of your recipe with actual ingredients, we won't have a meal to enjoy! So, last but not least, we need to call our new function by passing it an argument to modify.

Let's pass our write_sentence() function the "honeycrisp" string as an argument:

```
>>> write_sentence("honeycrisp")
honeycrisp is my favorite kind of apple.
```

The power of functions is that we can execute the function not just for one string, but for any other string. Next we run the function two times, each time using a different string as the argument of our function:

```
>>> writesentence("royal gala")
royal gala is my favorite kind of apple.
>>> writesentence("granny smith")
granny smith is my favorite kind of apple.
```

As this example shows, we can make a new sentence over and over again using our function with different strings.

We have now discovered the power of functions—a set of instructions that can be reused multiple times. However, even though you can now create a function to execute on demand, calling the function in every instance you want to use it can still be a chore, especially if you need to use it hundreds or thousands of times. Next you'll learn about another concept that will allow you to automatically run code multiple times: loops.

Using Loops

Loops allow us to perform actions multiple times. For our purposes, we'll use loops to go through a list and perform an action for each item. To do this, we'll use a for loop.

To illustrate the power of loops, let's revisit our apple pie recipe. Imagine we have four apples and we need to peel every single one. If we had a robot that could help us with our chores (the future is nigh!), we could write a for loop that instructs the robot to go through our bucket of apples and peel each one. We might give our robot helper an instruction like this: *for each apple in our bucket of apples, peel the apple!*

In actual robot language (Python), we have to follow a formula to create a for loop. The construction looks more like this:

```
for apple in list_of_apples:
    This is where we would specify what our robot would do
```

Let's run through a working Python example to see how this formula works. First, we need to define the list we want to loop, or *iterate*, through. Then, we need to *declare* a for loop by telling Python what list to loop through:

```
>>> apples = ["honeycrisp", "royal gala"]
>>> for apple in apples:
        new_string = "I'm peeling the " + apple
        print(new_string)
```

```
I'm peeling the honeycrisp
I'm peeling the royal gala
```

As we did earlier, we first define our list of apples—in this case, two strings. Then comes our for loop. To iterate through each item in the list, we need to temporarily store the item in a variable. We do this by storing each item in our apples list inside the variable apple one at a time. We'll see how this works soon.

Similar to a function, a for loop is often followed by a set of instructions. It will execute these instructions for every item in our list. Like functions, for loops also use a colon to tell Python when the instructions start, and indentation to tell Python which code belongs to the loop.

In the loop, we concatenate the variable apple to another string and store the resulting string in a variable called new_string. Then, we instruct our code to print the new string we just created.

The for loop executes the same instructions for each item in the list one at a time, so the interactive shell prints out two new strings. First, the for loop assigns the apple variable to the first item in the apples list, so apple is the string "honeycrisp". Then, the for loop executes the code inside of it, which prints the first string, "I'm peeling the honeycrisp". This is one iteration of the for loop. Once the for loop has finished its first iteration, it checks if there are more items in the apples list and, if there are, it assigns apple to the next item. In this case, that's the string "royal gala". Then, the for loop runs the code inside it again, which prints "I'm peeling the royal gala". This is the second iteration of the loop. The for loop will continue down the list of items and run the code for each item until it runs out. Since apples contains only two items, the for loop finishes looping after two iterations.

We'll see loops often when collecting data on the web. As we programmatically harvest data points online, we'll put data like headlines or time-stamps into a list and run functions on each one by iterating through them with lists. For example, the timestamps for any given tweet might be stored as long strings like 2019-01-22 06:58:44, so we may want to write a function to separate the date from the time when it was published. Using a loop allows us to operate that function on every single date instead of having to do the work manually for every timestamp.

Using Conditionals

Last but not least, let's talk about logic. Loops can help us automatically go through a large amount of data and perform actions on each one, but every item is treated the same. What should our script do when we encounter an item that should *not* be treated the same? This is where conditionals come in.

Conditionals tell Python to run code based on whether a condition has been met. One of the most often used conditionals are if clauses, which tell Python that if a condition is true, it should do one thing. If this condition is *not* met, an else clause tells Python to run some other code. While if clauses can be used by themselves, an else clause must always be paired with an if clause.

We usually use conditionals with *logical operators*—symbols that allow us to determine whether a condition is true or false. For example, in math class you've probably used the greater than sign (>) to make statements. For example, the statement 5 > 9 means "five is greater than nine." Since five isn't actually larger than nine, the statement is false. Logical operators in Python work in a similar way, except that some of the operator's symbols are different. For example, when you test for equality in math, you use a single equal sign (=), but because Python uses single equal signs for assignment statements, the operator to check whether two values are equal in Python is instead two equal signs (==).

Table 1-1 contains a list of operators that you can use with conditional statements.

Table 1-1: Logical Operators

Operator	What it does	Example
==	If the values to the left and right of the operator are equal, then the condition is true.	("pie" == "cake") is not true.
!=	If the values to the left and right of the operator are not equal, then the condition is true.	("pie" != "cake") is true.
>	If the value to the left of the operator is greater than the value to the right, then the condition is true.	(4 > 10) is not true.
<	If the value to the left of the operator is less than the value to the right, then the condition is true.	(4 < 10) is true.
>=	If the value to the left of the operator is greater than or equal to the value to the right, then the condition is true.	(4 >= 10) is not true.
<=	If the value to the left of the operator is less than or equal to the value to the right, then the condition is true.	(4 <= 10) is true.

Now that you know the basics of how if clauses and conditional statements work, let's look at an example. We'll tell Python to give us some pie if a food variable contains "pie" or to print something else when food isn't equal to "pie". First, assign the string "pie" to the variable food. Then enter the if operator followed by a condition. In this case, the condition is food == "pie", meaning the condition is that the variable food has the value "pie", followed by a colon :. An if clause uses indentation to signify scope, just like functions and loops do. Use the TAB key to indent the line that follows your if clause. Any indented code following the colon is now considered part of what Python will execute if the condition food == "pie" is met. In this case, if food == "pie" then Python will print the string "Give me some pie!". Then, using the operator else and a colon, we tell Python what it should do if the condition food == "pie" is *not* met. Again, use the TAB key to write out these instructions, so Python understands that the indented code contains instructions it should execute if the initial condition is not met. In this case, we want Python to print the string "I'm not hungry".

```
>>> food = "pie"
>>> if food == "pie" :
        print("Give me some pie!")
    else:
        print("I'm not hungry")

Give me some pie!
```

When we run this code in our interactive shell, it should print the string "Give me some pie!" because our condition (if food == "pie") is met.

The data we'll harvest on social media can be irregular, which might cause errors if our code isn't written to handle idiosyncrasies. An if clause is a great way for us to build "worst-case scenarios" into our data-gathering scripts to handle these situations. Let's say we wanted to use Python to gather the description for a list of 100 different Facebook groups. Since it's not mandatory for administrators to write up a description for their groups, some groups may have descriptions and others may not. If you use a for loop to go through the entire list of groups, Python will look for a description for every group, even those that may not have one. This may confuse the Python script. In those cases, it can be useful to write to use conditionals to instruct Python: if the group has a description, Python should gather that information, else it should record a generic string like "This group does not have a description" in lieu of a description.

Summary

This book covers a lot of ground. While you won't be able to become an expert in every web language—frontend or backend—this chapter hopefully has helped you understand the basic ways in which web languages function. In many ways, learning a programming language is akin to learning a spoken language: first we have to learn some of the most common words and grammar, and then we can expand our vocabulary and become more fluent. Think of the function names and HTML tags you just learned about as the vocabulary of the coding languages, and the concepts like conditionals, loops, and if clauses as the grammar. These fundamentals will help you read the scripts we write in the coming chapters, and as we move from example to example, you'll be able to build on this foundation to become a more fluent coder.

In the next chapter, we'll explore application programming interfaces (APIs) as a data source, and you'll use your newfound Python knowledge to request and access data from the YouTube API.

2

WHERE TO GET YOUR DATA

When we use social media, our actions leave a trace. A like on Facebook, a retweet on Twitter, a heart on Instagram—each of these actions represents a data point that is recorded on the internet somewhere. By agreeing to these companies' terms of services, we allow them to store this data, which they in turn may make available to the public.

Companies allow third parties to tap into these data troves via an *application programming interface (API)*. An API is like a middleman between the social media platform and the developers who wish to access information from it.

In this chapter, I'll explain in more detail what APIs are and what kind of data you can harvest through them, using YouTube as a practical example.

What Is an API?

On the most basic level, an API is an interface that allows programmers to access other developers' code. Some programmers use APIs to access data on an online platform so they can make their own apps. For example, a third-party developer might use the official Instagram app's API to allow users to post images to their Instagram feed outside of the app. In other words, the Instagram API allows the developer to connect their own code to a user whose account is managed by Instagram.

As we'll discuss shortly, an API also enables developers to make requests for data using a *script*, a program that communicates with servers and databases on the web.

To better understand how an API works, let's consider an analogy. Imagine you're a customer in a restaurant. An API is like the waiter, who gives you a set of options, takes your order, fetches your meal, and brings it to you. The restaurant owner determines what is available on the menu. She also controls how the dish is presented and portioned. The menu details what you can order, the name for each dish, and how it's generally prepared.

In our context, the social media company represents the restaurant owner, developers (or *clients*) represent the customers, and the dishes on the menu represent the data we're trying to gather. A client is any technology that we use to surf the web, like a browser or another application on a phone or desktop.

Whether or not a company like Facebook or Twitter offers an API is entirely up to it: it can make data available through one or multiple APIs, or it may opt to not give out any data at all. And even if the company does allow third parties to access its data stores, it often limits the available data and can change what data it shares at any point. Public outrage over privacy concerns, new laws and regulations aimed at protecting people's data, and news events involving social media companies all play into the decisions companies make about their data offerings. Some companies may even charge for access to their data.

To find out what kind of information each company offers developers through its APIs, you usually have to read through its *documentation*, which is a fancy word for an instruction manual. Unfortunately, documentation isn't standardized and can make even some of the most experienced researchers feel disoriented, especially if they are beginning coders. This is in part because the text is often aimed at application developers rather than researchers, marketers, or other nondevelopers.

The best way to find out what information a company makes available is by simply searching the company's API on Google.

Using an API to Get Data

Now that you have a rough idea of how an API works, we'll look into how to use one to access data.

As mentioned earlier, third parties request data from APIs using a script. These scripts are often text files that are executed or run by a machine like your computer. Think of a script like a little robot that performs tasks for you. The robot can communicate with an API, request data from it, read the data it receives, and create a spreadsheet from the data.

Scripts often communicate with APIs through URLs like the ones you use to access websites. Using a URL to communicate with an API is known as a *URL-based API call* (which I'll shorten to *API call*). As with most other URLs, you can paste an API call into any browser, and the browser will return the text-based data that you requested. When you use a script to make an API call, your script receives the information that would have been shown in your browser.

Let's look at Google's YouTube API as an example. You can use this API to access a plethora of data, including the description of a YouTube channel or number of views it has received over time. You tell the API what data you want by including it in the URL. For this exercise, we'll request a data feed of posts published by the BuzzFeed Tasty YouTube page. To do so, we'll use this API call: *https://www.googleapis.com/youtube/v3/search?channelId=UCJFp8u SYCjXOMnkUyb3CQ3Q&part=snippet*.

Each part of the URL serves a different purpose. Two types of strings make up an API call: a *base*, which indicates the API you're using, and various *parameters*, which tell the call what data you want to harvest and convey information about you (that is, the party requesting the information). In our earlier analogy, the base represents the restaurant where we're dining, and the parameters are the individual menu items we can pick.

NOTE *The structure of the API call is dependent on the individual API. To find out how to structure your calls to retrieve the information you need, you should consult the API's documentation. You'll see how to do that in more detail in "Refining the Data That Your API Returns" on page 41.*

In this example, the API base is *https://www.googleapis.com/youtube/*. It directs the browser or the Python script to Google's YouTube API. The next part of the call is a parameter that tells Google what version of the API we want to use. Social media websites update from time to time, and when they do, they also need to update their APIs. The version is separated from the base by a forward slash. In this example, we want to use version *v3* of the API. (Since these versions update frequently, you should consult the documentation to make sure you're using the latest version.) The next parameter is *search*, which specifies that we'll be searching for YouTube videos.

Then, we specify what we're searching for. In this case, we're looking for videos from the BuzzFeed Tasty channel, which has the YouTube channel ID *UCJFp8uSYCjXOMnkUyb3CQ3Q*. You can often find a channel ID at the end of the URL for a YouTube channel. The Tasty channel URL, for instance, is *https://www.youtube.com/channel/UCJFp8uSYCjXOMnkUyb3CQ3Q*. To use the channel ID parameter, we type out the name of the parameter, *channelId*, followed by an equal sign (=) and the long channel ID. The entire parameter looks like this (note that there are no spaces): *channelId=UCJFp8uSYCjX OMnkUyb3CQ3Q.*

Next we need to specify what *kind* of data we want to access through the API. To add another parameter, we insert an ampersand (&) followed by the parameter *part*, which indicates that we're about to specify which part of the YouTube video data we want to retrieve. In this case that's *snippet*, which refers to information about channels and videos (such as a video's description or a channel's title) that Google's YouTube API provides.

Now that we have a URL, we're ready to make our first call to the API! In the next chapter we'll make this call through a Python script, but for now, just paste the API call into a browser. This allows you to see the API response instantaneously. Once you do that, your browser should return the message in Listing 2-1.

```
{
 "error": {
  "errors": [
   {
    "domain": "usageLimits",
    "reason": "dailyLimitExceededUnreg",
    "message": "Daily Limit for Unauthenticated Use Exceeded. Continued use
requires signup.",
    "extendedHelp": "https://code.google.com/apis/console"
   }
  ],
  "code": 403,
  "message": "Daily Limit for Unauthenticated Use Exceeded. Continued use
requires signup."
 }
}
```

Listing 2-1: The code that the API call returns in the browser. Your response may look slightly different.

Listing 2-1 is your first API response! The response is structured in *JavaScript Object Notation (JSON)*, a format that APIs use to deliver data. We'll discuss JSON in more detail in the coming pages.

If you take a closer look at the response, you'll see the word error, indicating that something went wrong and the API couldn't fetch the requested posts from the BuzzFeed Tasty channel.

Working with code often involves reading and understanding error messages. As a beginner, you might feel like you're spending the vast majority of your time testing and fixing code. You'll often make mistakes before finding the right approach, but the more experience you gain, the easier it will be to fix those mistakes.

In most cases, error messages will give you clues about what went wrong. If you inspect the API error response more closely, you can see that it sent a "message" and an error notification: "Daily Limit for Unauthenticated Use Exceeded. Continued use requires signup."

To fix this error, we need an *API key*, which is a method of identifying yourself to an API. YouTube and other websites with APIs want to know who's using their API, so they sometimes require you to sign up for developer *credentials*, a form of identification that developers use to gain API access. Credentials are similar to a username and password. In exchange for access to their APIs, social media companies keep track of users in case someone abuses the API.

Getting a YouTube API Key

For social media networks like YouTube, you'll usually get credentials on the platform's website. Let's try getting credentials from YouTube now. To sign up for Google's YouTube developer credentials, you'll first need to have a Google account. If you don't have one already, create one at *https://www.google.com*. Once you've done that, sign in and navigate to a separate page that Google has set up for developers: *https://console.developers.google.com/apis/credentials*.

Follow the instructions from Google to create credentials and, in particular, an API key.

NOTE *For some APIs, you may encounter the term* app *or* application, *which refers to a software or phone app. This is because many developers signing up for credentials will use the API to create third-party apps. In our case, we're using the API to gather data, but we still need to sign up the same way as an app developer.*

This should create a generic API key for you. The default name for your key is "API key," but you can rename it by double-clicking the key name. I named mine *data gathering credentials*.

Once you have the key, navigate to the Library page. Google offers a variety of APIs, so you'll need to enable access to the specific API you want. To do this, navigate to **YouTube Data API v3** and click **Enable**. Now you're ready to access YouTube through your API key!

The key is connected to your Google account and acts much like a username and password that will allow you to access the Google API. Thus, you should treat this information with the same care and caution you would treat any other username and password. In the past, developers who write and publish scripts to code-sharing platforms like GitHub have accidentally published their credentials online. If you make the same mistake, it can have serious consequences. For instance, someone may abuse your credentials, and that may bar you from accessing services in the future.

Retrieving JSON Objects Using Your Credentials

Now that you have user credentials, let's access the API again using a URL. Though every API is different, APIs commonly have you enter your API credentials directly into your API call. If you find that isn't the case for any APIs you use in the future, check the documentation to see where you should enter your credentials. For Google's YouTube API, you add your API key into the URL as its own parameter after the parameters you specified for your original API call. Enter the following URL, replacing *<YOUTUBE _API_KEY>* with your API key: *https://www.googleapis.com/youtube/v3/search ?channelId=UCJFp8uSYCjXOMnkUyb3CQ3Q&part=snippet&key=<YOUTUBE _API_KEY>*.

Now you should receive an API response that contains data! Listing 2-2 is a sample of the data that the API call returned in my browser. Since the BuzzFeed page is constantly changing, your data will probably look slightly different, but it should be structured in the same way.

```
{
 "kind": "youtube#searchListResponse",
 "etag": "\"XI7nbFXulYBIpLOayR_gDh3eu1k/WDIU6XWo6uKQ6aM2v7pYkRa4xxs\"",
 "nextPageToken": "CAUQAA",
 "regionCode": "US",
 "pageInfo": {
  "totalResults": 2498,
  "resultsPerPage": 5
 },
 "items": [
  {
   "kind": "youtube#searchResult",
   "etag": "\"XI7nbFXulYBIpLOayR_gDh3eu1k/wiczu7uNikHDvDfTYeIGvLJQbBg\"",
   "id": {
    "kind": "youtube#video",
    "videoId": "P-Kq9edwyDs"
   },
   "snippet": {
    "publishedAt": "2016-12-10T17:00:01.000Z",
    "channelId": "UCJFp8uSYCjXOMnkUyb3CQ3Q",
    "title": "Chocolate Crepe Cake",
    "description": "Customize & buy the Tasty Cookbook here: http://bzfd.
it/2fpfeu5 Here is what you'll need! MILLE CREPE CAKE Servings: 8 INGREDIENTS
Crepes 6 ...",
    "thumbnails": {
     "default": {
      "url": "https://i.ytimg.com/vi/P-Kq9edwyDs/default.jpg",
      "width": 120,
      "height": 90
     },
     "medium": {
      "url": "https://i.ytimg.com/vi/P-Kq9edwyDs/mqdefault.jpg",
      "width": 320,
      "height": 180
     },
     "high": {
      "url": "https://i.ytimg.com/vi/P-Kq9edwyDs/hqdefault.jpg",
      "width": 480,
      "height": 360
```

```
    }
   },
   "channelTitle": "Tasty",
   "liveBroadcastContent": "none"
  }
 },
 {
  "kind": "youtube#searchResult",
  "etag": "\"XI7nbFXulYBIpLOayR_gDh3eu1k/Fe41OtBUjCV35t68y-E21BCpmsw\"",
  "id": {
   "kind": "youtube#video",
   "videoId": "_eOA-zawYEA"
  },
  "snippet": {
   "publishedAt": "2016-02-25T22:23:40.000Z",
   "channelId": "UCJFp8uSYCjXOMnkUyb3CQ3Q",
   "title": "Chicken Pot Pie (As Made By Wolfgang Puck)",
   "description": "Read more! - http://bzfd.it/1XPgzLN Recipe! 2 pounds
cooked boneless, skinless chicken, shredded Salt Freshly ground black pepper 4
tablespoons vegetable ...",
   "thumbnails": {
    "default": {
     "url": "https://i.ytimg.com/vi/_eOA-zawYEA/default.jpg",
     "width": 120,
     "height": 90
    },
    "medium": {
     "url": "https://i.ytimg.com/vi/_eOA-zawYEA/mqdefault.jpg",
     "width": 320,
     "height": 180
    },
    "high": {
     "url": "https://i.ytimg.com/vi/_eOA-zawYEA/hqdefault.jpg",
     "width": 480,
     "height": 360
    }
   },
   "channelTitle": "Tasty",
   "liveBroadcastContent": "none"
  }
 },

--snip--
```

Listing 2-2: Sample data returned by the YouTube API

You'll notice that the API response is still JSON. It might look over-whelming at first, but if we convert the JSON data into a more familiar form—a spreadsheet—it looks like Figure 2-1. If you read through some of the strings in the API response, you can see that the data is a snap-shot of five videos from the BuzzFeed Tasty YouTube channel.

	A	B	C	D	E	F	G	H
1	kind	etag	id__kind	id__videoId	snippet__publishedAt	snippet__channelId	snippet__title	snippet__description
2	youtube#search Result	"Xl7nbFXuIYBIp L0ayR_gDh3eu 1k/wiczu7uNikH DvDfTYeIGvLJ QbBg"	youtube#video	P-Kq9edwyDs	2016-12-10T17:00:01.0 00Z	UCJFp8uSYCjXOM nkUyb3CQ3Q	Chocolate Crepe Cake	Customize & buy the Tasty Cookbook here: http://bzfd.it/2fpfeu5 Here is what you'll need! MILLE CREPE CAKE Servings: 8 INGREDIENTS Crepes 6 ...
3	youtube#search Result	"Xl7nbFXuIYBIp L0ayR_gDh3eu 1k/Fe41OtBUjC V35t68y-E21BC pmsw"	youtube#video	eOA-zawYEA	2016-02-25T22:23:40.0 00Z	UCJFp8uSYCjXOM nkUyb3CQ3Q	Chicken Pot Pie (As Made By Wolfgang Puck)	Read more! - http://bzfd.it/1XPgzLN Recipe! 2 pounds cooked boneless, skinless chicken, shredded Salt Freshly ground black pepper 4 tablespoons vegetable ...

Figure 2-1: The JSON data as a spreadsheet (image shows only part of the spreadsheet)

Data formatted in JSON can look very confusing and complex at first, so let's break each part down to get a better sense of our data's structure. JSON data is always stored between two braces ({}). Each post is stored as a *JSON object*, and the data points that are part of each object are stored as *key-value pairs*. For example, the first post contains the following data point:

```
"publishedAt"❶: "2016-12-10T17:00:01.000Z"❷
```

The string before the colon is referred to as a *key* ❶, and the string after the colon is a *value* ❷ associated with that key. The key is the category of our data—you can think of it like the header of a spreadsheet column. The value represents the actual data, like a string, an integer, or a float. To understand how each data point is formatted, you'll need to look it up in the API documentation. In this example, the key is called `"publishedAt"`, which, according to YouTube's documentation, describes the time and date a post or comment was created. The value in our example, `"2016-12-10T17:00:01.000Z"`, is a timestamp. This timestamp is formatted in UTC, a standardized way of storing date and time information in one string.

How an API serves data is determined by the social media platform offering the data. That also means that Google determines the keys for our data. For instance, Google decided to call the date and time when a post was published `publishedAt` instead of `date` or `published_on`. Those idiosyncrasies are specific to Google and its API.

Next, let's look at one whole JSON object in our data set (Listing 2-3).

```
{❶
        "publishedAt": "2016-12-10T17:00:01.000Z",❷
        "channelId": "UCJFp8uSYCjXOMnkUyb3CQ3Q",
        "title": "Chocolate Crepe Cake",
        "description": "Customize & buy the Tasty Cookbook here: http://bzfd.
it/2fpfeu5 Here is what you'll need! MILLE CREPE CAKE Servings: 8 INGREDIENTS
Crepes 6 ...",
--snip--
},❸
```

Listing 2-3: A snippet with information about a YouTube video titled Chocolate Crepe Cake

As you can see, information for each YouTube video is stored between a set of braces ❶, and each JSON object is separated by a comma ❸. Within these braces are four keys ("publishedAt", "channelId", "title", "description") and their associated values ("2016-12-10T17:00:01.000Z", "UCJFp8uSYCjXOMnk Uyb3CQ3Q", " Chocolate Crepe Cake", "Customize & buy the Tasty Cookbook here: http://bzfd.it/2fpfeu5 Here is what you'll need! MILLE CREPE CAKE Servings: 8 INGREDIENTS Crepes 6 ...", respectively), which are displayed in pairs as they were in the previous example. Each key-value pair is also separated from the other pairs by a comma ❷.

Let's zoom out even more and look at the original code snippet from Listing 2-2 again (see Listing 2-4).

```
{
 "kind": "youtube#searchListResponse",
 "etag": "\"XI7nbFXulYBIpLOayR_gDh3eu1k/WDIU6XWo6uKQ6aM2v7pYkRa4xxs\"",
 "nextPageToken": "CAUQAA",
 "regionCode": "US",
 "pageInfo": {
  "totalResults": 2498,
  "resultsPerPage": 5
 },
 "items": [
  {
   "kind": "youtube#searchResult",
   "etag": "\"XI7nbFXulYBIpLOayR_gDh3eu1k/wiczu7uNikHDvDfTYeIGvLJQbBg\"",
   "id": {
    "kind": "youtube#video",
    "videoId": "P-Kq9edwyDs"
   },
   "snippet": {
    "publishedAt": "2016-12-10T17:00:01.000Z",
    "channelId": "UCJFp8uSYCjXOMnkUyb3CQ3Q",
    "title": "Chocolate Crepe Cake",
    "description": "Customize & buy the Tasty Cookbook here: http://bzfd.
it/2fpfeu5 Here is what you'll need! MILLE CREPE CAKE Servings: 8 INGREDIENTS
Crepes 6 ...",
    "thumbnails": {
     "default": {
      "url": "https://i.ytimg.com/vi/P-Kq9edwyDs/default.jpg",
      "width": 120,
      "height": 90
     },
     "medium": {
      "url": "https://i.ytimg.com/vi/P-Kq9edwyDs/mqdefault.jpg",
      "width": 320,
      "height": 180
     },
     "high": {
      "url": "https://i.ytimg.com/vi/P-Kq9edwyDs/hqdefault.jpg",
      "width": 480,
      "height": 360
     }
    },
```

```
      "channelTitle": "Tasty",
      "liveBroadcastContent": "none"
     }
    },
    {
     "kind": "youtube#searchResult",
     "etag": "\"XI7nbFXulYBIpLOayR_gDh3eu1k/Fe41OtBUjCV35t68y-E21BCpmsw\"",
     "id": {
      "kind": "youtube#video",
      "videoId": "_eOA-zawYEA"
     },
     "snippet": {
      "publishedAt": "2016-02-25T22:23:40.000Z",
      "channelId": "UCJFp8uSYCjXOMnkUyb3CQ3Q",
      "title": "Chicken Pot Pie (As Made By Wolfgang Puck)",
      "description": "Read more! - http://bzfd.it/1XPgzLN Recipe! 2 pounds
cooked boneless, skinless chicken, shredded Salt Freshly ground black pepper 4
tablespoons vegetable ...",
      "thumbnails": {
       "default": {
        "url": "https://i.ytimg.com/vi/_eOA-zawYEA/default.jpg",
        "width": 120,
        "height": 90
       },
       "medium": {
        "url": "https://i.ytimg.com/vi/_eOA-zawYEA/mqdefault.jpg",
        "width": 320,
        "height": 180
       },
       "high": {
        "url": "https://i.ytimg.com/vi/_eOA-zawYEA/hqdefault.jpg",
        "width": 480,
        "height": 360
       }
      },
      "channelTitle": "Tasty",
      "liveBroadcastContent": "none"
     }
    },

--snip--
```

Listing 2-4: Sample data returned by the YouTube API, revisited

Now you should be able to see that all the posts are nested inside a pair of brackets ([]). (Note that Listing 2-4 above is truncated in this book, and while you should be able to see the opening and closing brackets in the results of your API call, you can only see the opening brackets in these pages.) All of this data, in turn, is preceded by the string "items" and then followed by a colon. This signifies that the key "items" contains a list of data points—in this case, the videos from BuzzFeed's Tasty YouTube channel. The "items" key-value pair is stored between one more set of braces ({}), which makes up the entire JSON object.

Now you know how to request data from an API and how to read the JSON response it returns, so let's see how we can tailor the returned data to fit our needs.

Answering a Research Question Using Data

You may have noticed that the data our API call returns is fairly sparse. If we don't specify what kind of data we're asking for, the API assumes that we want only basic information and gives us default data points, but this doesn't mean that we're limited to that data. For example, look at Listing 2-5, which contains information from one of the videos returned from the API call in Listing 2-2.

```
{
  "kind": "youtube#searchResult",
  "etag": "\"XI7nbFXulYBIpLOayR_gDh3eu1k/wiczu7uNikHDvDfTYeIGvLJQbBg\"",
  "id": {
   "kind": "youtube#video",
   "videoId": "P-Kq9edwyDs"
  },
  "snippet": {
   "publishedAt": "2016-12-10T17:00:01.000Z",
   "channelId": "UCJFp8uSYCjXOMnkUyb3CQ3Q",
   "title": "Chocolate Crepe Cake",
   "description": "Customize & buy the Tasty Cookbook here: http://bzfd.
it/2fpfeu5 Here is what you'll need! MILLE CREPE CAKE Servings: 8 INGREDIENTS
Crepes 6 ...",
    "thumbnails": {
     "default": {
      "url": "https://i.ytimg.com/vi/P-Kq9edwyDs/default.jpg",
      "width": 120,
      "height": 90
     },
     "medium": {
      "url": "https://i.ytimg.com/vi/P-Kq9edwyDs/mqdefault.jpg",
      "width": 320,
      "height": 180
     },
     "high": {
      "url": "https://i.ytimg.com/vi/P-Kq9edwyDs/hqdefault.jpg",
      "width": 480,
      "height": 360
     }
    },
    "channelTitle": "Tasty",
    "liveBroadcastContent": "none"
   }
  },
```

Listing 2-5: A sample response to an API call that contains only basic information about a video

This data item corresponds to the video on BuzzFeed's Tasty channel in Figure 2-2.

Figure 2-2: A screenshot of the video represented by Listing 2-5

There's more data on display in the online video—for instance, the number of views and comments—than what we received through the API. This information and much more is available through the API, but we need to think about the *kind* of data we want to get and what questions we want to answer with it. Specifically, we need to do two things. First, we need to set the goal for our research. This is possibly one of the most important but least considered steps. Having a clear set of questions or a hypothesis for your research will inform how you collect your data. Second, we should consult the API documentation to see if the data we need to meet our research goal is available.

A good example of this approach is the BuzzFeed news story "Inside the Partisan Fight for Your News Feed" (*https://buzzfeed.com/craigsilverman/ inside-the-partisan-fight-for-your-news-feed*), a project for which Craig Silverman, Jane Lytvynenko, Jeremy Singer-Vine, and I gathered 4 million posts from 452 different Facebook pages through Facebook's Graph API. With millions of data points, we couldn't simply analyze all the data. We'd end up overwhelmed and wouldn't be able to find any meaningful patterns or trends. To start our analysis, we first needed to narrow down the information we wanted to use.

Since more and more news organizations are relying on third parties like Facebook to reach their audiences, this project took a deep look into how these organizations—both new and old—compare to one another on Facebook. We decided to analyze the popularity of left- and right-leaning news organizations based on their number of followers and the engagements (reactions and comments) each page garnered. Once we narrowed the data down into two categories, we graphed the information over time, as shown in Figure 2-3.

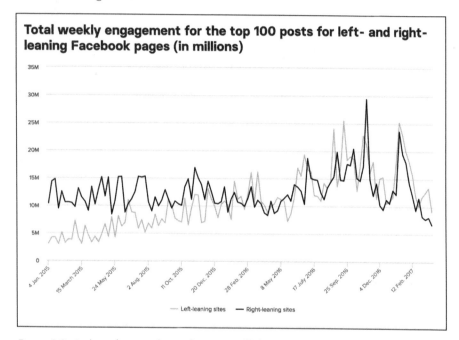

Figure 2-3: A chart showing the performance of left- and right-leaning Facebook pages analyzed by BuzzFeed News

We can see that engagement of left-leaning Facebook pages increased over time. In order to find answers to your research questions, then, you need to be able to not only access information but also filter it.

If we wanted to do a similar analysis of, say, the popularity of BuzzFeed's Tasty channel content over time, we would start by thinking about the categories of data that may help us answer that question. For example, we have multiple ways to measure the popularity of a video, such as the number of views, likes, dislikes, and comments. We'd need to decide which measure we want to use.

In some cases, the visual layout of a social media platform's posts is a good way to determine how to answer your research questions. For example, Figure 2-4 can give us an idea of what kind of data to look for in our popularity analysis of BuzzFeed's Tasty channel.

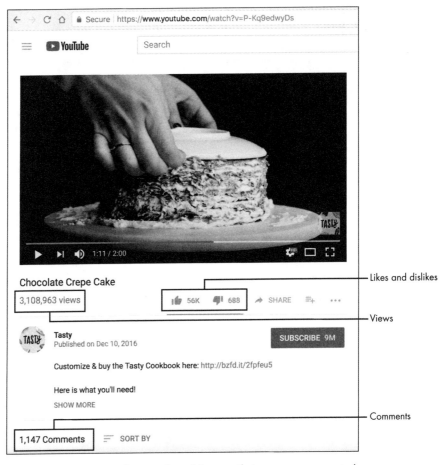

Figure 2-4: An annotated screenshot of the post that we saw represented as data in Listing 2-5

The best way to understand the nature of BuzzFeed's content may be by looking at its video properties (like the headline and the description that accompanies each video). For example, we could use the number of views and upvotes or downvotes as a way to measure a video's popularity. Last but not least, we could use the video timestamps to determine what content is performing well over time.

Now, how do we access some of this data? This is when we look through the API's documentation to find out whether the information is available. As mentioned earlier, a behemoth company like Google offers a number of APIs with various sets of documentation. We're interested in YouTube's Data API, which has documentation at *https://developers.google.com/youtube/*. Each API is organized differently, so you'll want to read the introduction or overview of any API you start using. Let's review some of the basics of Google's YouTube API before covering how to use it.

Refining the Data That Your API Returns

There are various parameters we can use to further narrow down or specify the kind of information we want to collect. Go to YouTube's API documentation at *https://developers.google.com/youtube/v3/docs/search/list* and scroll down to the Parameters table. The left column lists the parameters by name, and the right column provides a description and usage guidelines. When you look for data, read the description of each parameter and find one that matches the type of information you want to access. Let's say we wanted to narrow the results of our API to only videos that mention the word *cake*. To refine our API call, we would use the parameter *q* (short for *query*) and then enter the term we are searching for. This means you would enter *https://www.googleapis.com/youtube/v3/search?channelId=UCJFp8uSYCj XOMnkUyb3CQ3Q&part=snippet&key=YOUR_API_KEY&q=cake* into your browser.

Let's break this call down. The first part is similar to the first API call we made earlier in the chapter. We're accessing the search API *search?* and specifying through the parameter *channelId* that we want to restrict our search to videos from the BuzzFeed Tasty channel. Next, we enter our API key like before, followed by the ampersand (*&*) indicating that we're about to add a parameter, *q*. Then we use an equal sign (=) and specify the search term *cake* for the API to return. When you enter this API call into your browser, you should get a JSON response containing only videos with the word *cake* in the description or title.

Great! You've now learned how to use parameters to tailor your API data requests.

Summary

Understanding how to access specific data from an API call is an important task to understand both technically and conceptually. While every API has its own parameters, limitations, and authentication processes, I hope this chapter has equipped you with the tools to successfully navigate the various approaches each API requires. In the next chapter, I'll show you how to access and refine data using a Python script.

3

GETTING DATA WITH CODE

By now, you've seen how to call an API through your browser to access specific data. Next, you'll learn how to make these calls through a Python script and how to read data, store it, and write it into a file.

Previously, we typed lines of Python directly into an interactive shell that interpreted them, helping convey instantly how Python works. But as we're moving toward more complicated uses of Python, we'll need to shift gears and start using a text editor to write Python scripts.

You can write scripts in a free text editor preinstalled on your computer, such as TextEdit on Mac or WordPad on Windows, but it's better to write and edit code in a text editor designed for developers. These text editors have *syntax highlighting*, which colors code to make it easier to read. A good, free text editor I recommend is Atom, which you can download at *https://atom.io*.

Writing Your First Script

Now we can write a script! Let's start by organizing our files. Create a folder in a memorable place and name it *python_scripts*. For both Mac and Windows, I recommend saving it in the *Documents* folder. Then open a text editor and create a blank file (in Atom, select **File ▸ New File**).

Save this file in your *python_scripts* folder (**File ▸ Save As...**) with the name *youtube_script.py*. The file extension *.py* tells the text editor that the language in the text file is Python.

When you're naming your files, a good rule of thumb is to use all lower-case and to make sure the name describes what the script actually does. You can't use spaces in a script's filename or start the name with a number. So, if your filename gets very long, separate the individual words with under-scores or dashes instead of spaces (as we've done with *youtube_script.py*). Python is case sensitive, so referring to the same file using different capital-ization or making typos can result in broken code and a lot of headaches.

Now enter the following code into *youtube_script.py* and then save it:

```
print("This is my first Python script!")
```

Next we'll need to open a command line interface (CLI), which we used to access the Python interactive shell in Chapter 1. CLIs allow you to use lines of code to navigate through your computer's files. You can move files from one folder to another, create and delete files, and even access the internet through them. A CLI can run scripts as well.

Running a Script

Open your CLI like you did in Chapter 1, using the Terminal for Mac or the Command Prompt for Windows. In order to run a script, you need to navigate to the *directory*, or folder, that contains it. On a Mac, you can run the ls command, which stands for *list*, to see where you are on your hard drive. On Windows, you can run the dir command, which stands for *direc-tory*. When you run these commands, your CLI should list the files within the directory where it's currently located, as shown in Figure 3-1.

Now you need to navigate into the folder you created earlier, *python _scripts*. This can be a stumbling block at first if you're used to navigating folders using icons. To access a folder in a CLI, instead of clicking icons we need to specify a *filepath*, which is the path of folders leading to the file we want to access. On Mac this is usually the name of the folders separated by forward slashes, and on Windows it's typically the name of the hard drive followed by the folder names separated by backslashes. For example, if you saved your *python_scripts* folder inside the *Documents* folder on Mac or Windows, the paths for each folder should be *Documents/python_scripts* and *C:\Documents\python_scripts*, respectively. If you saved your folder in a dif-ferent location, you can also navigate to the file's folder in Finder (Mac) or File Explorer (Windows) and copy the path displayed in the window.

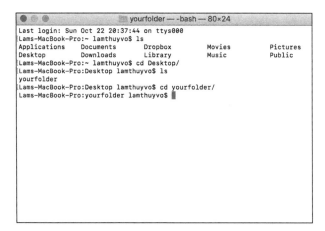

Figure 3-1: The listing for the current directory

To navigate to a folder through the CLI, you use the command cd (which stands for *change directory*), followed by the path of your folder. For example, if you stored your folder in the *Documents* folder on a Mac, run this command:

```
cd Documents/python_scripts
```

For Windows, you would run this command:

```
cd C:\Documents\python_script
```

Once you are in the folder that contains your Python script, you'll need to use another command to run the script. Enter this command in the CLI for Mac:

```
python3 youtube_script.py
```

For Windows, enter:

```
python youtube_script.py
```

On Macs, the command python3 tells your CLI that you're about to run a script written in Python (version 3), and youtube_script.py is the name and extension of the file you want the CLI to run.

We're taking off! This is what you should see in the CLI after running the script:

```
This is my first Python script!
```

The script executes the print() function you entered in the previous section. Now that you've seen how to run scripts, let's write one that will do what we want.

Planning Out a Script

Each script we run will perform a series of tasks. When you first start writing a script, you should list and describe these tasks to help organize your thoughts. This practice is sometimes referred to as *pseudocoding*. Pseudocoding is best done with *comments*, which are lines in your script that are purely for you or others reading your code, and aren't run by the computer. You can think of pseudocoding comments as a to-do list you'll use when coding later to remind yourself what each part of your code should do. The comments can also serve as descriptive notes to help others understand what your script does.

Let's start laying out a to-do list directly into the script. Create a comment in your *youtube_script.py* file by using a hashtag (#) and writing out a note, as shown in Listing 3-1.

```
# Import all needed libraries
# Open the URL and read the API response
# Identify each data point in your JSON and print it to a spreadsheet
```

Listing 3-1: Pseudocoding the steps to perform in your script

Each hashtag tells Python that the rest of the text on the line is a comment. Listing 3-1 has three comments on three separate lines. To write our script, we'll need to first import some *libraries*, which are prepackaged code files. Then, we'll open a URL-based API call and read the response as we did in Chapter 2. Finally, we'll store the returned data in a spreadsheet so we can analyze it.

Now that we have an outline, we can run through each task and add the code that performs it.

Libraries and pip

Throughout your long and surely successful career as a data sleuth, you won't have to write every function you'll ever use. Python is open source, as you learned earlier, which means that many developers have written functions that we can use for free. Most, if not all, coders depend on code that someone else has written and published for others to use; this is known as a *coding library*. As you tackle more complicated tasks with Python, you'll need to install and use coding libraries.

There are two kinds of libraries:

- The libraries included in the *Python standard library*—the set of tools that comes with Python and is included by default when we install Python on our computer
- Third-party libraries, which we can use only once we've installed them on our computer

First, let's discuss the libraries that are automatically installed with Python, and were written by its developers. Here are some of the most common libraries that we'll use:

csv Allows us to read and write *.csv* files, which can be opened as an Excel spreadsheet or Google Sheet. *CSV* stands for *comma-separated values*, which is a common way to format data.

json Enables us to read data that has been formatted in JSON.

datetime Allows our computers to understand and translate date formats and enables us to reformat them as needed.

Before we can use a library, we need to import it, which is like downloading an ebook onto your tablet before you can read it. To load a library, you use the Python keyword `import` and then specify the library's name, such as csv. For example, to load the csv library into the interactive shell, you would enter the following:

```
import csv
```

Using Python libraries from the wider Python community is a little trickier. Most of these libraries can be found on *PyPI* (the Python Package Index; *https://pypi.python.org/pypi*), a site where you can browse through the descriptions and code of libraries other people have uploaded for public use.

The easiest way to get these libraries is through `pip`, a library that was written to help developers manage other libraries (how meta!). You can install `pip` using the instructions at *https://pip.pypa.io/en/stable/installing/*.

Once you've installed `pip`, you can use it to install any library listed on PyPI. To install a library, enter this simple formula into your CLI (replace *library_name* with the name listed on PyPI):

```
pip install library_name
```

These are some of the PyPI libraries we use in this book:

requests Allows us to open websites using a URL.

beautifulsoup4 Helps us read the HTML and CSS code of websites.

pandas Enables us to parse millions of rows of data, modify it, apply math to it, and export the results of our analysis.

To follow the exercises in this book, install these libraries by running the following commands in your CLI one by one, pressing ENTER after each (make sure you're connected to the internet when you do this!):

```
pip install requests
pip install beautifulsoup4
pip install pandas
```

We'll tackle how to use each library as we go through the book's exercises.

Now that we know how to access libraries, let's deploy them in our script! Returning to our Python script *youtube_script.py*, let's go to the part of our pseudocode that contains the comment about importing all needed libraries. We'll use two of the libraries mentioned earlier that come preinstalled with Python, json and csv. We'll also use the requests library that we just installed, which allows us to open URLs. Enter the code from Listing 3-2 into *youtube_script.py*.

```
import csv
import json

import requests
--snip--
```

Listing 3-2: Importing the libraries we need in our script

You can see that we're using the keyword import to load each library—that's all there is to it! Now let's move on to the next task in our to-do list: opening the URL to make the API call.

Creating a URL-based API Call

In order to make our API call, we'll use the requests library we just imported, as shown in Listing 3-3.

```
--snip--
import requests

api_url = "https://www.googleapis.com/youtube/v3/search?part=
snippet&channelId=UCJFp8uSYCjXOMnkUyb3CQ3Q&key=YOUTUBE_APP_KEY"❶

api_response = requests.get(api_url)❷
videos = json.loads(api_response.text)❸
```

Listing 3-3: Making an API call using the requests library

First, we'll need to create the URL, which we do by creating the variable api_url and assigning it to a URL similar to the one we used in Chapter 2 ❶ (we dropped the parameter for videos that include the term cake and put the snippet specification before the channel ID, something that will come in handy later in "Storing Values That Change in Variables" on page 57). Now that we've set up the URL, we can use the requests library to connect to the internet, make the API call, and receive the API's response.

To access a function from any library, we need to refer to it by using the library's name—in this case, requests. Then we *chain* the function to the library name by preceding the function with a period. In this case, we'll use the function get(), which takes a URL string as an argument and makes a request to that URL. In Python, we call functions that belong to a library by typing the library's name, followed by a period, and finally the function name. For example, the get() function is part of the requests library, so we write requests.get() to call it.

We stored the string of the URL we want to access in the variable api_url, so we pass that to the get() function. The response library then offers us a number of options to receive our response. Then we store this API response in a variable called api_response ❷.

Last but not least, we call the loads() function from the json library ❸, which helps us translate the plain api_response text into JSON keys and values. The loads() function requires text but by default, the requests library returns an HTTP status code, which is generally a numbered response like 200 for a working website or 404 for one that wasn't found. We need to access the text of our response, or in this case the JSON rendering of our data. We can do so by putting a period after api_response variable, followed by the option .text. The entire construction thus looks like this: json.loads(api_response.text) ❸. This converts the response of our API call into text for our Python script to interpret it as JSON keys and values. We'll look more closely at this line of code and what it does next section in this chapter.

As you can see, we're using a lot of descriptive variables in this script. This helps us break up the script into parts that we'll be able to track clearly.

Storing Data in a Spreadsheet

All right, items 1 and 2 of our pseudocode to-do list are complete—we've imported our libraries and received the API response. It's time to move on to the next step: retrieving the data points from the JSON to put into a spreadsheet. To do that, we'll use the csv library. First, though, let's see how we can create a *.csv* file and write information to it. Enter the code from Listing 3-4 into your Python script.

```
--snip--
videos = json.loads(api_response.text)

with open("youtube_videos.csv", "w") as csv_file:❶
    csv_writer = csv.writer(csv_file)❷
    csv_writer.writerow(["publishedAt",❸
                        "title",
                        "description",
                        "thumbnailurl"])
```

Listing 3-4: Creating the headers of the .csv file

To create the *.csv* file, we use the open() function ❶, which is built into Python and opens or creates a file based on the arguments given to it. The open() function takes two strings as arguments, each separated by a comma. The first argument is the name of the *.csv* file that we want to create or open, which in this example is "youtube_videos_posts.csv". The second argument specifies whether we want to read the file ("r"), write into the file and erase everything else that was in it before ("w"), or simply add more content to the file ("a"). In this case, we want to write a completely new file. While the open() function sounds like it can only open files, it is also smart enough to check whether a file with a name that matches the first argument already exists. If the open() function doesn't find one, Python will know to create a new *.csv* file. Next, we need to assign the file to a variable so we can reference the file in our code.

You may notice that instead of assigning the file directly to a variable using an equal sign, we use the open() function in a with statement. A with statement opens a file and closes it automatically once we've finished modifying it. We construct a with statement by writing the keyword with, followed by the open() function. Then we use the word as followed by a variable name, like csv_file, which we'll use to refer to the file we're opening. The with statement ends with a colon, like the other types of statements you've learned about. After the colon, Python expects indented lines of code detailing a set of actions to be executed on the file. Once Python has executed those actions and the code is de-indented, the with statement will close the file.

Next we open the *.csv* file by using the csv library's writer() function, which allows us to write rows of data into the file ❷. To keep things simple, we'll start by writing just one row of data. The writer() function requires a *.csv* file as an argument, so we pass it csv_file. We store all of this in the variable csv_writer. Finally, we write our first row into the *.csv* file using the writerow() function, which takes a list of strings as an argument ❸. The first row of data should be the list of headers for our spreadsheet, describing the kind of content that each row will contain.

Now that we have a spreadsheet with headers, it's time to grab the data from the API response and write it into the *.csv* file!

For this task, we'll deploy our trusty old friend, the for loop, which we first encountered in Chapter 1. As we know, JSON data comes in sets of braces that contain various data points, and each data point comes in pairs of keys and values. We previously used a for loop to cycle through data in a list. Now, we'll use one to cycle through the data associated with each post and to access the data values using each data point's key.

In order to do this, first we'll need to look at how the JSON data is organized in Python. Let's step back to earlier in the code, when we loaded the JSON, as reproduced in Listing 3-5.

```
--snip--
api_response = requests.get(api_url)
videos = json.loads(api_response.text)❶

--snip--
```

Listing 3-5: Loading the JSON data

As you may remember, a loop requires a list of items to go through. In this case, we have a list of all our YouTube videos as JSON objects. We stored these posts into the videos variable earlier in our script ❶. Now, we can select videos using the for loop, but in order to access the post information we want, we'll need to navigate through the structure of the JSON object and see what the load() function does.

Converting JSON into a Dictionary

When Python loads JSON using the `json.load()` function, it converts the JSON data into a Python *dictionary*. A dictionary is similar to a list, but instead of simply storing multiple values, it stores values in key-value pairs—just like JSON! Let's see how this works with an example.

Fire up your interactive Python shell, and then enter the following:

```
>>> cat_dictionary = {"cat_name": "Maru", "location": "Japan"}
```

As you can see, we're using the variable `cat_dictionary`. Then we created a dictionary with the key names `cat_name` and `location` and paired them with the values `Maru` and `Japan`, respectively. Once you press ENTER, your interactive shell will assign this dictionary to the variable `cat_dictionary`. So far, so good. But how do you access each data item?

Remember each key is associated with a value. So, to access the data value stored with a key, first we need to type the name of the variable storing our dictionary, followed by the key name as a string inside square brackets. If we wanted to access the string `'Maru'` stored with the key `"cat_name"`, for instance, we would type the following:

```
>>> cat_dictionary["cat_name"]
>>> 'Maru'
```

Now let's access the stored JSON data using the script.

Going Back to the Script

Every website has JSON objects that are organized into key-value pairs, but not every site will use the same key names or overall JSON structure. In Chapter 2 you saw that YouTube's JSON is organized as shown in Listing 3-6.

```
"items"❶: [
  {
   "kind": "youtube#searchResult",
   "etag": "\"XI7nbFXulYBIpLOayR_gDh3eu1k/wiczu7uNikHDvDfTYeIGvLJQbBg\"",
   "id": {
    "kind": "youtube#video",
    "videoId": "P-Kq9edwyDs"
   },
   "snippet": {
    "publishedAt": "2016-12-10T17:00:01.000Z",
    "channelId": "UCJFp8uSYCjXOMnkUyb3CQ3Q",
    "title": "Chocolate Crepe Cake",
    "description": "Customize & buy the Tasty Cookbook here: http://bzfd.
it/2fpfeu5 Here is what you'll need! MILLE CREPE CAKE Servings: 8 INGREDIENTS
Crepes 6 ...",
     "thumbnails": {
      "default": {
       "url": "https://i.ytimg.com/vi/P-Kq9edwyDs/default.jpg",
       "width": 120,
       "height": 90
```

```
      },
      "medium": {
       "url": "https://i.ytimg.com/vi/P-Kq9edwyDs/mqdefault.jpg",
       "width": 320,
       "height": 180
      },
      "high": {
       "url": "https://i.ytimg.com/vi/P-Kq9edwyDs/hqdefault.jpg",
       "width": 480,
       "height": 360
      }
     },
     "channelTitle": "Tasty",
     "liveBroadcastContent": "none"
    }
   },
   {
    "kind": "youtube#searchResult",
    "etag": "\"XI7nbFXulYBIpLOayR_gDh3eu1k/Fe41OtBUjCV35t68y-E21BCpmsw\"",
    "id": {
    "kind": "youtube#video",
    "videoId": "_eOA-zawYEA"
    },
    "snippet": {
    "publishedAt": "2016-02-25T22:23:40.000Z",
    "channelId": "UCJFp8uSYCjXOMnkUyb3CQ3Q",
    "title": "Chicken Pot Pie (As Made By Wolfgang Puck)",
    "description": "Read more! - http://bzfd.it/1XPgzLN Recipe! 2 pounds
cooked boneless, skinless chicken, shredded Salt Freshly ground black pepper 4
tablespoons vegetable ...",
      "thumbnails": {
      "default": {
       "url": "https://i.ytimg.com/vi/_eOA-zawYEA/default.jpg",
       "width": 120,
       "height": 90
      },
      "medium": {
       "url": "https://i.ytimg.com/vi/_eOA-zawYEA/mqdefault.jpg",
       "width": 320,
       "height": 180
      },
      "high": {
       "url": "https://i.ytimg.com/vi/_eOA-zawYEA/hqdefault.jpg",
       "width": 480,
       "height": 360
      }
     },
     "channelTitle": "Tasty",
     "liveBroadcastContent": "none"
    }
   },
--snip--
```

Listing 3-6: YouTube's JSON data structure

In YouTube's case, all the video data is contained as a value under the "items" key ❶. This means that in order to access any video information, you'll need to navigate into the "items" key's values by selecting items using brackets and quotation marks: videos['items']. You can use either double quotes or single quotes for Python strings, so "items" is the same as 'items'.

Add the loop in Listing 3-7 to your own script.

NOTE   *This snippet shows code that is indented because it is still within the scope of the with open() statement that we began writing in Listing 3-4.*

```
--snip--
    if videos.get("items") is not None:❶
        for video in videos.get("items"):❷
            video_data_row = [
                        video["snippet"]["publishedAt"],
                        video["snippet"]["title"],
                        video["snippet"]["description"],
                        video["snippet"]["thumbnails"]["default"]["url"]
                    ]❸
            csv_writer.writerow(video_data_row)❹
```

Listing 3-7: Using a for loop to write the data into the .csv file

First we create an if statement that instructs our code to gather information only if the API call does indeed return our video items. The .get() function will return None if the API call returns no JSON structure with the "items" key (this helps us avoid errors that could interrupt our script for when we may have reached the limit of how much data YouTube allows us to gather) ❶. We then indent the code and create a for loop and access the post data using videos.get("items") ❷. Now that we have the loop set up, we can cycle through each video and store its data points as a list. Once we have a list of data points, we can write the full list to the .csv file. We need each data point to exactly match the order of the spreadsheet headers we created earlier in the script, or the data won't be organized correctly. This means that the list needs to comprise the video's publication date, title, description, and thumbnail URL, in that order.

Since each post is also organized into a dictionary, we create the list by selecting each value through its key: video["snippet"]["publishedAt"]. Then we put the values inside a list ❸. Last but not least, we can write each row into our spreadsheet using the writerow() function ❹, as we did when we wrote our spreadsheet headers. When you run the script, the for loop will run this code for each post in the JSON object.

Running the Finished Script

The finished script should look something like Listing 3-8.

```
import csv
import json
```

```
import requests

api_url = "https://www.googleapis.com/youtube/v3/search?part=
snippet&channelId=UCJFp8uSYCjXOMnkUyb3CQ3Q&key=YOUTUBE_APP_KEY"
api_response = requests.get(api_url)

with open("youtube_videos.csv", "w", encoding="utf-8") as csv_file:
    csv_writer = csv.writer(csv_file)
    csv_writer.writerow(["publishedAt",
                         "title",
                         "description",
                         "thumbnailurl"])
    if videos.get("items") is not None:
        for video in videos.get("items"):
            video_data_row  = [
                video["snippet"]["publishedAt"],
                video["snippet"]["title"],
                video["snippet"]["description"],
                video["snippet"]["thumbnails"]["default"]["url"]
                ]
            csv_writer.writerow(video_data_row)
```

Listing 3-8: The functioning script

Congratulations! We have officially written a script that harvests data from APIs for us.

Now that your script is ready, save it and then try running it by following the instructions in "Running a Script" on page 44. Once you run the script, you should find a *.csv* file named *youtube_videos.csv* in the same folder as your script. When you open the file in a spreadsheet program, it should contain YouTube video data that looks something like Figure 3-2.

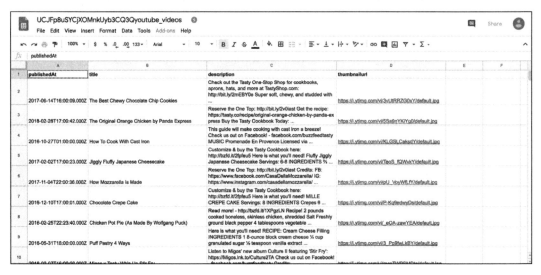

Figure 3-2: How our spreadsheet should look after being uploaded to a spreadsheet program like Google Sheets

While this script may work only with the YouTube API, it demonstrates the fundamental concepts you need to write a script that can harvest data from other platforms. Making a URL-based API call, reading and accessing JSON, and writing it into a *.csv* file are core skills that you'll use repeatedly for many data-gathering and web development tasks.

Dealing with API Pagination

We've now touched upon some basic aspects of data gathering through one API call, but if you inspect the spreadsheet you just created you may notice that the *.csv* file contains data only for a handful of posts.

Welcome to the problems posed by the ubiquity of social media data! Because loading hundreds or thousands of YouTube videos can strain the site's servers, we can't request all of the data we want at once. Depending on how many data points we request, we could even crash a page or server. To keep that from happening, a lot of API providers build in ways to slow down the data-grabbing process.

YouTube limits the data we can request through *pagination*, which divides data into multiple JSON objects. Think of it like a phone book (from the olden days) that contains thousands of entries. Instead of having all the entries on one *really* long page, you can leaf through a book of multiple pages.

In this exercise, you'll need to further explore YouTube's JSON object. We have already tapped into one part, which we accessed with the "data" key by using posts["data"]. If we look more closely at the JSON object we've been using, we'll see a second key after all the post data called "paging", which is shown in Listing 3-9.

```
{
 "kind": "youtube#searchListResponse",
 "etag": "\"XI7nbFXulYBIpLOayR_gDh3eu1k/WDIU6XWo6uKQ6aM2v7pYkRa4xxs\"",
 "nextPageToken": "CAUQAA",
 "regionCode": "US",
 "pageInfo": {
  "totalResults": 2498,
  "resultsPerPage": 5
 },
 "items": [
  {
   "kind": "youtube#searchResult",
   "etag": "\"XI7nbFXulYBIpLOayR_gDh3eu1k/wiczu7uNikHDvDfTYeIGvLJQbBg\"",
   "id": {
    "kind": "youtube#video",
    "videoId": "P-Kq9edwyDs"
   },
--snip--
```

Listing 3-9: The pagination data in the JSON object

When we run our script it only retrieves what's on the page in the "items" key, so to access more results, we need to open the next page. As you can see in Listing 3-9, the API response renders more JSON data, which is accessible with the key "nextPageToken" and contains two more dictionaries.

To access the next page, we can use the token that is provided with the "nextPageToken" key. How do we use this value? Every API handles pagination differently, so we should consult the YouTube API documentation. We learn that to jump to the next page of results, we'll need to add a new parameter to our API URL called "pageToken" and assign it the value provided with the "nextPageToken" key. Modify your script as shown in Listing 3-10.

```
--snip--
    csv_writer.writerow(["publishedAt",
                         "title",
                         "description",
                         "thumbnailurl"])
    has_another_page = True❶
    while has_another_page:❷
        if videos.get("items") is not None:
            for video in videos.get("items"):
                video_data_row  = [
                    video["snippet"]["publishedAt"],
                    video["snippet"]["title"],
                    video["snippet"]["description"],
                    video["snippet"]["thumbnails"]["default"]["url"]
                    ]
                csv_writer.writerow(video_data_row)
        if "nextPageToken" in videos.keys():
            next_page_url = api_url + "&pageToken="+videos["nextPageToken"]❸
            next_page_posts = requests.get(next_page_url)
            videos = json.loads(next_page_posts.text)❹
        else:
            print("no more videos!") has_another_page = False❺
```

Listing 3-10: Modifying the script to gather data from other pages

First we introduce a variable called has_another_page, which we assign the value True ❶. We'll use this variable to check whether there's another page where we can get data. This is a trick many developers use with conditional statements, like the if clauses we learned about in Chapter 1. The while statement ❷ is a type of loop that takes a conditional, like an if statement, and runs the code within it until the condition given to it is False. We'll use the has_another_page variable in the while statement and switch it to False ❺ when we've reached the end of our data stream and there are no pages left. The first few lines of the script are identical to the lines we wrote in Listing 3-8, except that we've now nested them in the while loop. The first time the while loop runs, it gathers data on the first JSON page just as it did before.

Once we've looped through each data object in the JSON on the first page, we check whether the JSON contains a value for a "nextPageToken" key. If no "nextPageToken" key exists, then there are no other pages for the script to load. If the "nextPageToken" key does exist, we'll store the string of the videos["nextPageToken"] link in a variable called next_page_url ❸. This corresponds to the data item "nextPageToken": "CAUQAA", which we saw in Listing 3-9 under "nextPageToken". We'll do another URL-based API call ❹ with this URL and store the response in the posts variable. With the next page of posts loaded, we return to the beginning of our loop and gather the next set of post data.

This loop will run until we've reached the end of our JSON output (in other words, the end of our "phone book"). We'll know that we've reached the last page once the API no longer displays a value for videos["nextPage Token"]. *That* is when we assign our variable has_another_page to False ❺ and end our loop.

What we covered in this exercise is quite a bit for beginners to take in, so don't worry too much if you need to reread it. The main concept to take away is that this is how paginations often work and how we as developers have to work around them: because data providers limit the amount of data we can get with each API URL, we have to programmatically "leaf" through the different pages of data we're permitted to access.

Templates: How to Make Your Code Reusable

We've done what we came here for: we got our data—and a lot of it! But wait! Now we need to take an extra step and clean up our code in a way that makes it reusable. In other words, we want to *template* the code, or turn the script into a template that we can use over and over again.

What does that mean? Well, we'll want a script that is not only reusable but also flexible enough to adapt to different kinds of scenarios. To template our script, first we look at which parts of it we may want to change when repurposing it.

What we want to potentially change are our credentials (if we want to give the code to someone else), the YouTube channel we want to access, and the kinds of data we want to gather. This is particularly helpful when we work on tight deadlines and often repeat tasks, or when we tend to experiment a lot with the kind of information we want to use for our research.

Storing Values That Change in Variables

One way we can make our code more flexible is by setting parameters as variables that we define at the beginning of the script. This way, all the changeable pieces of code are organized together in one easy-to-find place. Once we've defined each variable, we can then stitch them back together to form our API call. Take a look at Listing 3-11 to see how that would work.

```
--snip--
import csv
import json

import requests
```

```
channel_id = "UCJFp8uSYCjXOMnkUyb3CQ3Q" ❶
youtube_api_key = "XXXXXXX" ❷

base = "https://www.googleapis.com/youtube/v3/search?" ❸
fields = "&part=snippet&channelId=" ❹
api_key = "&key=" + youtube_api_key ❺
api_url = base + fields + channel_id + api_key ❻
api_response = requests.get(api_url)
posts = json.loads(api_response.text)

--snip--
```

Listing 3-11: Templating the script for reuse

At the top we define two more variables: the channel_id that is associated
with the YouTube channel of interest ❶ and the youtube_api_key variable to
store our API key as a string ❷. You can also see that we break up our API
URL into individual parts. First, we define the base of our API, which will
always be the same, and store it in the variable base ❸. Then we enter the
field parameters of the API as a separate string and store them in the variable fields ❹. Next we concatenate the YouTube API key youtube_api_key into
a string that we store in a variable called api_key ❺.

Lastly, we stitch these pieces back together into one long string that
makes up our URL-based API call ❻. This process allows us to modify parts
of our API call in the future, in case we want to add other parameters to the
query or use different credentials to access the API.

Storing Code in a Reusable Function

Another way we can template our code is by wrapping it into a function that
we can call again and again, as shown in Listing 3-12.

```
def make_csv(page_id): ❶
    base = "https://www.googleapis.com/youtube/v3/search?"
    fields = "&part=snippet&channelId="
    api_key = "&key=" + youtube_api_key
    api_url = base + fields + page_id + api_key
    api_response = requests.get(api_url)
    videos = json.loads(api_response.text)
    with open("%syoutube_videos.csv" % page_id, "w") as csv_file:
        csv_writer = csv.writer(csv_file)
        csv_writer.writerow(["post_id",
                             "message",
                             "created_time",
                             "link",
                             "num_reactions"])
        has_another_page = True
        while has_another_page:
            if videos.get("items") is not None:
                for video in videos.get("items"):
                    video_data_row = [
                    video["snippet"]["publishedAt"],
```

```
                    video["snippet"]["title"],
                    video["snippet"]["description"],
                    video["snippet"]["thumbnails"]["default"]["url"]
                    ]
                csv_writer.writerow(video_data_row)
        if "nextPageToken" in videos.keys():
            next_page_url = api_url + "&pageToken="+videos["nextPageToken"]
            next_page_posts = requests.get(next_page_url)
            videos = json.loads(next_page_posts.text)
        else:
            print("no more videos!")
            has_another_page = False
```

Listing 3-12: Putting code into the make_csv() *function*

Here we wrap all of our code into a function called make_csv(), which
takes the argument page_id. As we discussed in Chapter 1, a function is a
way to lay out a series of steps in code that we can repeatedly run by calling
the function later. First, we declare the make_csv() function and specify any
arguments we want it to take ❶, and then we enter all of the code we want
to include in the function. Everything you want to include in make_csv()
needs to be indented under the function declaration so that Python knows
which code is part of the function. Now that we have defined make_csv(),
we can execute it by calling its name and passing an argument in the function's parentheses.

The final reusable script should look like Listing 3-13.

```
import csv
import json

import requests

channel_id = "UCJFp8uSYCjXOMnkUyb3CQ3Q"❶
channel_id2 = "UCpko_-a4wgz2u_DgDgd9fqA"❷
youtube_api_key = "XXXXXXX"

def make_csv(page_id):❸
    base = "https://www.googleapis.com/youtube/v3/search?"
    fields = "&part=snippet&channelId="
    api_key = "&key=" + youtube_api_key
    api_url = base + fields + page_id + api_key
    api_response = requests.get(api_url)
    videos = json.loads(api_response.text)
    with open("%syoutube_videos.csv" % page_id, "w") as csv_file:
        csv_writer = csv.writer(csv_file)
        csv_writer.writerow(["publishedAt",
                            "title",
                            "description",
                            "thumbnailurl"])
        has_another_page = True
        while has_another_page:
            if videos.get("items") is not None:
```

```
                    for video in videos.get("items"):
                        video_data_row  = [
                        video["snippet"]["publishedAt"],
                        video["snippet"]["title"],
                        video["snippet"]["description"],
                        video["snippet"]["thumbnails"]["default"]["url"]
                        ]
                        csv_writer.writerow(video_data_row)
                if "nextPageToken" in videos.keys():
                    next_page_url = api_url + "&pageToken="+videos["nextPageToken"]
                    next_page_posts = requests.get(next_page_url)
                    videos = json.loads(next_page_posts.text)
                else:
                    print("no more videos!")
                    has_another_page = False
make_csv(channel_id)❹
make_csv(channel_id2)❺
```

Listing 3-13: The full template script

We use the variables channel_id ❶ and channel_id2 ❷ to hold the parts of
the script that are most likely to change. Then we define the make_csv() function, which holds the code we want to run ❸. Now we can run the function
by passing the channel_id ❹ and channel_id2 ❺ variables into the make_csv()
function. And that's it!

There are two additional things to note. First, YouTube limits the
amount of API calls per day one can make on a free account. This is
known as a *rate limit*. With this kind of API call, we can only get a few
hundred videos per channel, so if one channel has a lot of videos—more
than we can get through a free account—we may need to use different
API credentials to get data for the second channel. Secondly, the content
produced online may include different kinds of special characters—emoji
or characters in different languages, for example—that can be difficult
for specific versions of Python to understand or, as coders say, *encode*. In
those scenarios, Python may return a UnicodeEncodeError, a notification that
Python encountered content that it has trouble reading and writing.

NOTE   *Unicode (https://unicode.org/) is a specification that aims to represent every
character used in written human language, like a letter or an emoji, by assigning
each its own code. Think of it as a lookup table for your computer.*

While this was not an error I encountered when running our script
on Mac computers, Windows computers seemed to have issues with encoding some of the content we tried to ingest through API calls. Since API
calls return some of the latest data available from any given platform, each
response to your API call will be specific to the most recent information
from the API provider. This also means that, if you run into errors related
to the content you're trying to access through this API, you'll need to find
solutions closely tied to that particular content. To ensure you receive the

right results, it might be helpful to specify an encoding method for the data you're trying to collect. Listing 3-14 shows a small modification of the script that can help resolve issues for a few specific types of data.

```
--snip--

video_data_row  = [
    video["snippet"]["publishedAt"],
    video["snippet"]["title"].encode("utf-8")❶,
    video["snippet"]["description"].encode("utf-8")❷,
    video["snippet"]["thumbnails"]["default"]["url"].encode("utf-8")❸
]
```

Listing 3-14: Modifying the script to help retrieve the right results

In this code, we add the .encode() function to three values that we're accessing through different keys: the title, which we access with video["snippet"]["title"] ❶; the description of a video, which we access with video["snippet"]["description"] ❷; and the link for the video, which we access with video["snippet"]["thumbnails"]["default"]["url"] ❸. Inside the .encode() function's parentheses, we specify which kind of encoding method we want to use to better understand the data. In this case, we're using a common encoding type called utf-8 (UTF stands for *Unicode Transformation Format*, and 8 simply specifies that we're using 8-bit values to encode our information). Note that while this method may solve some encoding issues, since each error is specific to the content you're trying to collect, it may be worth reading up on other potential solutions. (You'll find a helpful tutorial at *https://docs.python.org/3/howto/unicode.html*.)

Having created our template code, we can use it for any YouTube channel we want. We can now run the make_csv() function for multiple pages or use different credentials. All we need to do is change the strings that are associated with the channel_id and channel_id2 variables or the youtube_api_key variable.

Templating your code is a great practice to follow after you've drafted a script that accomplishes your goals. This allows you to improve your code, repeat the tasks you've already programmed, and share your scripts with others who may be able to use them—we use other people's code, so why not return the favor?

Summary

This chapter has shown you how APIs work and how to mine data from them using a script. APIs are an essential tool for gathering data. Knowing how to tap into them and how to modify a script is more important than the script itself. That's because scripts can become outdated very quickly. The ways in which social media companies serve up data change all the time—they may implement new policies that restrict data access, the way Facebook did in 2015 by shutting down access to friends' data. Or companies may just change the ways in which they allow users to interact with their API, the way Instagram did when it discontinued access to its photo streams in 2013.

To learn more about scripts, visit *https://github.com/lamthuyvo/social -media-data-scripts*, which has scripts for social media data gathering, instructions on how to use them, and links to other resources.

In the next chapter, you'll see how to grab your data from Facebook and put it into a format your computer can understand.

4

SCRAPING YOUR OWN
FACEBOOK DATA

 Social media is becoming a digital vault for our lives and our memories; its servers store a history of our behavior that allows us to remember important events with incredible precision. A number of social media platforms allow us to download archives of our social media history as data files or HTML web pages. These archives may contain posts from our Facebook timelines, messages we send to each other, or every tweet we've ever posted.

In this chapter, you'll learn how to use Python to get data from our downloadable Facebook archives using an automated scraper. The scraper goes through each HTML element that contains the information we want to collect, extracts this information, structures it in rows, and then writes every row of data into a list or spreadsheet, just like we did when we wrote an API in Chapter 3. But this time we'll use a slightly different method to populate our spreadsheet: we'll be using a data *dictionary* to structure our data before we write it to a *.csv* file. This is a very helpful and widely adopted way to organize data, and it will expand your knowledge of the csv library we used in the previous chapter.

Your Data Sources

From the day you register an account, most (if not all) social media companies start storing data about you. You can see some of this data by scrolling backward on your Facebook and Twitter timelines or your Instagram feed.

Although most platforms allow users to download a lot of their personal data, it is often unclear how complete these data archives are. Social media companies determine how much and what kind of data they want to release to their users, just like they determine how much data they want to release publicly through an API. And on top of that, it can be a little tricky to figure out how to download your own data archive: options can be buried in the fine print of our user settings, and are not often visually distinguished.

Access to data archives varies from platform to platform and can be almost shockingly granular or similarly sparse. In May of 2018 the European Union's General Data Protection Regulation (GDPR) went into effect, requiring companies across the world to protect the privacy of their users, in part by giving them more control over their own data. While the laws were introduced to largely benefit users in the European Union, many social media companies have created easier pathways for anyone, in Europe or not, to download and view their own data.

In this chapter, we'll only tap into the data that's publicly available in downloadable social media archives. You'll learn about *web scraping*, the process of gathering and storing data from the web. Every website presents its own unique data challenges. For the purposes of this tutorial, we'll be looking at how to scrape data from Facebook, which is one of the most popular global platforms and offers various formats for us to analyze. If you do not have a Facebook account, you can find a sample file to scrape here: *https://github.com/lamthuyvo/social-media-data-book*.

Downloading Your Facebook Data

First we need to download our data. Many social media sites contain the instructions for downloading your archive, but they may be buried deep within the site. An easy way to find your archive is by entering this formula into your search engine of choice: *platform/language + verb + object*. For example, to find your Facebook archive, you'd search "Facebook download archive" or "Python scrape Facebook archive."

To download your Facebook archive, follow these steps:

1. Click the down arrow at the top right of any Facebook page and select **Settings**.

2. On the sidebar at the left, click **Your Facebook Information** below your General account settings.

3. Navigate to **Download Your Information** and click **View**.

4. This should open a new page with an option to create a file containing your archive. Keep the default settings (Date Range: All of my data; Format: HTML; and Media Quality: Medium). Click **Create File**.

Next, you should be prompted to enter your account credentials (confirming your password), and then Facebook should email you the link to a downloadable file.

The archive should download as a ZIP file. Place this file inside the folder you'll use for all the files related to this project. Unzip the downloaded file, and you should see multiple files and folders in a folder titled *facebook-<yourname>*. In my case, this folder is called *facebook-lamthuyvo*.

Double-click the file titled *index.html*, and your default browser should open the page. In your browser, you should see categories for the information you downloaded (ads, messages, friends, and so on) on the left side of the menu and an overview of your account information on the right side, as shown in Figure 4-1.

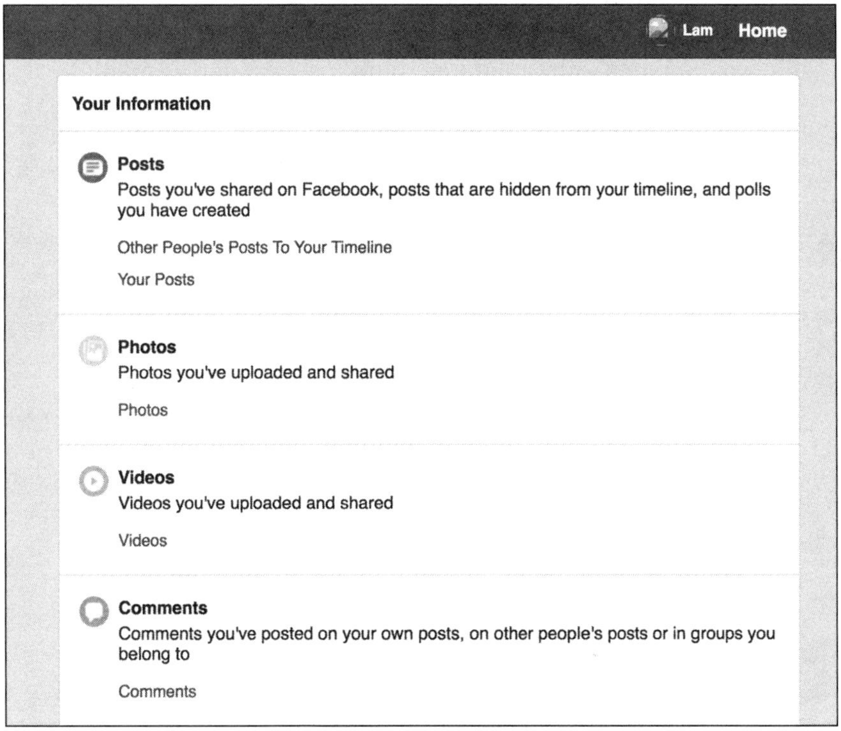

Figure 4-1: A Facebook archive profile page

This folder represents a more complete archive than what you might see when scrolling through your Facebook account online. Here, you'll find information like all of the telephone numbers you've ever registered with Facebook, a code associated with the facial recognition data Facebook uses to tag you and your friends, and the ads that you've clicked in the past three months. The archive profile page should give you an idea about the kind of information Facebook stores about your activities and online presence for its own purposes.

Reviewing the Data and Inspecting the Code

To introduce the process of scraping, we'll begin by looking at the ads you've clicked in the past three months.

Scraping generally proceeds as follows:

1. Look at the visual display of information in a web browser.
2. Inspect the code that contains this information.
3. Instruct your scraper to grab the information from this code.

So, to start, inside the *ads* folder of your Facebook archive, open *advertisers_you've_interacted_with.html*, the page that contains the titles and timestamps of every advertisement you've clicked in the past three months.

Once you've looked through your ad data, it's time to move on to the second step: inspecting the code. To do this, we'll use Chrome's built-in developer tools (we learned about these in Chapter 1). Start by right-clicking one of the listed advertisements and, in the drop-down list that opens, select **Inspect**. When the Web Inspector opens, it should highlight the code representing the ad you just right-clicked. Figure 4-2 shows the Web Inspector view in Chrome.

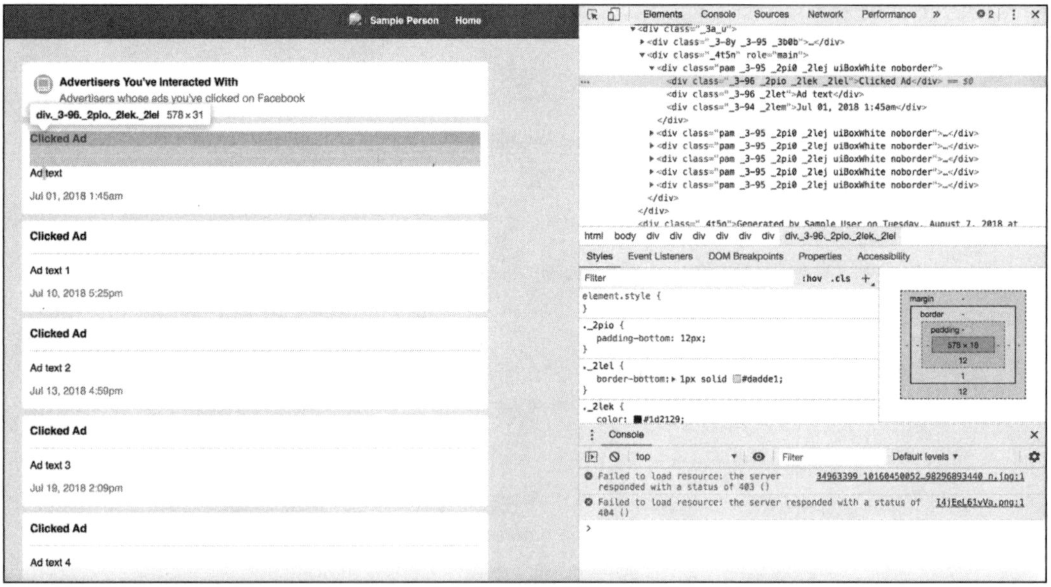

Figure 4-2: Chrome's Web Inspector view

Recall that web pages are HTML files that contain information inside of HTML tags styled with CSS IDs and classes. When a page renders repetitive content—like posts that are featured on our news feeds or the advertisers listed in our data archive—it will likely use the same pattern of HTML tags and CSS classes to display each piece of information. In order to harvest the data contained in those HTML tags, we have to recognize and understand these patterns.

Structuring Information as Data

In this case, all the ads are inside an overall <div> tag, which has the class attribute _4t5n and the role attribute main. Listing 4-1 contains HTML code that displays a sample Facebook ad as it might be stored in an archive.

```
<div class="_4t5n" role="main">
<div class="pam _3-95 _2pi0 _2lej uiBoxWhite noborder">
    <div class="_3-96 _2pio _2lek _2lel">Clicked Ad</div>
    <div class="_3-96 _2let">Ad name 1</div>
    <div class="_3-94 _2lem">Jul 01, 2019 1:45am</div>
</div>
<div class="pam _3-95 _2pi0 _2lej uiBoxWhite noborder">
    <div class="_3-96 _2pio _2lek _2lel">Clicked Ad</div>
    <div class="_3-96 _2let">Ad name 2</div>
    <div class="_3-94 _2lem">Jul 10, 2019 5:25pm</div>
</div>
<div class="pam _3-95 _2pi0 _2lej uiBoxWhite noborder">
    <div class="_3-96 _2pio _2lek _2lel">Clicked Ad</div>
    <div class="_3-96 _2let">Ad name 3</div>
    <div class="_3-94 _2lem">Jul 11, 2019 5:25pm</div>
</div>

--snip--
</div>
```

Listing 4-1: Sample code for Facebook ads

Listing 4-1 includes an HTML <div> tag with the classes _3-96 and _2let (note that each individual class within a pair of quotation marks is separated by a space). This <div> tag contains the title of the Facebook ad that the user clicked. A second <div> tag with the classes _3-94 and _2lem contains the time-stamp indicating when the user clicked on the ad.

If we created a spreadsheet based on this HTML, it might look like Figure 4-3.

	A	B	C
1	advertisement	timeaccessed	
2	Ad name 1	Jul 01, 2019 1:45 AM	
3			
4			
5			
6			
7			
8			
9			
10			
11			
12			
13			
14			

Figure 4-3: A sample spreadsheet after we've scraped some of the data

We've used two headers, *advertisement* and *timeaccessed*, to categorize and structure the data. Note that there are many ways to do this; we could have chosen only to look at the titles of the ad, or to separate the timestamp into *date* and *time_of_day* columns. Data collection is a creative process, and the solution you find will always depend on the specific project and data you're working with.

In Figure 4-3 we started creating our spreadsheet by manually copying the data straight from the web page. Though you can scrape the web like this, as you can imagine it would take a lot of time and effort. Almost all web scraping is done automatically. So, in the next section, we'll use Python to set up an automatic scraper.

Scraping Automatically

As with a script, you can think of a scraper as a little robot who will perform repetitive tasks for you. And like the script we used in Chapter 3, the scraper fetches data and puts it into a spreadsheet for you—except that it gets data from HTML pages instead of from an API response.

Unlike JSON, HTML data can be tricky to work with, as it's not always structured in data-friendly ways. Going in with a plan, then, will help us identify which parts of a website may best be structured as data. As we did with our API script, let's start by writing down our list of tasks as pseudo-code, making each task a separate comment, as in Listing 4-2.

```
# import libraries
# open our page
# grab all the information for the ads
# put all the ad data into an list
# create a csv file
# write each line into a csv file
```

Listing 4-2: The plan for our script

Next we'll import the libraries we need, shown in Listing 4-3.

```
# import libraries
import csv

from bs4 import BeautifulSoup
```

Listing 4-3: Importing our libraries

For this script we need two libraries: csv, which comes built into Python, and Beautiful Soup, a library an independent developer wrote for other Python developers to use. Beautiful Soup allows our scraper to read and understand HTML and CSS.

Because it isn't built into Python, we'll need to install Beautiful Soup separately before using it. We covered the library installation process in Chapter 1. In this case, you can install the library using the pip command **pip install beautifulsoup4** (beautifulsoup4 refers to the fourth version of Beautiful Soup, which is the latest and most improved version of the library). After you install any library, the best way to understand and use it is to look up its documentation. You can find the documentation for Beautiful Soup at *https://www.crummy.com/software/BeautifulSoup/bs4/doc/*.

Now that Beautiful Soup is installed and imported, we can put it to use. Normally, Python doesn't understand what tags are, so when it opens an HTML page, the information is just a long string of characters and spaces like this:

```
<div class="pam _3-95 _2pi0 _2lej uiBoxWhite noborder">
    <div class="_3-96 _2pi0 _2lek _2lel">Clicked Ad</div>
    <div class="_3-96 _2let">See how Facebook is changing</div>
    <div class="_3-94 _2lem">Jul 01, 2018 1:45am</div>
</div>
```

Beautiful Soup takes in HTML and CSS code, extracts the useful data, and turns it into objects Python can work with—a process known as *parsing*. Imagine Beautiful Soup as X-ray goggles that allow our scraper to see through the HTML coding language and concentrate on the content we are really interested in (bolded in the following code):

```
<div class="pam _3-95 _2pi0 _2lej uiBoxWhite noborder">
    <div class="_3-96 _2pi0 _2lek _2lel">Clicked Ad</div>
    <div class="_3-96 _2let">See how Facebook is changing</div>
    <div class="_3-94 _2lem">Jul 01, 2018 1:45am</div>
</div>
```

We'll use Beautiful Soup to turn the HTML code into a list that will hold the name of each ad and the time it was accessed. First, though, create a file in the same folder that contains your archive and save it as *ad_scraper.py*, then set up the basic structure of your code in *ad_scraper.py* as shown in Listing 4-4.

```
import csv

from bs4 import BeautifulSoup

# make an empty array for your data
❶ rows = []
# set foldername
❷ foldername = "facebook-lamthuyvo"
# open messages
with open("%s/ads/advertisers_you've_interacted_with.html" % ❸foldername)
as ❹page:
    soup = ❺BeautifulSoup(page, "html.parser")
```

Listing 4-4: Creating an empty list and opening our file

First, we create the rows ❶ variable, which we'll eventually fill with our data. Then we create the foldername variable ❷ to hold the name of the folder where our data currently resides, which allows us to easily modify our script in the future if we want to scrape someone else's archive ❸. Then we open the HTML file and store its information in the page variable ❹. Lastly, we pass page into the BeautifulSoup() function ❺. This function parses the HTML into a list of elements that we can work with; specifically, it turns the page into a Beautiful Soup object so the library can differentiate between HTML and other content. The second argument, "html.parser", which we passed into BeautifulSoup(), tells Beautiful Soup to process page as HTML.

Analyzing HTML Code to Recognize Patterns

Earlier in this chapter, we saw that each ad name is encased in <div> tags with the classes _3-96 and _2let. The timestamp associated with the ad is stored in a <div> tag that has the classes _3-94 and _2lem.

You'll notice in Listing 4-1 that some of these classes, like _3-96, may be used for other <div> tags, like the subheading containing the words Clicked Ad. Because classes are used to style <div> elements that can be used over and over, we'll need to identify the CSS classes and tags that are *unique* to the type of information we want to scrape. That is, we need to be able to instruct our script to grab content only from the <div> tags that contain information about the ads we clicked. If we told our script to grab information from <div> tags without specifying classes, we would end up with a lot of extraneous information since <div> tags are used for numerous content types across the page.

Grabbing the Elements You Need

To get just the content we want, first we need to add some code that selects the parent (outer) <div> tag containing all the ad names and timestamps we want to grab. Then we'll go into that parent <div> tag and search through each <div> tag, one by one, to collect the relevant information for each of the ads we clicked on.

Listing 4-5 shows the script that accomplishes this.

```
import csv

from bs4 import BeautifulSoup
--snip--
    soup = BeautifulSoup(page, "html.parser")
    # only grab the content that is relevant to us on the page using the class
named "contents"
    contents = soup.find("div", ❶class_="_4t5n")
    # isolate all the lists of ads
  ❷ ad_list = contents.find_all( "div" , class_="uiBoxWhite")
```

Listing 4-5: Selecting a specific <div> using Beautiful Soup

First, we look for a <div> tag with the class _4t5n ❶, which we know from Listing 4-1 will contain all the <div> tags with the ad information we want to scrape. We look for this tag by applying the find() function to soup, which is the HTML that we parsed earlier in our code. We'll then assign (using the equal sign) the results of this function to the variable contents.

To find a <div> tag that has a specific class, the find() function requires two arguments. First, it needs to know which kind of HTML tag it's looking for. In this case, we're looking for <div> tags, which we specify through the string "div" (make sure you keep the quotes around the word div).

But if we ran the code with only the "div" argument using soup.find ("div"), our script would not return the right <div> tag for us. Instead, our scraper would go through the entire HTML file, find each <div> tag, and then render only the last one it found.

The find() function is designed to go through the entire code, identifying every <div> tag it finds in the code stored in the soup variable until it gets to the end. Thus, because find() is meant to find only one <div> tag, it keeps only the very last one—not all the other ones it cycled through.

To find not just any <div> tag but the one that has the _4t5n class, then, we need to pass a second argument, class_="_4t5n" ❶, into the find() function. Specifying what class the <div> tag uses helps us grab only the <div> tag that we're interested in.

Once we have a <div> containing all the ad <div>s stored in contents, we can go through contents, select every <div> tag that contains ad information, and store those <div>s in a list. We can do this by applying the find_all() function to the contents class ❷. We use find_all(), not find(), to return every <div> tag with the uiBoxWhite class. The function should now return the results as a list, which we store in the ad_list variable.

Extracting the Contents

Once we have the list of advertisements, we need to grab each ad's title and timestamp. To do this, we'll loop through each <div> tag in ad_list using a for loop and extract its contents. Listing 4-6 shows how to do this in Python.

```
--snip--
    ad_list = contents.find_all("div", class_="uiBoxWhite")
❶ for item in ad_list:
        ❷ advert = item.find("div", class_="_2let").get_text()
        ❸ timeaccessed = item.find("div", class_="_2lem").get_text()
```

Listing 4-6: Extracting the contents of HTML <div> tags

First, we write a statement that introduces the for loop ❶. The line for item in ad_list: means that we'll go through the list item by item, storing the current item in the item variable, and then run the process we specify in the lines following the for loop. In this case, item holds a <div> tag with the uiBoxWhite class.

Then we'll grab a <div> tag with the class _2let from item and store it in the advert variable ❷. Notice, though, that we didn't just use find(); we also chained another function onto find() by calling get_text() at the end of the line. Python and libraries like Beautiful Soup allow you to modify the results of one function by calling another function at the end of it, a process known as *chaining*. In this case, the find() function allows us to grab a <div> that may look like this:

```
<div class="_3-96 _2let">See how Facebook is changing</div>
```

Then we apply the get_text() function to get the text contained inside the <div> tag:

```
See how Facebook is changing
```

We repeat this process to extract the timestamp information from the <div> tag that uses the _2lem class ❸.

Whew, we just made our scraper do a ton of work! Let's revisit our HTML code so we know what information the scraper just parsed:

```
❶ <div class="_4t5n" role="main">
❷ <div class="pam _3-95 _2pi0 _2lej uiBoxWhite noborder">
     <div class="_3-96 _2pi0 _2lek _2lel">Clicked Ad</div>
  ❸ <div class="_3-96 _2let">See how Facebook is changing</div>
  ❹ <div class="_3-94 _2lem">Jul 01, 2018 1:45am</div>
   </div>
   <div class="pam _3-95 _2pi0 _2lej uiBoxWhite noborder">
     <div class="_3-96 _2pi0 _2lek _2lel">Clicked Ad</div>
     <div class="_3-96 _2let">Ad name 2</div>
     <div class="_3-94 _2lem">Jul 10, 2018 5:25pm</div>
   </div>
   <div class="pam _3-95 _2pi0 _2lej uiBoxWhite noborder">
     <div class="_3-96 _2pi0 _2lek _2lel">Clicked Ad</div>
     <div class="_3-96 _2let">Ad name 3</div>
     <div class="_3-94 _2lem">Jul 11, 2018 5:25pm</div>
   </div>

   --snip--
   </div>
```

To recap: our scraper first found the <div> tag that contained all ads ❶, turned each ad into a list item ❷, and then went through each ad, extracting its title ❸ and timestamp ❹ from each nested <div> tag.

Writing Data into a Spreadsheet

Now we know how to use our scraper to get the information we need. But we haven't told our little robot what to do with this information just yet. This is where *.csv* files can be helpful—it's time to tell our scraper to turn the data it's been reading into a spreadsheet that we humans can read.

Building Your Rows List

We need to instruct our script to write every row of data into a spreadsheet, just like we did when we wrote an API. But this time we'll do so by creating a Python *dictionary*, a data structure that allows us to assign specific data points (values) to specific data categories (keys). A dictionary is similar to JSON in that it maps a value to a key.

In its simplest form, a dictionary looks like this:

```
row = {
    "key_1": "value_1",
    "key_2": "value_2"
    }
```

In this example, I define a variable called row using a pair of braces ({}). The data in the dictionary is inside those braces (note that I added some line breaks and spaces to make the dictionary more legible).

In a dictionary, our values are stored in pairs of keys and values. In this case, there are two keys, "key_1" and "key_2", and each is paired with a value, "value_2" and "value_2". Each key-value pair is separated by a comma, making this a list of two different pairs. Imagine keys as column headers in a spreadsheet. In this example, the string key_1 would represent the column header, and value_1 would be one of the cells in that column. If this structure looks familiar, it's no accident: this is how JSON data is structured. In some ways, you can look at Python dictionaries as blueprints for data that may be structured in the JSON format.

To return to our specific example, let's create a dictionary for our data and append it to our *.csv* file, as shown in Listing 4-7.

```
--snip--
for item in ad_list:
    advert = item.find("div", class_="_2let").get_text()
    timeaccessed = item.find("div", class_="_2lem").get_text()
 ❶ row = {
     ❷ "advert": ❸advert,
     ❷ "timeaccessed": ❸timeaccessed
        }
 ❹ rows.append(row)
```

Listing 4-7: Writing data to the .csv file

The keys "advert" and "timeaccessed" ❷ are strings that represent the types of data we want to collect—the equivalent of column headers in our spreadsheet. Each key is paired with a variable: the "advert" key goes with the advert variable and the "timeaccessed" key with the timeaccessed variable ❸. Recall that we used these variables earlier to temporarily store the text we extracted from each HTML element using Beautiful Soup. We store this dictionary in the row variable ❶.

Once we have our row, we need to store it with the other rows. This is where the rows variable we defined at the top of our script comes into play. During each iteration of the for loop, we add another row of data to the rows list by using the append() function ❹. This allows us to grab the latest values from each list item, assign those values to the appropriate keys, and append the keys and values to our `rows` variable. This entire process allows us to accumulate a new row of data with each loop, ensuring that we extract information about every single ad we clicked on and that we populate the `rows` list with this data so we can write it into a *.csv* file in the next step.

Writing to Your .csv File

Last but not least, we need to open a *.csv* file and write each row to it. As stated before, this process is a little bit different from what you saw in Chapter 3. Instead of using the simple `writer()` function the csv library offers, we'll be using `DictWriter()`, a function that knows how to handle dictionaries. This should help us avoid any careless mistakes, like accidentally swapping our column values.

Listing 4-8 shows the code to create the *.csv* file.

```
--snip--
❶ with open("../output/%s-all-advertisers.csv" % foldername, "w+") as csvfile :
❷     fieldnames = ["advert", "timeaccessed"]
      writer = csv.DictWriter(csvfile, fieldnames=fieldnames) ❸
      writer.writeheader() ❹
      for row in rows: ❺
          writer.writerow(row) ❻
```

Listing 4-8: Turning data into a .csv file

First, we create and open a new file ❶ using the string *facebook-<lamthuyvo> -all-advertisers.csv* (you replaced my username, *lamthuyvo*, with yours earlier, as shown in Listing 4-4), which is a concatenation of the `foldername` variable and the name of the folder containing the *.csv* file. Then we open the *.csv* file and refer to it as `csvfile`. Next, we create a variable called `fieldnames` to store a list of strings ❷, which correspond to the keys we defined in our dictionary in Listing 4-7. This is important because we then use the `DictWriter()` function ❸ to instruct Python to write data based on a dictionary containing the keys we specified in `fieldnames`. The `DictWriter()` function requires the parameter `fieldnames` to know what the column headers of our *.csv* file will be and which parts of our data rows it should access. In other words, the field names that we list and store in our `fieldnames` variable represent the parts of the data we want the `DictWriter()` function to write into our *.csv* file.

We then use the `writeheader()` function ❹ to write the first row of our *.csv* file, the headers for each column. Since `writer` already knows those field names from the previous line, we don't need to specify anything, and our *.csv* file should now look like this:

```
advert,metadata
```

All that's left is to add our data. By looping through each row in `rows` ❺, we can write each row of data into our spreadsheet ❻.

Finally, once we stitch all the pieces together, our script should look like Listing 4-9.

```
import csv

from bs4 import BeautifulSoup

rows = []
foldername = "facebook-lamthuyvo"

with open("%s/ads/advertisers_you've_interacted_with.html" % foldername) as
page:
    soup = BeautifulSoup(page,  "html.parser")
    contents = soup.find("div", class_="_4t5n")
    ad_list = contents.find_all( "div" , class_="uiBoxWhite")

    for item in ad_list:
        advert = item.find("div", class_="_2let").get_text()
        metadata = item.find("div", class_="_2lem").get_text()
        row = { "advert": advert,
                "metadata": metadata
            }
        rows.append(row)

with open("%s-all-advertisers.csv" % foldername, "w+") as csvfile:
    fieldnames = ["advert", "metadata"]
    writer = csv.DictWriter(csvfile, fieldnames=fieldnames)
    writer.writeheader()

    for row in rows:
        writer.writerow(row)
```

Listing 4-9: The complete scraper script

Looks good! Let's try it out.

Running the Script

At the beginning of this chapter, you saved your file as a script called
ad_scraper.py in the same folder that contains your Facebook archive. Now
you can run it like you would any other Python script. In the console, navigate to that specific folder. For Mac users, run the following command:

```
python3 ad_scraper.py
```

On Windows machines, run this code instead:

```
python ad_scraper.py
```

Once you run the script, your scraper should go through every ad
you've clicked in the past three months, and you should see a file whose
name ends with *-all-advertisers.csv*. This file should contain the title and
timestamp for every ad listed in the archive page *advertisers_you've_interacted
_with.html*. This data will help you better understand your behavior on

Facebook; for example, you can use it to learn on what days or in which months you clicked on a lot of ads. Or you could look into what ads you may have clicked multiple times.

The example in this chapter represents a very simple version of web scraping: the HTML page we scraped was one we could download (not one we had to open by connecting to the internet), and the amount of data we scraped from the page was not large.

Scraping simple HTML pages like those of our archive is a good introduction to the basic principles of web scraping. Hopefully, this exercise will help you transition to scraping websites that are more complicated—whether it's web pages that are hosted online and that change frequently, or HTML pages with much more complicated structures.

Summary

In this chapter, you learned how to inspect an HTML page from your Facebook archive to find patterns in the code that allow you to structure what you see on the page as data. You learned how to use the Beautiful Soup library to read in the HTML page, identify and grab the <div> tags that contain the information you want to collect, store that information in rows of data using a dictionary, and lastly, write that dictionary to a *.csv* file using the DictWriter() function. But more importantly, you learned how to extract information from a web page and write it into a data file that you can feed into various analytical tools like Google Sheets or into a Python-rendering web app like Jupyter Notebook—two tools we'll see in later chapters. This means we have now taken information that was locked into a web page and transformed it into a format that is much easier to analyze!

In the next chapter, we'll build on what you've learned here by applying similar processes to scrape a website that is live on the internet.

5

SCRAPING A LIVE SITE

 Seen through the eyes of a data sleuth, almost every piece of online content is a treasure trove of information to be collected. Think of a series of Tumblr posts, or the comments for a business listed on Yelp. Every day, people who use online accounts produce an ever-growing amount of content that is displayed on websites and apps. Everything is data just waiting to be structured.

In the previous chapter, we talked about web scraping, or extracting data from HTML elements using their tags and attributes. In that chapter we scraped data from archive files we downloaded from Facebook, but in this chapter we'll turn our attention to scraping data directly from sites that are live on the web.

Messy Data

Websites are made for people who consume them, not for people like us who want to mine them for data. For this reason, many websites have features that, while they make it easier for consumers to read and use them, may not be ideal for our data sleuthing purposes.

For instance, a Facebook post with 4,532 reactions may show an abbreviated label of 4.5K reactions. And, instead of displaying a full timestamp and data, Facebook often shows only how many hours ago a post was created. Especially on social media platforms, online content is often optimized to be helpful and interesting, but not necessarily to have complete information.

For our purposes, this means that the data we harvest can be irregular, messy, and potentially incomplete. It also means that we may need to find some ways to work around a website's structure to grab information.

You may wonder why we would put this much work into getting data when there might be an API available. In some cases, data that is easily accessible on a live website isn't offered through an API. Twitter, for instance, allows us to look at three months' worth of data when scrolling through feeds, but only lets us access approximately 3,200 tweets through the API. On Facebook, data related to public groups and pages is available through the API, but it may differ from what populates our news feeds.

For one BuzzFeed News story, we analyzed 2,367 posts from the Facebook news feeds of Katherine Cooper and Lindsey Linder, a politically divided mother/daughter pair, to show them just how different their online worlds are. Cooper and Linder said that on Facebook their political differences led to heated and ugly spats, which wouldn't occur when they talked offline. Looking at the respective feeds helped us illuminate how each woman's information universe was shaped by whose posts appeared most frequently (see Figure 5-1).

This information was tailored to each Facebook account, meaning that it was available only through looking at Linder and Cooper's Facebook news feeds.

NOTE *You can read the article, "This Conservative Mom and Liberal Daughter Were Surprised by How Different Their Facebook Feeds Are," from BuzzFeed News at* https://www.buzzfeed.com/lamvo/facebook-filter-bubbles-liberal-daughter-conservative-mom/.

Figure 5-1: A graphic of whose posts show up the most on Linder's and Cooper's feeds, respectively

Ethical Considerations for Data Scraping

Social media companies set data restrictions based on what they deem appropriate for their business interests, for their users' privacy concerns, and for other reasons. To some degree, scraping is a way around these restrictions.

The decision to scrape a website, however, should not be taken lightly. Scraping information from websites or republishing scraped data without permission may be against a company's terms of service, and can get you banned from the platform or, worse, result in legal action.

So when is it okay to grab data from a website?

There are various considerations both for the decision to scrape data from live sites and for how we structure our web scrapers. Data journalist Roberto Rocha, in his blog post "On the Ethics of Web Scraping" (*https://robertorocha.info/on-the-ethics-of-web-scraping/*), listed four questions that may serve as a good guideline:

1. Can I take this data?
2. Can I republish this data?
3. Am I overloading the website's servers?
4. What can I use this data for?

We are certainly not the first, nor will we be the last, people who have had an interest in scraping information from live websites. Given that fact, companies will likely have policies written around the practice, often in the form of two documents:

*   The robots exclusion protocol
*   The terms of service

Next we'll dig deeper into both policies, starting with the robots exclusion protocol, often referred to as the *robots.txt* file.

The Robots Exclusion Protocol

The robots exclusion protocol is a text file that is usually hosted on the platform's servers. You find it by typing in a website's URL, such as *http://facebook.com/*, and appending *robots.txt* to the end, like so: *http://facebook.com/robots.txt*.

Many website and platform owners use this document to address *web robots*—programs and scripts that browse the web in automated ways, or, put more simply, that aren't humans. These robots are often also referred to as *crawlers*, *spiders*, or, if you prefer a slightly more poetic term, *web wanderers*. The robots exclusion protocol file is structured in a standardized way and basically acts like a rule book for web robots that are trying to visit the website.

Not every scraper will abide by these rules. Spambots or malware may disregard the protocol, but in doing so they risk being booted from a platform. We want to make sure that we respect the rules of each website so we don't suffer the same fate.

A very basic *robots.txt* file may look like this:

```
User-agent: *
Disallow: /
```

And follows this structure:

```
User-agent: [whom this applies to]
Disallow/Allow: [the directory or folder that should not be crawled or scraped]
```

The term *user-agent* specifies whom a rule applies to. In our example, the user-agent is *, which means that the rule applies to any robot, including one we might write. *Disallow* means that the robot may *not* crawl the directory or folder listed. In this case, the forward slash (/) specifies that the robot may not crawl anything within the *root* folder of the website. The root folder contains all the files of the website, meaning that this *robots.txt* file forbids all robots from crawling any part of the site.

This does not imply that it's impossible to scrape data from the site. It just means the site frowns upon scraping, and doing so might get us into trouble with the site owners.

The *robot.txt* file can have more specific rules, too. Facebook's *robots.txt* file, for instance, includes clauses that apply specifically to a user-agent named Googlebot (see Listing 5-1).

```
--snip--
User-agent: Googlebot
Disallow: /ajax/
Disallow: /album.php
Disallow: /checkpoint/
Disallow: /contact_importer/
Disallow: /feeds/
Disallow: /file_download.php
Disallow: /hashtag/
Disallow: /l.php
Disallow: /live/
Disallow: /moments_app/
Disallow: /p.php
Disallow: /photo.php
Disallow: /photos.php
Disallow: /sharer/
--snip--
```

Listing 5-1: Facebook's more complex robots.txt file

This means that the robot named *Googlebot* is not allowed to access any parts of the Facebook website that include the URLs *facebook.com/ajax/*, *facebook.com/album.php*, *facebook.com/checkpoint/*, and so on.

The Terms of Service

A website's *terms of service* document is another way to find out whether a website owner allows robots to crawl or scrape their site. Terms of service may specify what web robots are allowed to do, or how information from the website may or may not be reused.

Social media users produce data that is very valuable and important to the companies that provide these online services. Our sharing behavior, browsing, and search history allows platforms to build data profiles for users and market products to them. There's a clear economic incentive for many social media companies to disallow others from collecting this data.

Companies also must protect a user's data and privacy. If a spambot or other problematic robot collects user information, it may alienate the platform's users and cause them to leave the service. For these two reasons, and various others, social media companies take their terms of service very seriously.

Technical Considerations for Data Scraping

On top of the ethical considerations around web scraping, there are also technical factors to consider. In the previous chapter, we scraped data from a web archive that we downloaded to our local machine. This means we did not use our script to connect to the internet and were not accessing live websites.

Once we *do* open a website using a scraper, we should consider how that could impact the server that hosts the content. Every time we open a website, we are accessing information that is hosted on a server. Each request requires the scripts of the website to fetch data, put it into HTML format, and transfer it to our browser. Each of these actions costs a tiny fraction of money—the same way transferring several megabytes of information on a mobile phone costs us money.

It's one thing to open up a website in a browser, wait for it to load, and scroll through it the way a human user would. It's another to program a robot to open 1,000 websites in the span of a few seconds. Imagine a server having to deal with a thousand of these transfers at one time. It might collapse under the speed and weight of these requests—in other words, the server would become *overloaded*.

This means that when we write a scraper or a robot, we should slow it down by instructing it to wait a few seconds between opening each website. You'll see how to do this later in the chapter when we write our scraper.

Reasons for Scraping Data

Last but not least, it can be helpful to think about the reasons we need information. There's no surefire way to avoid conflict with the companies that own and operate the platforms, the websites we wish to scrape, and the content that people publish, but having well-thought-out reasons for scraping can be beneficial if we decide to ask social media companies for permission to harvest data from their websites or if we decide to go ahead and scrape a site at our own risk.

Being transparent and clear about why you are scraping information can help companies decide whether to allow you to continue. For example, academics researching human rights abuses on Facebook may be able to make a better case for scraping certain Facebook profiles for noncommercial purposes, while companies republishing scraped data for a commercial service that would compete with Facebook are more likely to face legal consequences for their actions. There are myriad factors that affect what laws govern the act of scraping information—your location, the location of your company or organization, the copyright of the content that is posted, the terms of services of the platform you're trying to scrape, the privacy issues that your data collection may raise—all of which have to be part of your decision-making process when you want to scrape information. Each case for data collection is distinct enough that you should make sure to do the legal and ethical research before you even start to write code.

Keeping in mind those ethical and technical considerations, now we'll get started scraping data from a live website.

Scraping from a Live Website

For this example, we'll scrape a list of women computer scientists from Wikipedia, which has a *robots.txt* file that allows for benign robots to scrape their content.

The URL of the page we'll scrape, shown in Figure 5-2, is *https://en.wikipedia.org/wiki/Category:Women_computer_scientists*.

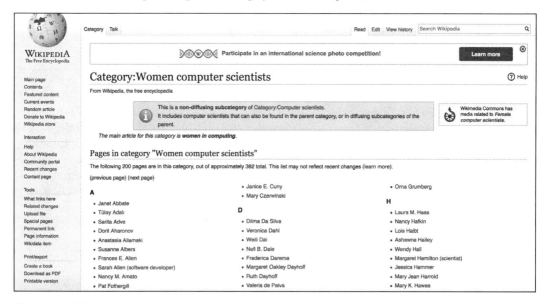

Figure 5-2: Wikipedia's list of women computer scientists

As we did in previous chapters, we begin our script by loading all the libraries we need. Open your text editor and save a new file called *wikipediascraper.py* in a folder you can easily access. Then enter the code from Listing 5-2 into that file.

```
# Import our modules or packages that we will need to scrape a website
import csv

from bs4 import BeautifulSoup
import requests

# make an empty array for your data
rows = []
```

Listing 5-2: Setting up the script

We import the `csv`, `requests`, and `beautifulsoup4` libraries, which we used in previous chapters. Up next, as we did in our previous script, we assign the variable `rows` the value of an empty list, to which we'll add our rows of data later.

Then comes a slightly new task: opening up a live website. Again, the process is very similar to what we did in Chapter 2 when we opened an API feed based on a URL, but this time we'll open up the Wikipedia page that contains the information we want to harvest. Enter the code from Listing 5-3 into your Python file.

```
# open the website
url = "https://en.wikipedia.org/wiki/Category:Women_computer_scientists"❶
page = requests.get(url)❷
page_content = page.content❸

# parse the page with the Beautiful Soup library
soup = BeautifulSoup(page_content, "html.parser")
```

Listing 5-3: Retrieving content from the URL

The first variable we set, `url` ❶, is a string that contains the URL we want to open with our script. Then we set the variable `page` ❷ to contain the HTML page, which we open using the `requests` library's `get()` function; this function grabs the site from the web. After that, we use the `content` ❸ property from `requests` to encode the HTML of the page we just opened and ingested in the previous line as bytes that are interpretable by Beautiful Soup. Then we use Beautiful Soup's HTML parser to help our script differentiate between HTML and the site's content.

Analyzing the Page's Contents

Just as we did with the HTML pages of our Facebook archives, we need to analyze the HTML tags that contain the content we want to harvest through our Python script.

As before, the Web Inspector is a helpful tool that allows us to isolate the relevant code. In this case, we want a list of women computer scientists that was assembled by Wikipedia writers and editors, which we can see in Figure 5-3.

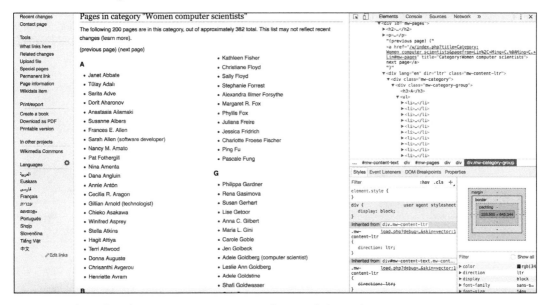

Figure 5-3: The Wikipedia page we want to scrape, shown with the Web Inspector open

As you can see on the page, the computer scientists' names are subdivided into lists sorted by each woman's last name and displayed in alphabetical order. In addition to that, our lists are spread onto two pages. We can access the second page by clicking a next page link.

To reveal which elements contain our content, we can right-click a name on the list we want to scrape and access the HTML of the page. Remember we're interested in detecting patterns that we can take advantage of when collecting our data.

Right-click on a name in the "A" group and select the option in the drop-down menu that says "Inspect." This should change the view inside the Web Inspector: the HTML view should jump to the part of the code that contains the name in the "A" group that you selected and highlight the tag that contains it. Websites can be very long and contain hundreds of HTML tags, and Inspect allows you to locate a specific element you see on the page in the HTML of the website. You can think of it as the "You Are Here" marker on a map.

Now that you have located where one of the names in the "A" group is located in the HTML, you can start examining the HTML tag structure that contains all the other names in the "A" group a little closer. You can do that by scrolling through the code until you reach the parent <div> tag, <div class="mw-category-group">, which highlights the corresponding section of the page, as shown in Figure 5-4. This tag holds the list of last names beginning with "A."

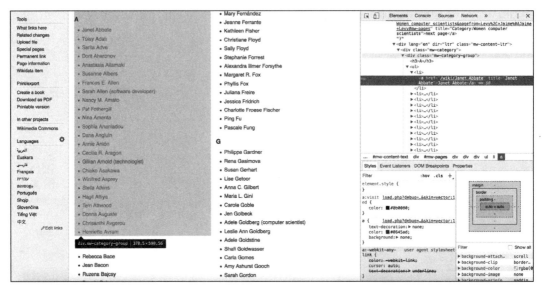

Figure 5-4: The parent tag of the list of women computer scientists filed under the highlighted letter "A"

Now right-click the parent tag and choose **Edit as HTML**. This should allow you to copy and paste the parent tag and every HTML tag that is nested inside the parent tag, as shown in Figure 5-5.

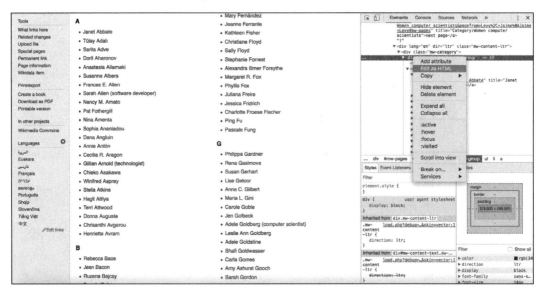

Figure 5-5: Selecting Edit as HTML

If you paste the code we just copied into an empty file in your text editor, it should look like Listing 5-4.

```
<div class="mw-category-group"><h3>A</h3>
<ul><li><a href="/wiki/Janet_Abbate" title="Janet Abbate">Janet Abbate</a></li>
```

```
<li><a href="/wiki/T%C3%BClay_Adal%C4%B1" title="Tülay Adalı">Tülay Adalı</a></li>
<li><a href="/wiki/Sarita_Adve" title="Sarita Adve">Sarita Adve</a></li>
<li><a href="/wiki/Dorit_Aharonov" title="Dorit Aharonov">Dorit Aharonov</a></li>
<li><a href="/wiki/Anastasia_Ailamaki" title="Anastasia Ailamaki">Anastasia Ailamaki</a></li>
<li><a href="/wiki/Susanne_Albers" title="Susanne Albers">Susanne Albers</a></li>
<li><a href="/wiki/Frances_E._Allen" title="Frances E. Allen">Frances E. Allen</a></li>
<li><a href="/wiki/Sarah_Allen_(software_developer)" title="Sarah Allen (software
developer)">Sarah Allen (software developer)</a></li>
<li><a href="/wiki/Nancy_M._Amato" title="Nancy M. Amato">Nancy M. Amato</a></li>
<li><a href="/wiki/Pat_Fothergill" title="Pat Fothergill">Pat Fothergill</a></li>
<li><a href="/wiki/Nina_Amenta" title="Nina Amenta">Nina Amenta</a></li>
<li><a href="/wiki/Dana_Angluin" title="Dana Angluin">Dana Angluin</a></li>
<li><a href="/wiki/Annie_Ant%C3%B3n" title="Annie Antón">Annie Antón</a></li>
<li><a href="/wiki/Cecilia_R._Aragon" title="Cecilia R. Aragon">Cecilia R. Aragon</a></li>
<li><a href="/wiki/Gillian_Arnold_(technologist)" title="Gillian Arnold (technologist)">Gillian
Arnold (technologist)</a></li>
<li><a href="/wiki/Chieko_Asakawa" title="Chieko Asakawa">Chieko Asakawa</a></li>
<li><a href="/wiki/Winifred_Asprey" title="Winifred Asprey">Winifred Asprey</a></li>
<li><a href="/wiki/Stella_Atkins" title="Stella Atkins">Stella Atkins</a></li>
<li><a href="/wiki/Hagit_Attiya" title="Hagit Attiya">Hagit Attiya</a></li>
<li><a href="/wiki/Terri_Attwood" title="Terri Attwood">Terri Attwood</a></li>
<li><a href="/wiki/Donna_Auguste" title="Donna Auguste">Donna Auguste</a></li>
<li><a href="/wiki/Chrisanthi_Avgerou" title="Chrisanthi Avgerou">Chrisanthi Avgerou</a></li>
<li><a href="/wiki/Henriette_Avram" title="Henriette Avram">Henriette Avram</a></li></ul></div>
```

Listing 5-4: The Wikipedia HTML without indentation

As you can see here, the HTML code on websites is often rendered with little to no indentation or spaces. That's because the browser reads code from top to bottom and each line from left to right. The fewer spaces there are between different lines of code, the faster the browser can read them.

However, this pared-down code is much harder for humans to read than indented code. Using spaces and tabs allows coders to indicate hierarchies and nesting within different parts of the code. Since most web pages *minify*, or minimize, code to cater to browsers, we sometimes need to *unminify* it. It will be much easier for us to read and understand the hierarchy and patterns of the HTML elements that contain our desired information if this code is indented.

There are plenty of free tools on the web that reintroduce indentation and spaces to minified code, including Unminify (*http://unminify.com/*). To use these tools, you often just need to copy the minified HTML, paste it into a window that the tool provides, and click a button to unminify it!

Listing 5-5 shows the same code from Listing 5-4, now unminified.

```
<div class="mw-category-group">❶
    <h3>A</h3>❷
    <ul>❸
    ❹ <li><a href="/wiki/Janet_Abbate" title="Janet Abbate"❺>Janet Abbate</a></li>
        <li><a href="/wiki/T%C3%BClay_Adal%C4%B1" title="Tülay Adalı">Tülay Adalı</a></li>
        <li><a href="/wiki/Sarita_Adve" title="Sarita Adve">Sarita Adve</a></li>
        <li><a href="/wiki/Dorit_Aharonov" title="Dorit Aharonov">Dorit Aharonov</a></li>
        <li><a href="/wiki/Anastasia_Ailamaki" title="Anastasia Ailamaki">Anastasia Ailamaki</a></li>
```

```
        <li><a href="/wiki/Susanne_Albers" title="Susanne Albers">Susanne Albers</a></li>
        <li><a href="/wiki/Frances_E._Allen" title="Frances E. Allen">Frances E. Allen</a></li>
        <li><a href="/wiki/Sarah_Allen_(software_developer)" title="Sarah Allen (software
developer)">Sarah Allen (software developer)</a></li>
        <li><a href="/wiki/Nancy_M._Amato" title="Nancy M. Amato">Nancy M. Amato</a></li>
        <li><a href="/wiki/Pat_Fothergill" title="Pat Fothergill">Pat Fothergill</a></li>
        <li><a href="/wiki/Nina_Amenta" title="Nina Amenta">Nina Amenta</a></li>
        <li><a href="/wiki/Dana_Angluin" title="Dana Angluin">Dana Angluin</a></li>
        <li><a href="/wiki/Annie_Ant%C3%B3n" title="Annie Antón">Annie Antón</a></li>
        <li><a href="/wiki/Cecilia_R._Aragon" title="Cecilia R. Aragon">Cecilia R. Aragon</a></
li>
        <li><a href="/wiki/Gillian_Arnold_(technologist)" title="Gillian Arnold
(technologist)">Gillian Arnold (technologist)</a></li>
        <li><a href="/wiki/Chieko_Asakawa" title="Chieko Asakawa">Chieko Asakawa</a></li>
        <li><a href="/wiki/Winifred_Asprey" title="Winifred Asprey">Winifred Asprey</a></li>
        <li><a href="/wiki/Stella_Atkins" title="Stella Atkins">Stella Atkins</a></li>
        <li><a href="/wiki/Hagit_Attiya" title="Hagit Attiya">Hagit Attiya</a></li>
        <li><a href="/wiki/Terri_Attwood" title="Terri Attwood">Terri Attwood</a></li>
        <li><a href="/wiki/Donna_Auguste" title="Donna Auguste">Donna Auguste</a></li>
        <li><a href="/wiki/Chrisanthi_Avgerou" title="Chrisanthi Avgerou">Chrisanthi Avgerou</
a></li>
        <li><a href="/wiki/Henriette_Avram" title="Henriette Avram">Henriette Avram</a></li>
    </ul>
</div>
```

Listing 5-5: The Wikipedia code with indentation

As you can see, the content of the HTML page contains the parent
<div> tag with the class mw-category-group ❶, a headline inside an <h3> tag ❷
containing a letter of the alphabet, an unordered list in a <ul> tag ❸, and
<li> tags ❹ inside that list that contain all the women whose last names
start with the letter specified in the <h3> heading—in this case, A. There
are also links to each woman's Wikipedia page associated with each name
and <li> tag ❺.

Storing the Page Content in Variables

Given what we know now about the code, let's recap what we have to do
after opening the page:

1. Grab every unordered list of names from the first page.
2. Extract information from each list item, including the name of the
   woman computer scientist, the link to her profile, and the letter she is
   categorized under.
3. Create a row of data based on this information and write each row into
   a *.csv* file.

To help us visualize what this data set may look like and how we would
organize it, the spreadsheet in Figure 5-6 structures our data based on
our instructions.

A	B	C
name	link	letter_name
Janet Abbate	/wiki/Janet_Abbate	A
Tülay Adalı	/wiki/T%C3%BClay_Adal%C4%B1	A
Sarita Adve	/wiki/Sarita_Adve	A
Dorit Aharonov	/wiki/Dorit_Aharonov	A
Anastasia Ailamaki	/wiki/Anastasia_Ailamaki	A
Susanne Albers	/wiki/Susanne_Albers	A
Frances E. Allen	/wiki/Frances_E._Allen	A
Sarah Allen (software d	/wiki/Sarah_Allen_(software_developer)	A
Nancy M. Amato	/wiki/Nancy_M._Amato	A
Pat Fothergill	/wiki/Pat_Fothergill	A
Nina Amenta	/wiki/Nina_Amenta	A
Dana Angluin	/wiki/Dana_Angluin	A

Figure 5-6: A mockup spreadsheet that can help us structure our scraper

Okay, now we're ready to begin writing the part of our script that grabs information from our HTML!

We'll start by grabbing every alphabetical list with our script. Go back to your Python file and enter the code in Listing 5-6.

```
--snip--
soup = BeautifulSoup(page_content, "html.parser")
content = soup.find("div", class_="mw-category")❶
all_groupings = content.find_all("div", class_="mw-category-group")❷
```

Listing 5-6: Using Beautiful Soup to retrieve the HTML

In this code, we use the find() ❶ function to find a <div> tag that contains the class mw-category. This is the overall <div> tag that contains the content we want to scrape, as we saw earlier when looking at our page through the Web Inspector. We'll assign this value—meaning that entire HTML block containing all the lists—to the variable content. The next line puts all the <div> tags containing the class mw-category-group ❷ into the variable all_groupings. This task is best accomplished using the function find_all(), which searches the HTML for elements based on characteristics that we specify and creates a list of them for us. We pass the find_all() function two arguments: the string "div", which tells find_all() what kind of HTML element we want it to find, and the class_ argument "mw-category-group". This means that the find_all() function will fetch every <div> that has the class "mw-category-group" and create a list of them. The variable all_groupings, then, will hold a list of HTML elements that contains a list of names sorted alphabetically, as well as the first letter of each woman's last name.

Up next, we need to cycle through each alphabetical list and collect the names from each one, as shown in Listing 5-7. Enter this code into your Python file as well.

```
--snip--
all_groupings = content.find_all("div", class_="mw-category-group")
for grouping in all_groupings:❶
```

```
    names_list = grouping.find("ul")❷
    category = grouping.find("h3").get_text()❸
    alphabetical_names = names_list.find_all("li")❹
```

Listing 5-7: Collecting each name using a for loop

First we need to write a for loop ❶ to go through each of the group-ings we just added to our variable all_groupings. Then we gather the unor-dered list tag <ul> ❷ inside each alphabetical list using the grouping.find() function and put all the lists inside a variable we've defined, names_list. Next, we gather the headline tag <h3> using the grouping.find() function again ❸. The code grouping.find("h3") contains all the <h3> headlines, but all we need for the purposes of our *.csv* file is the text associated with each headline. To gather the text, we use the get_text() function to extract the letter belonging to each group. We can do all of this in one line and store the results in the variable category. Last but not least, we grab every single list item tag <li> inside the <ul> unordered lists. Since we stored all the <ul> groupings in names_list, we can simply use the find_all() function directly on the variable ❹. This should allow us to get the letter and a list of all associated names.

The last step of the script is to create a row of information that contains the name, the link, and the letter connected to each name, as shown in Listing 5-8.

```
--snip--
    category = grouping.find("h3").get_text()
    alphabetical_names = names_list.find_all("li")

    for alphabetical_name in alphabetical_names:❶
        # get the name
        name = alphabetical_name.text❷
        # get the link
        anchortag = alphabetical_name.find("a",href = True)❸
        link = anchortag["href"]❹
        # get the letter
        letter_name = category
```

Listing 5-8: Assigning each name's information to variables to prepare for creating a row in a .csv file

This is perhaps the first time our code gets a little more complicated: we need to write a loop inside another loop! First we had to loop through each alphabetical list. In the code in Listing 5-8, we are now writing another for loop ❶ inside the loop we wrote in Listing 5-7—very meta! In Listing 5-8's nested loop, we cycle through every alphabetical name within the list of list item tags <li> that is currently stored in the variable alphabetical_names.

Each <li> list item tag contains a name, which we extract using the text attribute ❷. This list item also contains links, which we grab using two other functions. To grab the anchor tag <a>, we use the find() func-tion ❸. The find() function has two parameters. The first parameter is the tag we want to find, which is simply "a" for the anchor tag. The second parameter is *optional*, meaning that we don't always have to pass an argument to it. Optional parameters have a default value that we can change when needed. In this case, the optional parameter is href, which is usually set to the value False by default. By setting href = True, we tell the function to grab an anchor tag only if the tag has an href attribute, or link, associated with it. Otherwise—that is, if we don't pass the optional parameter an argument—the find() function will grab every anchor tag by default.

We store the anchor tag we retrieve inside the variable anchortag, which now would contain all the information from the anchor tag we retrieved. We want to get the link inside the anchor tag, so we need to access the tag's href value, which is stored in the tag as an attribute. We do this by grabbing the href attribute using brackets containing the string "href" ❹. Afterward, as we did in the previous chapter, we create a dictionary that we can use to structure the data we gather, as shown in Listing 5-9.

```
--snip--
        # make a dictionary that will be written into the csv
        row = {"name": name,❶
               "link": link,❷
               "letter_name": letter_name}❸
        rows.append(row)❹
```

Listing 5-9: Creating a dictionary to store data

We'll create one row of data every time the for loop iterates. In the first line of code, we assign the variable row a dictionary, using braces that we open in line ❶ and close in line ❸. Then we proceed to assign each key (name ❶, link ❷, and letter_name ❸) the value that holds the corresponding data we gathered earlier in the script. In the end, we append the row of data to our list variable rows ❹.

The script you have written thus far should look like Listing 5-10.

```
# Import our modules or packages that we will need to scrape a website
import csv

from bs4 import BeautifulSoup
import requests

# make an empty list for your data
rows = []

# open the website
url = "https://en.wikipedia.org/wiki/Category:Women_computer_scientists"
page = requests.get(url)
page_content = page.content
# parse the page through the BeautifulSoup library
soup = BeautifulSoup(page_content, "html.parser")
content = soup.find("div", class_="mw-category")
all_groupings = content.find_all("div", class_="mw-category-group")
for grouping in all_groupings:
    names_list = grouping.find("ul")
    category = grouping.find("h3").get_text()
```

```
    alphabetical_names = names_list.find_all("li")
    for alphabetical_name in alphabetical_names:
        # get the name
        name = alphabetical_name.text
        # get the link
        anchortag = alphabetical_name.find("a",href=True)
        link = anchortag["href"]
        # get the letter
        letter_name = category
        # make a data dictionary that will be written into the csv
        row = { "name": name,
                "link": link,
                "letter_name": letter_name}
        rows.append(row)
```

Listing 5-10: The entire script you have written so far

This script works great it you want to gather data only from one page, but it's not as useful if you need to collect data from dozens or even hundreds of pages. Remember how I keep emphasizing that we should write reusable code? We finally have a use case for this in our exercise!

Making the Script Reusable

We now have a script that will grab the names of every woman computer scientist on a single page. But the page contains only half of the names, because there are so many significant women computer scientists that Wikipedia had to divide the list into two web pages.

This means, to get the complete list, we need to grab the rest of the names from the next page. We can do this by wrapping all the code we just wrote into a function that we can reuse, like the one shown in Listing 5-11.

```
# Import our modules or packages that we will need to scrape a website
import csv

from bs4 import BeautifulSoup
import requests

# make an empty list for your data
rows = []

❶ def scrape_content(url):
  ❷ page = requests.get(url)
    page_content = page.content
    # parse the page through the BeautifulSoup library
    soup = BeautifulSoup(page_content, "html.parser")
    content = soup.find("div", class_="mw-category")
    all_groupings = content.find_all("div", class_="mw-category-group")
    for grouping in all_groupings:
        names_list = grouping.find("ul")
        category = grouping.find("h3").get_text()
        alphabetical_names = names_list.find_all("li")
        for alphabetical_name in alphabetical_names:
```

```
# get the name
    name = alphabetical_name.text
    # get the link
    anchortag = alphabetical_name.find("a",href=True)
    link = anchortag["href"]
    # get the letter
    letter_name = category
    # make a data dictionary that will be written into the csv
    row = { "name": name,
            "link": link,
            "letter_name": letter_name}
    rows.append(row)
```

Listing 5-11: Putting the script into a function for reuse

To reproduce Listing 5-11 in your own file, first remove the following line of code from your current script:

```
url = "https://en.wikipedia.org/wiki/Category:Women_computer_scientists"
```

You no longer need to assign the url variable a value because we need to run the code on multiple URLs.

Next, at ❶, we tell Python that we're creating a function called scrape _content() that takes the argument url. Then we add the rest of the code at ❷ that makes up the contents of the scrape_content() function. All of the code in the function is the same as the code you wrote in Listing 5-10, except now it is indented. (If the code editor that you're using didn't automatically indent your code, you can usually highlight every line of code you want to include in your function and press TAB.) You'll notice that at ❷, we open a URL using the requests.get(url) function. The url variable in the function refers to the url at ❶.

In plain English, we just gave Python an instruction manual for all the things we want to do when we call the function scrape_content(url). We'll replace the url argument with an actual URL that we want our script to open and scrape. For example, to run the function on the Wikipedia page, we just add the following line to our script:

```
scrape_content("https://en.wikipedia.org/wiki/Category:Women_computer_scientists")
```

However, we need to run the function multiple times. If we want to run it on one or two URLs, this works great, but we'll likely need to run it on hundreds of URLs. To run it for more than one URL, we can create a list that contains each URL as a string; that way, we can loop through the list to run the function for each link. To do this, add the code in Listing 5-12 to your script after the code from Listing 5-11.

```
# open the website
urls = ❶["https://en.wikipedia.org/wiki/Category:Women_computer_scientists",
"https://en.wikipedia.org/w/index.php?title=Category:Women_computer_scientists
&pagefrom=Lin%2C+Ming+C.%0AMing+C.+Lin#mw-pages"]
```

```
def scrape_content(url):
--snip--
            rows.append(row)
for url in urls:❷
    scrape_content(url)❸
```

Listing 5-12: Running the function on URLs using a loop

The variable urls ❶ holds a list of two strings: the URL of the first
Wikipedia page, which holds the first half of the names of women computer scientists, and then the link for the second page that holds the rest
of the names. Then we write a for loop that cycles through every URL in
our urls list ❷ and runs the scrape_content() function ❸ for each URL. If
you wanted to run the scraper on more Wikipedia list pages, you would
simply add those as links to the urls list.

Now that we have put all our data into our rows variable, it's time for us
to output our data as a spreadsheet. Add the lines of code in Listing 5-13 to
your script, which will do the job.

```
--snip--
# make a new csv into which we will write all the rows
with open("all-women-computer-scientists.csv", "w+") as csvfile:❶
    # these are the header names:
    fieldnames = ["name", "link", "letter_name"]❷
    # this creates your csv
    writer = csv.DictWriter(csvfile, fieldnames=fieldnames)❸
    # this writes in the first row, which are the headers
    writer.writeheader()❹
    # this loops through your rows (the array you set at the beginning and
have updated throughtout)
    for row in rows:❺
        # this takes each row and writes it into your csv
        writer.writerow(row)❻
```

Listing 5-13: Create a .csv file from the collected data

As we did before, we use the with open() as csvfile ❶ statement to
create and open an empty *.csv* file called *all-women-computer-scientists.csv*.
Since we're using a dictionary to gather our data, we need to specify a
list of header names for our spreadsheet ❷ and then use the DictWriter()
function from the csv library ❸ to write each header into the first row ❹.

Finally, we need to loop through each row that we compiled in the rows
list ❺ and write each row into our spreadsheet ❻.

Practicing Polite Scraping

Almost done! We have now written a working script that can gather data
efficiently. But there are two things that we should consider adding to the
script both to be transparent about our efforts and to avoid overloading the
servers that host the data we want to scrape.

First, it's always helpful to provide contact details for your scraper so
the owner of the website you're scraping can contact you if any issues arise.

In some cases, if your scraper is causing trouble, you may be booted from a website. If a website owner has the ability to contact you and tell you to adjust your scraper, however, you're more likely to be able to continue your work on the site.

The Python library we installed for this scraper, requests, comes with a helpful parameter called headers, which we can set whenever we access a page from the web. We can use it to create a data dictionary to hold information that is important for the website owner to know. Add the code from Listing 5-14 to your scraper, substituting your own information for mine.

```
--snip--
headers = {❶"user-agent" : "Mozilla/5.0 (Macintosh; Intel Mac OS X 10_12_6)
AppleWebKit/537.36 (KHTML, like Gecko) Chrome/65.0.3325.162 Safari/537.36",
            ❷ "from": "Your name example@domain.com"}
--snip--
    page = requests.get(url, headers=headers)❸
```

Listing 5-14: Adding headers to your scraper

The code from Listing 5-14 has to be placed *after* the first few lines of our script where we import the libraries, since we need to load the requests library before we can leverage it. Since the headers are variables you set up and won't change throughout the script, you can place them near the top of your script, ideally right after the import lines. The line that calls up the page we want to scrape, page = requests.get(url, headers=headers), is a modification of a line you've already written. Replace the line that currently reads page = requests.get(url) with the new page calling code. This alerts the website owner of your information each time you request to load the URL of the website you want to scrape.

The information assigned to the headers variable is information you exchange with a server when you open a URL through a script. As you can see, all of this information is, once more, structured in JSON with strings that represent keys ("user-agent","from") and values ("Mozilla/5.0 (Macintosh; Intel Mac OS X 10_12_6) AppleWebKit/537.36 (KHTML, like Gecko) Chrome/65.0.3325.162 Safari/537.36","Your name example@domain.com").

First, we can give the website owner information about the kind of user-agent ❶ we're using. While this information is not necessary for bots, it may allow your scraper to open websites that normally can't be opened outside of a web browser. Your scraper can also use the different browsers your computer already has installed to access websites. The user-agent header can communicate information about the browser capabilities our bot might use to open a page within a browser (in this example we don't do this, but this may be a useful habit to adopt early on when you write other bots). To find out what other user-agents you use, you can find various online tools, including one here: *https://www.whoishostingthis.com/tools/user-agent/*.

Then we can specify who we are ❷ within a string assigned to the key from. In this case, you can write your name and an email address into the string to serve as your contact information. To use these headers, we assign them to the headers parameter in the requests.get() ❸ function.

Last but not least, we should also avoid overburdening the servers that host the websites we are scraping. As mentioned earlier, this often happens when a scraper opens multiple pages in rapid succession without taking a break between each request.

For that purpose we can use a library called time, which is part of Python's standard library, so it's already installed. Add the code from Listing 5-15 to your script.

```
--snip--
# Import our libraries that we will need to scrape a website
import csv
import time❶

from bs4 import BeautifulSoup
import requests
time.sleep(2)❷
```

Listing 5-15: Adding pauses in the scraper's code

To use the time library, first we need to import it ❶. Then, we can use a function from it called sleep() ❷, which basically tells our scraper to take a break. The sleep() function takes a number as an argument—an *integer* (whole number) or *float* (number with decimals)—which represents the amount of time, measured in seconds, for the break. In line ❷, our script is instructed to wait for 2 seconds before resuming and scraping data.

If we now stitch together all of the code snippets we've written throughout this chapter, our script should look like Listing 5-16.

```
# Import our modules or packages that we will need to scrape a website
import csv
import time

from bs4 import BeautifulSoup
import requests

# Your identification
headers = {"user-agent" : "Mozilla/5.0 (Windows NT 6.1) AppleWebKit/537.36
(KHTML, like Gecko) Chrome/41.0.2228.0 Safari/537.36;",
          "from": "Your name example@domain.com"}

# make an empty array for your data
rows = []

# open the website
urls = ["https://en.wikipedia.org/wiki/Category:Women_computer_scientists",
"https://en.wikipedia.org/w/index.php?title=Category:Women_computer_scientists
&pagefrom=Lin%2C+Ming+C.%0AMing+C.+Lin#mw-pages"]

def scrape_content(url):
    time.sleep(2)
```

```
        page = requests.get(url, headers= headers)
        page_content = page.content
        # parse the page through the BeautifulSoup library
        soup = BeautifulSoup(page_content, "html.parser")
        content = soup.find("div", class_="mw-category")
        all_groupings = content.find_all("div", class_="mw-category-group")
        for grouping in all_groupings:
            names_list = grouping.find("ul")
            category = grouping.find("h3").get_text()
            alphabetical_names = names_list.find_all("li")
            for alphabetical_name in alphabetical_names:
                # get the name
                name = alphabetical_name.text
                # get the link
                anchortag = alphabetical_name.find("a",href=True)
                link = anchortag["href"]
                # get the letter
                letter_name = category
                # make a data dictionary that will be written into the csv
                row = { "name": name,
                        "link": link,
                        "letter_name": letter_name}
                rows.append(row)

for url in urls:
    scrape_content(url)

# make a new csv into which we will write all the rows
with open("all-women-computer-scientists.csv", "w+") as csvfile:
    # these are the header names:
    fieldnames = ["name", "link", "letter_name"]
    # this creates your csv
    writer = csv.DictWriter(csvfile, fieldnames=fieldnames)
    # this writes in the first row, which are the headers
    writer.writeheader()

    # this loops through your rows (the array you set at the beginning and
have updated throughtout)
    for row in rows:
        # this takes each row and writes it into your csv
        writer.writerow(row)
```

Listing 5-16: The completed scraper script

To run and test your scraper, make sure you are connected to the internet and save your file. Open up your command-line interface (CLI), navigate to the folder that contains the file, and then run one of the following commands in your CLI based on the version of Python you're using. On Mac, use this command:

```
python3 wikipediascraper.py
```

On a Windows machine, use this command:

```
python wikipediascraper.py
```

This should produce a *.csv* file in the folder that contains your *wikipediascraper.py* file.

Summary

All in all, these practices have taught you not only the power of scraping but also the ethical ramifications that your actions may have. Just because you have the capability to do something does not always mean you have free rein to do so. After reading this chapter, you should have all the knowledge you need to gather data *responsibly*.

Happy scraping!

PART II

DATA ANALYSIS

6

INTRODUCTION TO DATA ANALYSIS

The past few chapters were dedicated to finding and gathering data. But now that we have our data, what should we do with it? This chapter will help you understand how to perform simple data analyses.

In many ways, the term *data analysis* describes a very basic action: interviewing a data set. As with any interview, this means you ask questions of your data set. Sometimes these questions aren't particularly complicated, and you can answer them by, say, sorting a column from its largest to smallest value. Other times they're more complex and you need to run multiple analyses to answer them.

This chapter will introduce you to the basic concepts of data analysis through Sheets, a web-based program that Google account holders can access for free. The majority of the features we discuss are also available in Microsoft Excel.

While many of the methodologies and tools we use in this chapter can easily be replicated in Python, it's helpful for beginners to concentrate on the conceptual steps of the analysis before getting too wrapped up in writing code. In other words, it's useful to work out analyses in an interface like Sheets or Excel before executing them as code. To that end, in this chapter we'll walk through the data analysis process using various methods to examine the activity of two Twitter accounts.

The Process of Data Analysis

One common assumption is that data sets are infallible collections of facts that we can just use in our research the same way we received it. Often what we think of as data sets is just *summary data*. But the findings in summary data come from rather messy, wildly varying replies to surveys or other databases of *raw data*—that is, data that has not been processed yet.

Data tables provided by organizations like the US Census Bureau often have been cleaned, processed, and aggregated from thousands— if not millions—of raw data entries, many of which may contain several inconsistencies that data scientists worked to resolve. For example, in a simple table listing people's occupations, these organizations may have resolved different but essentially equivalent responses like "attorney" and "lawyer."

Likewise, the raw data we look at in this book—data from the social web—can be quite irregular and challenging to process because it's produced by real people, each with unique quirks and posting habits. We'll have to summarize it to find the trends and anomalies that answer the questions we're asking. This kind of processing isn't necessarily complicated and difficult; often it just means that we have to go through some tedious yet fairly simple tasks.

There are a few primary methods involved in the process of analyzing data. The ones we'll see in this chapter were adapted from Amanda Cox and Kevin Quealy's New York University data journalism class, available at *http://kpq.github.io/nyu-data-journalism-2014/classes/sort-filter-aggregate-merge/*.

Modifying and formatting   Data is almost never organized consistently or in the format we need. By modifying and formatting it, we can more easily compare values.

Aggregating   We can query our formatted data by applying simple math to it, known as *aggregation*. Aggregating data can take the form of finding the sum of all values within a data column, or it can mean counting the instances of a given value, like how often a name appears in a spreadsheet.

Sorting and filtering   We might simply want to ask our data what the largest or smallest value in any given column or category is. We can often answer these basic questions by sorting and filtering our data. For instance, by sorting a spreadsheet in descending order, we can easily see the largest values at the top of our spreadsheet. Through filtering, we can find out which rows share a particular value.

Merging   One of the most effective techniques to compare two data sets is merging them, or combining them into one set.

In the abstract, these methods may not be very intuitive, but here we'll use them to investigate and better understand the activities of two types of Twitter users: those of an automated bot account, and those of a human.

Bot Spotting

The social web is populated both by real people like you and me, who are on social media to connect with their friends, and by *bots*, which are automated accounts controlled through code. Bots publish content as instructed by scripts (many of which are written in Python!). These bots are not always malicious: some automated accounts publish delightful haikus, and others send you the latest headlines from a news organization.

In this chapter, you'll learn how to use Google Sheets to examine the social media data of a Twitter account that experts at the Digital Forensic Research Lab have identified as a bot. We'll then compare this data to the activity of a real social media user.

NOTE *For more details about the Digital Forensic Research Lab and their research, see https://www.digitalsherlocks.org/.*

Our analysis closely resembles a BuzzFeed News analysis on spotting automated accounts by identifying various characteristics that a Twitter bot may display. Figure 6-1 shows two of the charts BuzzFeed made to illustrate the difference between bot and human activity.

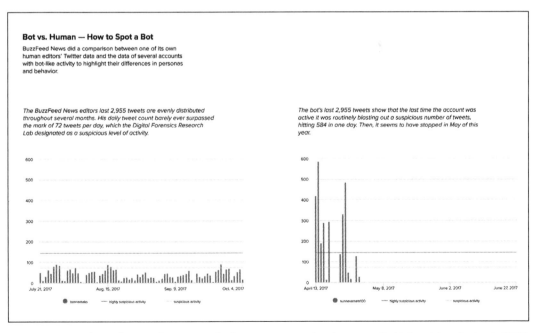

Figure 6-1: Two charts showing the activity of a human compared to the unusually high activity of a bot in 2017

Economically or politically motivated people can use bots to start online debates and steer conversations toward specific topics. In the worst-case scenario, large numbers of bots can be used to grossly exaggerate how many people hold a certain opinion.

While there's no surefire way to nail the identity of false or deceptive online actors, one of the most telltale signs of a bot is when an account tweets more than is humanly possible. So, in this exercise, we want to look at daily activity levels for both a bot and a real human. We'll import, clean, format, and analyze a data set of posts collected from the Twitter account @sunneversets100. In doing so, we'll get acquainted with the helpful tools that Google Sheets offers.

Okay, ready to start bot spotting? Let's go.

Getting Started with Google Sheets

In order to use Sheets, you need a Google account. If you don't already have one, you can sign up for free at *https://accounts.google.com/SignUp*. Once you have an account, navigate to Google Drive (*https://drive.google.com/*), which is cloud-based storage that allows you to organize all your files.

Organizing your data is very important. Like coding, data analysis can take multiple tries to get right, and can involve several steps. Data organization, then, is not just for the sake of neatness but also for the sake of accuracy. The more organized we are, the easier it will be for us to trace our steps, modify our methodology, and reproduce our analysis in the future.

Let's start by making a folder in our Google Drive to store any files related to our data analysis. It's always good practice to keep each of your projects in a folder. Similar to how comments in our scripts are like notes to our future selves about our thought process at the time, the different files and folders we create are a way to help us navigate our analysis. Folders and comments allow us and others to more easily replicate our work, and can complement any other notes we may write up to document the steps of our data analyses. To create a folder, select **New ▸ Folder**.

Next we need to name the folder. Having a clear naming convention for data folders and files is a great way to make sure we and observers alike can clearly understand the folder's purpose. The naming convention you adopt for your projects is up to you, but be consistent. I usually name folders using the date and a few keywords that show what the folder contains, like this: *mmddyyyy-related-keywords*. For this exercise, let's use that convention and name our new folder *04062019-social-media-exercises*.

Now let's create a new spreadsheet file. If you are not already in the new folder, double-click it through the left-hand navigation of Google Drive. When you create a file, it should automatically be stored inside that folder.

To start a new spreadsheet, select **New ▸ Google Sheets ▸ Blank Spreadsheet**. This should pop up a new tab in which the browser loads the new spreadsheet (see Figure 6-2). If you have previously used Microsoft's Excel software, the window should look familiar.

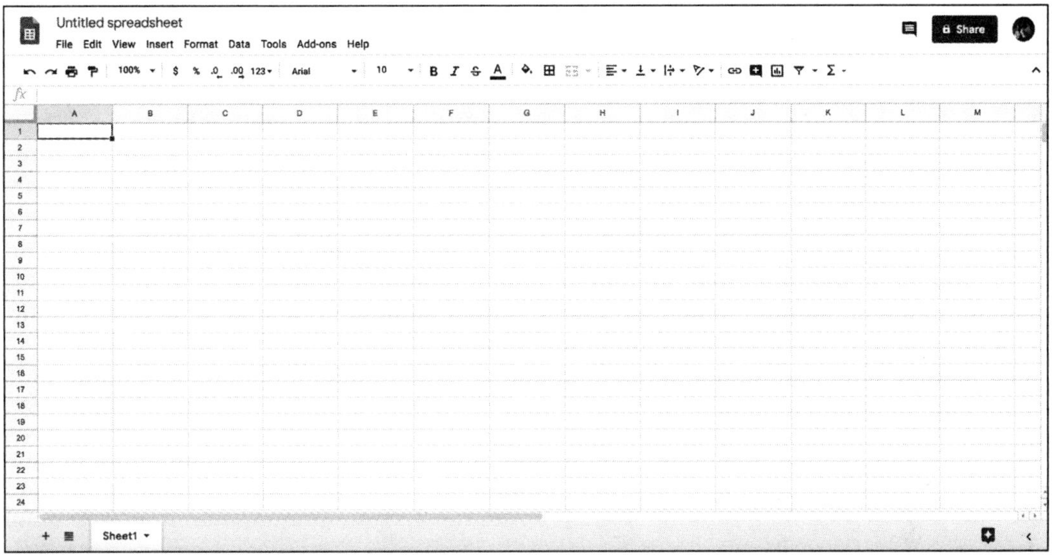

Figure 6-2: A blank spreadsheet

Let's name our spreadsheet file using the same convention we used for the *04062019-social-media-exercises* folder: *04062019-tweet-analysis-@sunneversets100*.

Next, we need to populate our spreadsheet with data. For this exercise, we'll use data from @sunneversets100, a Twitter account that tweets political news, downloaded from the Twitter API (find more information on Twitter's API here: *https://developer.twitter.com/*). These tweets were collected using the social media data scripts, which you can find along with a detailed rundown on how to use them, at *https://github.com/lamthuyvo/social-media-data-scripts/*. The data is collected from the API as a *.csv* file, which is a type of file Google Sheets knows how to interact with to generate a spreadsheet.

To start the import, go to **File ▶ Import ▶ Upload**. When prompted, choose the **Upload** function, navigate to the folder where you downloaded the @sunneversets100 data, and upload the *.csv* sheet.

Google Sheets should ask you to select import options. Select **Import Location**, **Separator Type**, and **Convert to Numbers and Dates**. Select **Replace Current Sheet** as your import location—this is how we populate our current empty sheet with the Twitter data. Because the data is formatted as a *.csv* file, select **Comma** as the separator. (You can also allow Sheets to automatically detect the separator, which will often work just as well.) Finally, when Sheets asks to convert text to numbers and dates, select **No**.

Understanding how text conversion works is important when it comes to data analysis, be it in Sheets, Python, or any other tool. Formatting or, as Sheets refers to it here, "converting text," is vital for programming languages. Software like Sheets recognizes the difference between a string (in other words, text) and other types of data like integers, floats (numbers), or datetimes. While we humans can determine whether a value represents a date, number, or word based on how it's written, most software and programming languages can't automatically do the same, so they often need to make a sophisticated guess. If we were to select Yes under the import option Convert Text to Numbers and Dates, Google Sheets would do just that: it would try to guess which value is a number, date, or word. This is a step we shouldn't automate. For instance, we'd want to interpret ZIP codes as text, not as numbers, since ZIP codes act like labels for an area even though they contain only numbers. If we left it up to Google Sheets, though, it would likely convert them to numbers and potentially lose information (ZIP codes starting with a zero would lose that first digit, for example). When it comes to guesswork, leave as little as possible to automation.

Once you've followed all the preceding steps, you should have a spreadsheet that looks like Figure 6-3.

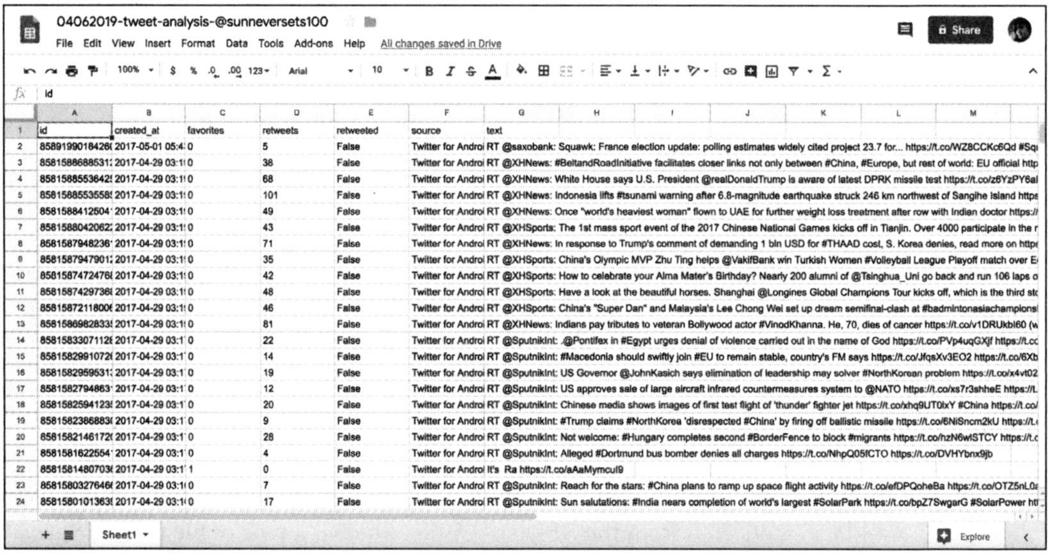

Figure 6-3: Imported and unchanged data in a spreadsheet

All right! Now we're ready to do some data processing!

Modifying and Formatting the Data

To effectively use the Sheets functions, we need to make sure that Sheets is interpreting each data column properly. This is where *formatting* comes in handy. However, before you start changing your spreadsheet, we need to do one of the most important steps in data analysis: make a copy of the original, unchanged data set.

Humans are fallible. We should always triple-check our data manipulations and calculations, but we should also make sure we can go back to the original data set in case we make a mistake along the way. While Google Sheets, like other Google products, automatically tracks your changes as you work (see File ▸Version History), you should always keep a copy of the data in a format that is easily accessible and allows you to reference it as you do your analyses. That way, you won't need to pull up older versions of your spreadsheet when you want to see how the data originally looked.

The easiest way to do this is to create a copy of the sheet for each step of the data analysis and rename it accordingly. This can be particularly helpful when we create, change, or remove values or entire columns from our data set. Destructive modifications of our data may be hard to undo later, so tracking our steps through multiple sheets can make things easier in the long run.

First, go to the bottom of the sheet, double-click the **Sheet 1** sheet tab, and give it a name describing the content. In this case, we rename the first sheet **raw data**. Then, to duplicate the sheet, click the arrow by the sheet name and select **Duplicate** from the menu that pops up, as shown in Figure 6-4.

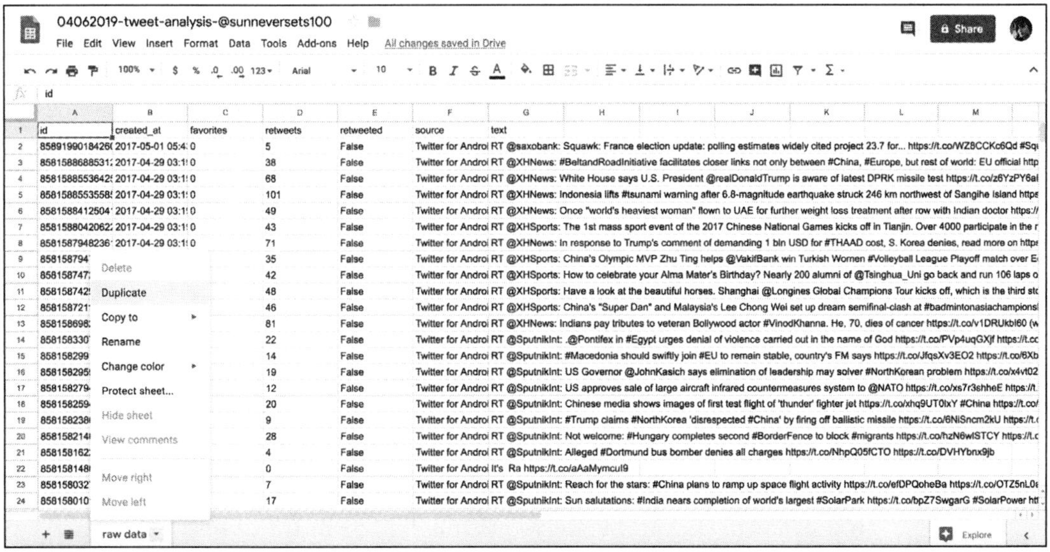

Figure 6-4: Duplicating sheets

This should open a second sheet, which we can also rename. For this exercise, call it **step 1: modify and format**. This is the spreadsheet we'll use to apply our formatting. In the step 1 spreadsheet, select the column that contains the counts of favorites for each tweet by clicking the letter above the column header (in this case, the values we're interested in are the timestamps in column B). The entire column should be highlighted blue. Then, select **Format ▸ Number ▸ Number**, as shown in Figure 6-5.

This transforms every value in that column from a string to a number. You'll need to repeat these steps for the retweets column, which also contains numbers.

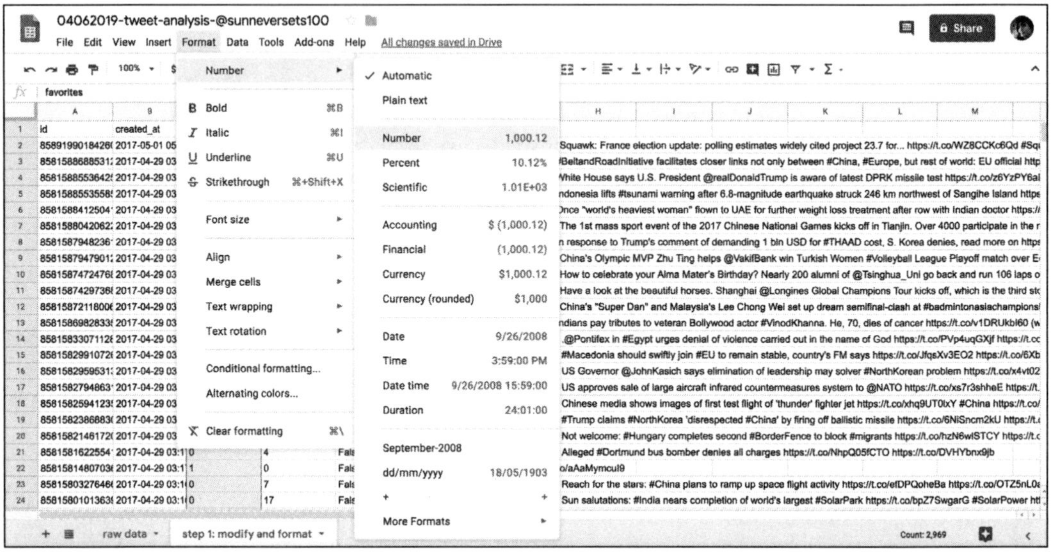

Figure 6-5: Spreadsheet formatting options

Note that the timestamp that we get from the API is very granular and representative of how Twitter structures and stores it in databases. Granularity in data is great. It allows us to aggregate our data in various ways: we can see the exact time when the tweet was sent, down to the second, or look at the date when the tweet was published. To access these different kinds of data summaries, though, first we'll need to modify our data.

As I've mentioned, data analysis often consists of the tedious and sometimes groan-inducing process of getting the data into the right format. Particularly for data created by humans, this means that we need to clean data before we can compare values. For example, if we were collecting tweet text data, we may need to resolve various spellings of the same word (for example, "gray" versus "grey") or remove misspellings and typos. For data that is collected through code or by robots, we may need to modify the data by separating it into various parts or finding different ways to combine it. In the case of the timestamp data, for example, we may want to separate the date of a tweet's publication from the time of day when it was sent.

Let's quickly recall what our task is: we are analyzing a suspected bot's Twitter activity to distinguish it from human activity. We can do this by looking at the average number of times per day the suspected account @sunneversets100 tweets. Experts say that bot activity is unusually high compared to human tweeting. According to the Digital Forensic Research Lab, tweeting 72 or more times per day is suspicious, and tweeting 144 or more times per day is *highly* suspicious. Now we can use Sheets to determine whether @sunneversets100's activity levels are suspiciously high.

Currently, our timestamp data displays both the date and the time to the second that a tweet was posted, like this: 2017-05-01 05:43:57. We can get a daily tally of tweets @sunneversets100 published by counting how many times any given date shows up in our raw data. To accomplish this task, we'll use a Sheets feature called pivot tables. But to use pivot tables, first we have to create a new column that contains only the date that each tweet was posted. We need to modify the column containing the entire timestamp by removing the hours, minutes, and seconds so we're left with only the dates.

One simple way to separate the data is to use the Split Text to Columns tool under the Data menu. This built-in tool looks for repeating characteristics within column values. Once it detects a pattern, it will try to split the value into two columns. Patterns could include things like a first and a last name separated by a comma (like "Smith, Paul") or, in this case, a date and a time separated by a space.

To use the tool, first we'll create an empty column to the right of our created_at column. Right-click the letter above the created_at column and select **Insert 1 right** from the menu. Now we can use the Split Text to Columns tool without overwriting any other data. Click the letter of the column containing the timestamp data, and then select **Data ▸ Split Text to Columns.**

You'll be prompted to choose a separator through a small pop-up menu. The separator defaults to Detect Automatically, but since we've determined that the part separating our date and time is a space, we can choose **Space.** The tool should leave the values to the left of the separator in the current column and move the content to the right of the separator in the new column we just created.

This tool works best with data that has been formatted as plaintext, which Sheets interprets as a string. Remember when we first we imported our data and Sheets asked to convert the text to numbers and dates, we selected No. That ensured that each data cell would be interpreted as a string of characters rather than as numbers or dates. For this exercise, it is best to manipulate our values as strings before we format them as any other data types.

We'll often need to reformat entire columns to tell Sheets how to interpret each data type. We can only take advantage of date-based functions if a string is formatted as a date like those in the created_at column. Likewise, mathematical operations can be done only on values that have been formatted as numbers.

We don't need to change the format for the data values in our spreadsheet just yet. For housekeeping's sake, however, we should rename our new columns. Name the column with the newly isolated dates **date** and the column with the newly isolated times **time**.

Et voilà! We have split the values of one column into two and can now proceed to count how often a date occurs.

Aggregating the Data

We've now completed the basic steps to set up data for analysis. First, we imported the data into Sheets, and then we modified it so it's formatted in a way that allows us to analyze it. Now that the data is prepared, we can move on to the next step of the data analysis process: aggregating the data. We'll use two Sheets features to do so: pivot tables and formulas.

Using Pivot Tables to Summarize Data

Pivot tables are one of the most powerful features of Sheets. They allow us to summarize large amounts of detailed data and analyze it in various ways—for example, we can count the number of times a term occurs in a column or calculate the sum of numerical values based on a date or category. In other words, pivot tables give us a bird's-eye view of a large amount of data in an easy-to-navigate interface. They do so by creating a *summary table*, which includes statistical information about our raw data, like the total number of times a value occurs inside a column.

We can use pivot tables to find the frequency of each date in our Twitter data set. Since we know that each row in our data set represents information about an individual tweet, we can safely say that the number of times a specific date appears also represents the number of tweets the @sunneversets100 account published on any given day.

To do this analysis, first we need to select the data we want included in our pivot table. To select all the data in the *step 2: modify and format* sheet, click the rectangle above the first row and to the left of the first column. Then select **Data ▶ Pivot Table…** (see Figure 6-6) and select the option New Sheet when Sheets asks where to insert the Pivot table. This should open up a new sheet called *Pivot Table 1.*

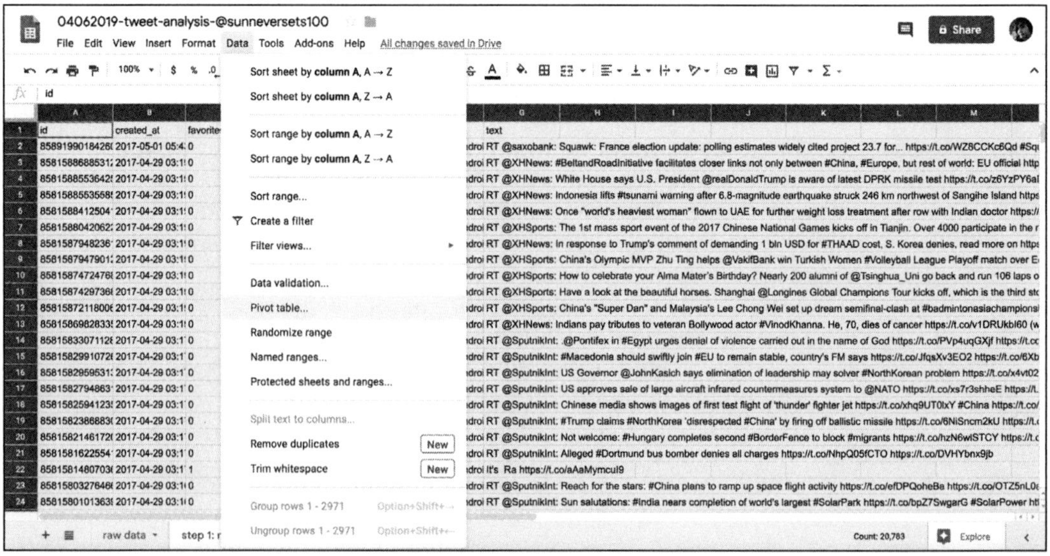

Figure 6-6: Accessing pivot tables in the Data menu

On the right-hand side of the newly created sheet, Sheets offers a number of options to populate our pivot table. We want to populate our rows with the dates we isolated in our column.

Select **Rows ▸ Add**, and then select the **date** column from the drop-down menu. Once you've selected the date column, Sheets creates a row for every date that occurs in the data set. Then we need to tell the pivot table what kind of values to display for the summarized dates. These values will appear in a column next to the dates.

We want to count how many times each unique date occurs. Click **Values ▸ Add**, choose the **date** column again, and select the kind of math you want Sheets to perform on the data. In this case, there are two options that sound like they might work for our analysis: COUNT and COUNTA. We'll choose **COUNTA** since COUNT works only with data formatted as a number. You can think of COUNTA as a tool that can count anything.

This creates a pivot table that summarizes the number of times a date occurs in the detailed data set (Figure 6-7). This pivot table allows us to make an initial assessment of the @sunneversets100 account. We know that an account tweeting 72 or more times a day is suspicious, and that an account tweeting 144 or more times is highly suspicious. Are there days when this account tweets 72 or more times a day? Certainly! Are there days when it tweets more than 144 times? Indeed! On the busiest day, the account tweeted *586 times.* That means @sunneversets100 tweeted roughly every 2.5 minutes over a 24-hour period, which doesn't sound like something a normal person would do if they just wanted to share their thoughts with the world.

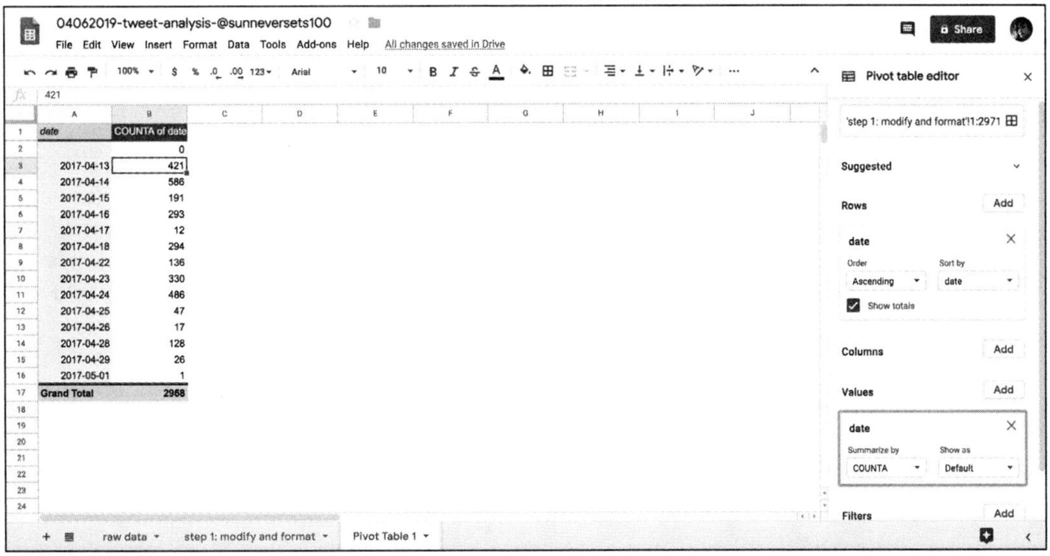

Figure 6-7: The pivot table we generated by using COUNTA to find the occurrences of each date

Using Formulas to Do Math

We just used a pivot table to answer an important question about our data: how often does a particular Twitter account tweet per day? Using this tool allowed us to look at the days when the bot tweeted a number of times that's considered suspiciously high for a human user. Tweeting behavior, however, can vary from day to day. Even if an account tweeted 72 or more times one day, that doesn't necessarily mean the account is *consistently* tweeting a suspicious number of times.

Let's say we need to also find the average number of tweets that the account published. We'll use a new feature to answer our question—welcome to the joy of formulas!

You can think of formulas as functions that are built into Sheets. Sheets distinguishes between ordinary data and formulas through an equal sign (=). All formulas consist of an equal sign followed by a function name and an open and closing parenthesis—for example, =lower(A2).

I often tell my students that if they are using formulas in Excel or Sheets, they are already doing rudimentary coding. Like Python functions, formulas have strict rules (that is, syntax), take arguments, and allow us to create new values based on the interaction between those rules and arguments.

For example, we used the Python len() function and passed it the string "apple pie" to find the length of that string in Chapter 1:

```
>>> len("apple pie")
9
```

Sheets has a formula called len that accomplishes exactly the same thing. To use it, open a new spreadsheet and enter the following into the top-left cell:

```
=len("apple pie")
```

The cell that you used to write your formula should display the number 9.

What's even more exciting is that we can pass spreadsheet cells to the formulas as arguments. We specify a cell as an argument by finding its coordinates on the spreadsheet using its column letter and its row number, which can be found at the top and the left-hand side of the spreadsheet, respectively.

Next, enter **apple pie** into the second cell in the first column. This means the cell is in column A and row 2. We can find the length of this string by replacing "apple pie" with the cell coordinates A2 in the formula stored in the first cell, like so (note that we do not use quotation marks when we use cell coordinates):

```
=len(A2)
```

We can also pass multiple cells to some formulas. The syntax to select multiple cells changes depending on which cells we're trying to select.

To return to our data analysis, we want to find the average number of posts tweeted by the @sunneversets100 account. We can use the aptly named =average() formula to do so.

The =average() formula takes a group of cells and finds the average of their values. The formula allows you to select individual cells or cells in ranges. For example, we can get the average of all the cells in our pivot table by passing the =average() formula a list of cells, each separated by a comma:

```
=average(B2,B3,B4,B5,B6,B7,B8,B9,B10,B11,B12,B13,B14,B15)
```

A clearer and more convenient way to use the =average() formula, though, is to use a colon to select a range of consecutive cells. The range starts in the cell specified before the colon and includes all cells through the cell specified after the colon.

To get the average of cells B2 through B15, for instance, we use this formula:

```
=sum(B2:B15)
```

To select an entire column, we can use the colon without any row specifications like this: =average(A:A). The same goes for rows: =average(2:2). Sheets also allows us to select cells from a different sheet of the same file by specifying the sheet name in quotation marks followed by an exclamation mark, like this: =average('Sheet 1'!A:A).

One last way to select cells is by using your cursor. Select an empty cell and start by writing the formula up until the opening parenthesis. For this exercise, we'll reuse the =len() formula, so enter **=len(**. Then use your cursor to select a cell that you want to pass to the formula. In this case, select the cell **A2**. This should autopopulate the formula with the cell coordinates. Add a closing parenthesis. The completed formula =len(A2) should display 9 so long as cell A2 contains the words "apple pie."

Now that you've seen how formulas work, you can go back to the Twitter analysis and apply what you have learned. Go back to your pivot table and enter the formula =average(B2:B15) into an empty cell. Once you hit return, you should see that the average number of tweets per day from the @sunneversets100 account is 212. Still suspiciously high!

Google Sheets comes with countless formulas like these. For instance, if we enter the formula =sum() into a cell and select a column of numbers, we can find the sum for those values.

One great thing about formulas is that we can copy and paste them into multiple cells to perform the same actions on several columns or rows of data. Even better, Sheets allows for smart copying and pasting. To see how that works, return to the *step 1: modify and format* sheet.

Say we wanted to measure the length of each tweet in our spreadsheet. We could create a new column to the right of column H, which contains each tweet's text. If we enter the formula =len(H2) into cell I2, copy the formula, and then paste it in all the rows following I2, Sheets is smart enough to figure out the length of each tweet, not just the tweet at H2 that the original formula refers to.

This is because Sheets doesn't copy just the actual letters of the formula; it has built-in logic that alters the formula's arguments in relation to the cell in which it is applied. In other words, Sheets remembers that we're trying to measure the length of the tweet right next to the cell that contains the formula, not the cell in position I2.

We cannot possibly cover every formula available through Sheets, but one handy tool to keep in mind for the future is the small helper window Sheets shows when it detects that you're using formulas. The window pops up when you begin entering a formula and usually displays information about what type of arguments the formula takes, shows you an example of how the formula may be used, and spells out what data the formula outputs, as shown in Figure 6-8. It's not a complete glossary of formulas, but it's a good place to start experimenting.

With pivot tables and formulas, you now have the tools to execute simple operations to answer questions about a data set in just a few clicks. More importantly, hopefully you've also seen that you can answer data queries in more than one way.

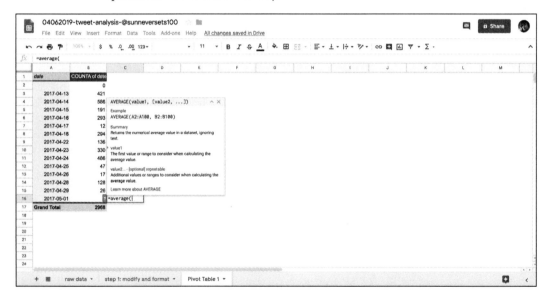

Figure 6-8: The pop-up formula helper window in Sheets

Sorting and Filtering the Data

Now that you know how to import, modify, and aggregate data, the next step is sorting and filtering the results in order to rank or isolate the data we're looking for.

Ranking data findings from largest to smallest or vice versa is a good way to assign a hierarchy to results and makes it much easier to communicate them. Within the context of our analysis, we can sort the data in our pivot table to get an idea of how often the suspected bot account tweeted on its busiest day. One way to do so is by creating a new sheet with our aggregate results and changing the entire sheet to a *filter view*.

First, select the findings of the pivot table by clicking and dragging your cursor across all the cells you want to include in the sorted table. Once you have the cells highlighted, copy the selection by right-clicking inside one of the highlighted cells and selecting **Copy** (or use the shortcut CMD-C for Mac, or CTRL-C for PC).

Then, as with the other steps, follow best practices by creating a new sheet to use for sorting the pivot table data. To populate this sheet with the pivot table results, we'll use a method called *paste special*.

Because copying in Sheets copies formulas and pivot table functionalities to the new spreadsheet, we won't be able to modify the actual values that are represented in our pivot table. Luckily for us, though, Sheets allows us to paste values based on the results of formulas and pivot tables. Right-click in the cell in the first row and first column of your new sheet and select **Paste Special ▸ Paste Values Only**. That should paste the values, rather than the formulas, into the cells. When you paste these values, they'll be stripped of any formatting. This means that the dates we copied and pasted into the new cells may be formatted as strings of integers. To format them into dates again, use your cursor to highlight the cells containing the dates, right-click inside one of the highlighted cells, and select **Format ▸ Number ▸ Date**.

Now we need to select the data we want to turn into a filter view. The easiest way to select all the data in the current sheet is to click the blank rectangle next to the first column and above the first row. Next, click the little arrow next to the filter icon (which looks like a funnel) and, with the cells selected, select **Create New Filter View** (Figure 6-9).

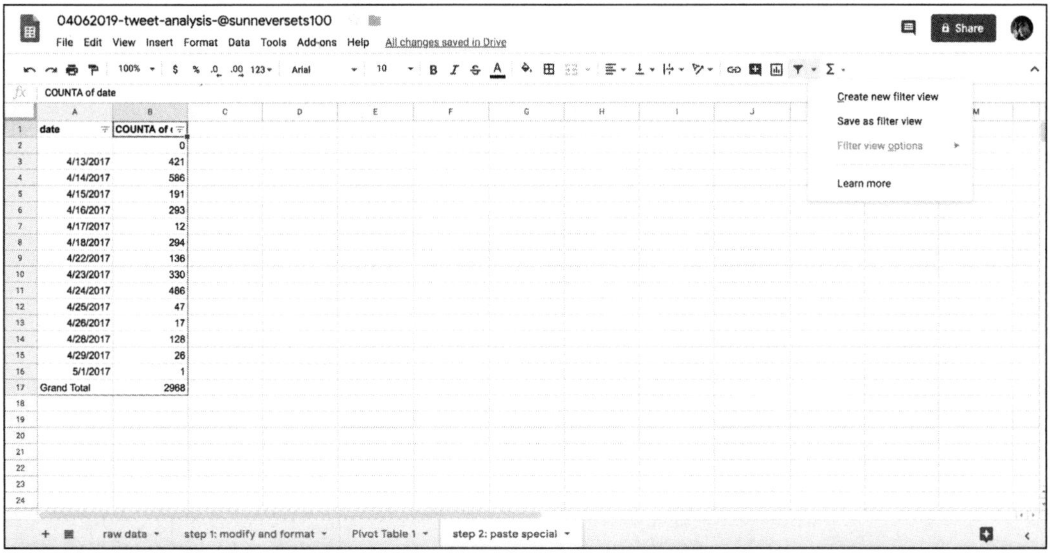

Figure 6-9: Filter view options in Google Drive

The Filter View tool allows us to access various functionalities for each column, such as filtering our data by values or conditions (for instance, we can filter our tables to display only values greater than 100). We can also sort the data. This tool doesn't modify our data set—it merely changes the order in which we see our data or which parts of it are visible (when we filter out values, we're not deleting them; they're just hidden while the filter is applied).

Let's look at our filter options. By clicking the triangle next to each column header, we can filter our spreadsheet to show only subsections of our overall data set. We can select and deselect values within each column and hide or show rows based on whether they contain each value.

Filtering can be helpful when we're interested in analyzing only a subset of our data. It's commonly used to isolate raw data based on a minimum or maximum threshold or on a certain time frame. The filter options can also help us ask more specific questions of our data set. In our tweet analysis, for instance, we may be interested only in tweets that have at least 100 retweets. Alternatively, we may want to look at tweets that were published within a specific month.

We can also filter values based on a condition, or *conditional*—a concept we explored earlier while discussing Python. Google Sheets has a number of handy conditionals built into its filter tool that allow us to filter our data based on fairly simple conditions. If we select the Filter by Condition ▸ Cell Is Not Empty option, for instance, our sheet will show only cells that have data (see Figure 6-10).

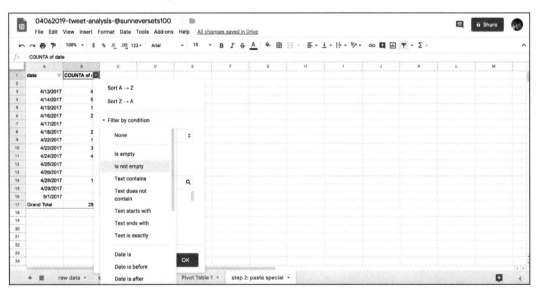

Figure 6-10: Filter options in Google Drive

Finally, we can sort our data using the Sort A→Z and Sort Z→A options. Sort A→Z allows us to sort our rows in *ascending* order: from smallest numerical value to largest, from earliest to latest date, or from

A to Z in alphabetical order. Sort Z→A sorts our data in *descending* order, which is the reverse of ascending order.

Sorting a data set may help you answer one of many research questions you have. For our Twitter analysis, this might include questions like these: What was the earliest tweet sent by this account? What was the latest? Which tweet garnered the most favorites? Which one got the most retweets? Try filtering the data to answer these questions.

Merging Data Sets

The last method we'll consider for our data analysis is *merging*, or *joining*, data sets. Comparing one data set to another is one of the most powerful ways of using tools like Sheets. By merging two sheets, we can easily compare values based on a common category.

We should be cautious about drawing major conclusions about the relationship between data sets, however. Correlation is not the same as causation. This means even though two data sets may seem like they have a relationship—that is, the data sets seem correlated—that doesn't mean that one data set *caused* the results in the other. Correlational and causational connections between data sets should be backed by other research from reports, experts, or field studies. But even the simplest comparisons between two or more data sets can be very illustrative.

So how do we join two tables in Sheets? We can use a handy formula called =vlookup() to help us cross-reference two spreadsheets and merge them based on a common value. We use this formula by referencing one value and looking it up in a table that serves as a dictionary.

For instance, to compare the tweet activity of @sunneversets100 to that of a Twitter account operated by an actual human—you—during the first two weeks of 2017, you can walk through the same steps you did for @sunneversets100 with your own account. If you don't have a Twitter account, you can make a copy of a spreadsheet (*https://github.com/lamthuyvo /social-media-data-book*), which has the information for the human-managed @nostarch account (*https://twitter.com/nostarch/*).

To merge the two spreadsheets, first create another tab within your spreadsheet. You'll soon populate the left column with the dates you're interested in—in this case, the data from the first half of 2017 since that's the time period when @sunneversets100 was tweeting. We can call this column merged_counts_sunneversets100_<*account*> where <*account*> is the name of the human-controlled Twitter account.

For a time series, we could enter a column header at the top called *date* and then fill in a date for each row. We'll start in cell A2 with the earliest date, 4/13/2017. Enter this date into the spreadsheet. Then in A3 enter **4/14/2017**. We want the rest of the rows in the columns to contain dates until we reach the last date that @sunneversets100 tweeted, 5/01/2017. Instead of entering each date individually, you can use some convenient Sheets functionality to fill in the rest of the column. Enter two dates, select them, and then mouse over the bottom-right corner of the second cell until your cursor turns into a little cross. Then either double-click or click and drag the cross down to row 20. Sheets will autopopulate the rows based on the pattern it detects in the first two cells.

Next we need to merge the pivot table of @sunneversets100's tweets with the sheet that contains our dates using the `=vlookup()` formula, which looks at a value in one table, looks up the value in another table, and then retrieves data based on this common value. Before we do that, though, set up a new column for @sunneversets100's daily tweet counts right next to the date column.

There are four arguments that the `=vlookup()` formula uses within its parentheses. First, it wants to know which value you want to look up:

```
=vlookup(A2, ...)
```

This is the value `=vlookup()` will look up in another table. In this case, the A2 cell should contain the first date in our series of dates, 4/13/2017.

For the second argument, the formula wants to know which range represents the reference table or dictionary where we'll look up our value.

```
=vlookup(A2, 'Pivot Table 1'!A:B, ...)
```

In our case, this is the range of values that represents the table where we'll look up the value in cell A2 (4/13/2017). We first specify as a string the name of the sheet containing our lookup table and the daily counts of tweets for @sunneversets100 (in this case, `'Pivot Table 1'`), followed by an exclamation mark (!), indicating that `'Pivot Table 1'` is the name of a different sheet. After that, just as we did when selecting cells earlier, we need to specify the columns where the values of our lookup table live, which in this case are columns A and B, represented in Sheets as `A:B`.

The range we selected should include the column we'll use to join our data sets (the dates in column A) as well as the values we want to use to populate our new and merged table (the counts in column B). In this case, we need to ensure that the column A contains the dates because we're trying to find the date represented in cell A2 (4/13/2017) within that column. With pivot tables, we always need to make sure that the first column in our range contains the values we're looking up.

Once Sheets finds the date represented in cell A2 (4/13/2017) in column A of our `'Pivot Table 1'`, it will inspect the row that contains the date 4/13/2017 and then look for a value in that row that it's supposed to transfer over to our merged data set. This is where the third argument of the `vlookup()` formula comes into play: `vlookup()` requires us to tell it which column contains the values we want to splice into our new merged table. And, to complicate things, it wants to know the column position relative to the first column of our range. In our case, this data lives in the column next to the date column and hence represents column number 2 within our range.

```
=vlookup(A2, 'Pivot Table 1'!A:B , 2, ...)
```

It may help to imagine Sheets going through these two tables like a directionless robot that wants really foolproof instructions on what to do. So far, with this formula, we've told Sheets to remember the date contained in cell A2 (4/13/2017). Then we told Sheets to wander over to Pivot Table 1 and sift through columns A and B to find the date 4/13/2017. Once it finds the row in column A that contains the date, we want it to go to the second column (or column 2) of the range that we selected via 'Pivot Table 1'!A:B.

Almost there! Last we need to explain to =vlookup() whether the range we're looking at has been sorted in the same order as the table we created for our data merge. In this case we choose FALSE (for safety's sake, it's good to default to FALSE, since selecting this option will return the correct results even if the lookup table *has* been sorted in the same order as the current table).

```
=vlookup(A2, 'Pivot Table 1'!A:B, 2, FALSE)
```

To run this formula across an entire column for the time frame we designated—April 13 to May 1, 2017—we can copy and paste it into the entire column. As mentioned before, Sheets allows for smart copying and pasting and will run each formula for each date, instead of just pasting the same formula verbatim into each cell, which would apply our formula only to cell A2.

Once you do this, the cells in the @sunneversets100 column should now contain a series of formulas.

If we replicate the process we followed for @sunneversets100 with the human Twitter account, we get a new merged table that allows us to see the data side by side, as shown in Figure 6-11.

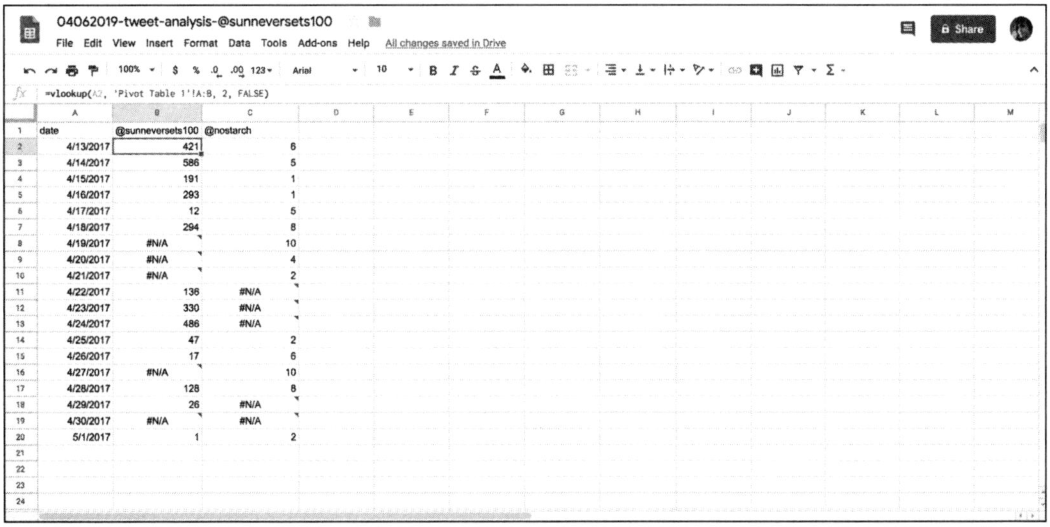

Figure 6-11: Our analysis, with errors rendered in cells where the vlookup() formula was unable to retrieve data from a lookup table

You can see that some of our results are #N/A, which means *not available* and indicates that our formula returned an error. This is because there's no data for some of the dates that we generated for our pivot tables. These are dates when the account @sunneversets100 or the human account didn't tweet.

To avoid these errors, we should fill the cells that currently contain #N/A with the numerical value 0. One way to do this is to modify our current formula so it can handle an error when one occurs. This is an important concept to keep in mind during your analyses, since this issue often recurs throughout a programmer's workflow.

Sheets provides a helpful formula called =iferror() that we can use here. The =iferror() formula takes two arguments. The first is the formula we want to run on the cell—in this case, vlookup(). Since we've already written that formula, we just have to nest it and its arguments inside our iferror() formula.

Here's how the iferror() formula should look with its first argument:

```
=iferror(vlookup(A2, 'Pivot Table 1'!A:B, 2, FALSE), ...)
```

NOTE   *We don't need the equal sign for the vlookup() formula here; we only need one at the beginning of a cell to indicate to Sheets that we're going to use a formula.*

The second argument iferror() takes is the value that Sheets should fall back to in case the first argument—in this case, our vlookup() formula—returns an error. For our purposes, we want that fallback value to be 0. That's because our pivot table aggregated the number of tweets only for dates in our data set on which tweets were published, and we want to include the other dates as well to eliminate the #N/A results.

The finished iferror() formula should look like this:

```
=iferror(vlookup(A2, 'Pivot Table 1'!A:B, 2, FALSE), 0)
```

Once we've replicated the formula across both columns, the merged table should show two columns side by side (see Figure 6-12).

As you can see, a bot tweets a lot more than the human account we analyzed. While this is not the most statistically representative analysis, this anecdotal data can still help us understand how automated accounts may compare to the accounts of real human beings.

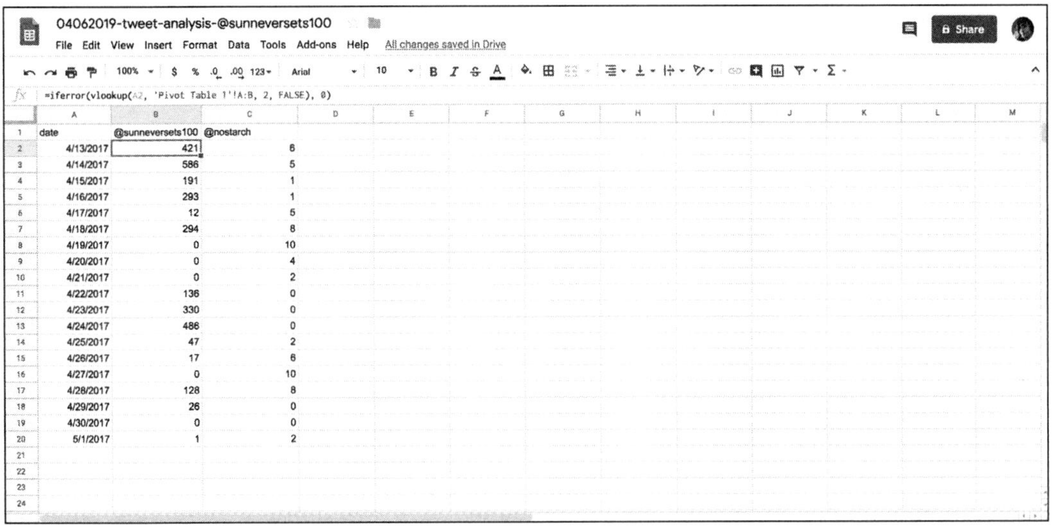

Figure 6-12: What our finished spreadsheet should look like

Furthermore, we've learned some very important principles. You now know you need to modify and format your data for a computer to truly understand it. You've learned how to aggregate raw data into larger summaries based on categories. You've learned that sorting and filtering your data can bring clarity to your analysis by showing hierarchy. And you've learned about the power of merging data sets. These concepts will play into a lot of the work you do both in Sheets and in Python. They should help guide your thought processes as you continue to develop your skills as a data analyst.

Other Ways to Use Google Sheets

This chapter introduced a number of different functionalities within Google Sheets, but the program has numerous other capabilities that we didn't have the space to discuss here. Google has a handy manual that walks through some of them here: *https://support.google.com/docs/answer/6000292?hl=en&ref _topic=2811806/*.

It may be worth digging further into other formulas available in Sheets. Some of the most popular formulas are often used to manipulate strings or to do math (you can find a long list of them here: *https://support.google.com /docs/table/25273/*).

Eventually, you may even want to write your own custom functions if you find yourself performing the same tasks over and over again. Here's a handy walk-through of how you can do that: *https://developers.google.com /apps-script/guides/sheets/functions/*.

Sheets is capable of dealing with a large number of simple analyses and has a wealth of resources available online, which may cover your needs. But it does have its limitations, especially when it comes to the amount of data it can handle before it freezes or slows. We'll look at the Python library pandas in a later chapter for analyses that resemble some of those we covered here, but on a much larger scale.

Summary

In this chapter, you saw how to conduct simple data analysis with Google Sheets: you learned how to import and organize data in Sheets, how to ask specific questions of a data set, and how to answer those questions by modifying, sorting, filtering, and aggregating the data.

In the next chapter, we'll build on the analysis we started in this chapter and learn how to better understand our findings with visuals. We'll use tools like conditional formatting and charts to interpret and communicate our results more efficiently.

7

VISUALIZING YOUR DATA

So far you've learned how to collect, process, and crunch data from social media. The next step of data analysis is to harness the power of *visualizations* to make better sense of your findings.

Visualizations are effective ways to understand data almost instantly. A chart, for instance, can help us grasp how our data behaves over time. A color-coded spreadsheet can deliver a clear picture of the range of values in a data set.

In this chapter, we'll discuss how to use visualizations with the Twitter bot data we analyzed in the previous chapter. We'll use charting tools and visual formatting in Google Sheets to gain a deeper understanding of this data.

Understanding Our Bot Through Charts

In Chapter 6, we used a standard developed by the Digital Forensic Research Lab to determine whether the Twitter user @sunneversets100 was an automated "bot" account rather than an actual person. As a reminder, tweeting 72 or more times per day is suspicious activity that indicates an account might be a bot, and tweeting 144 or more times a day is considered *highly* suspicious behavior. We found that there were many days when @sunneversets100 tweeted quite a bit more than either threshold.

At the end of that chapter, we also looked at how the bot's behavior compares to that of a normal person. Figure 7-1 shows the results.

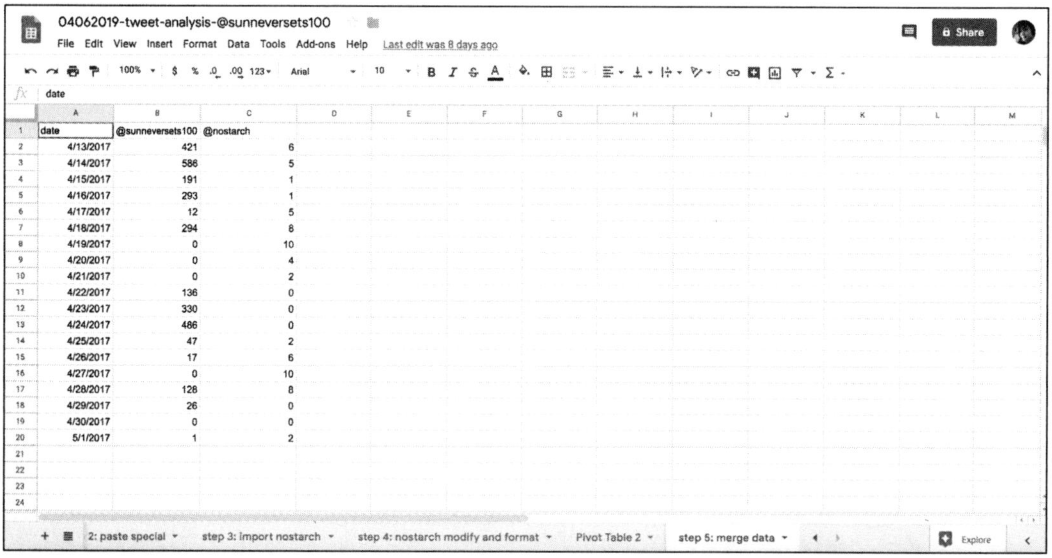

date	@sunneversets100	@nostarch
4/13/2017	421	6
4/14/2017	586	5
4/15/2017	191	1
4/16/2017	293	1
4/17/2017	12	5
4/18/2017	294	8
4/19/2017	0	10
4/20/2017	0	4
4/21/2017	0	2
4/22/2017	136	0
4/23/2017	330	0
4/24/2017	486	0
4/25/2017	47	2
4/26/2017	17	6
4/27/2017	0	10
4/28/2017	128	8
4/29/2017	26	0
4/30/2017	0	0
5/1/2017	1	2

Figure 7-1: A spreadsheet comparing the tweet activity of a suspected bot account with an account controlled by a person

The spreadsheet clearly shows that @sunneversets100 tweets a lot more than the user chosen as a comparison. But it can be difficult to comprehend how numbers compare to one another just by reading about the findings in text or looking at the values in a spreadsheet. This is where data visualizations like charts can help.

Choosing a Chart

Charts and data-driven graphics can give us an instant understanding of a larger context. We can use shapes (for example, circles, rectangles, or lines) and colors to compare values, including how they change over time. These visualizations can help our audiences see patterns or key findings at a glance.

Before we can use them, though, we need to learn about the different types of charts. Some chart types are known mostly within the circles of statisticians or data crunchers, while others are more familiar to the general public. With that in mind, it's important to recognize that any given chart may be very effective at conveying one type of data, but completely fail to convey another. For that reason, we need to consider *what* we want to show using the chart. As you learned earlier, data analysis is a bit like interviewing. Determining an answer for each question requires a slightly different set of tools, and asking questions of our data set can help us determine what kind of chart to use for finding answers.

Choosing the right chart can be tricky, but lucky for us, there are numerous guides that scholars and graphics editors have developed to help. One example is the one-page "Chart Suggestions—A Thought-Starter," a flowchart of some of the most common types of data visualizations, shown in Figure 7-2.

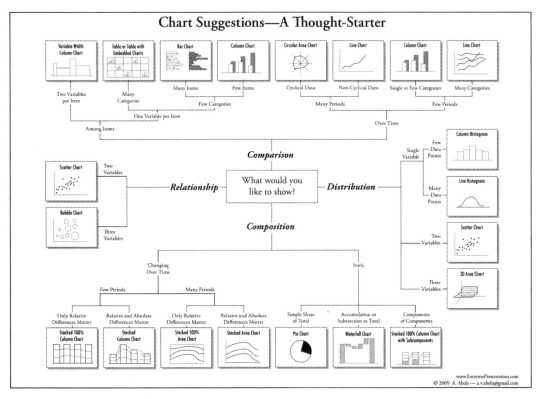

Figure 7-2: A guide developed by Andrew Abela, © Andrew V. Abela, 2012. Abela, A. Advanced Presentation by Design.

Let's break down the different chart types and how they are used. First, there are *comparisons* between different data sets. For instance, in our previous analysis we compared two data sets: one of a bot and one of a human.

One common comparison chart is a column chart like the one shown in Figure 7-3, which plots the merged pivot tables from Figure 7-1 (you'll learn how to make these charts later in this chapter).

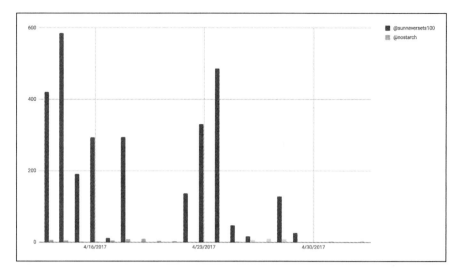

Figure 7-3: A column chart comparing the activities of a bot and a person

In addition to using charts to compare individual data points, you can use them to compare the *distribution*, or range of values, of a data set. Imagine dividing up your entire data set into buckets—for example, age brackets or grades (A to A–, B+ to B–, and so forth)—and then counting how many or what percentage of them occur in each bucket. That's a basic way to understand distributions.

Returning to the @sunneversets100 data, for instance, we could look at the distribution of retweets that each tweet received. In the "raw data" spreadsheet pictured in Figure 6-3 on page 106, you'll see that the retweet values range from 0 to 1–100, 101–200, 201–300, and so on.

Consulting the flow chart in Figure 7-2 for guidance again, we see that for data with a small distribution like ours, we should use a simple *column graph* like the one in Figure 7-4.

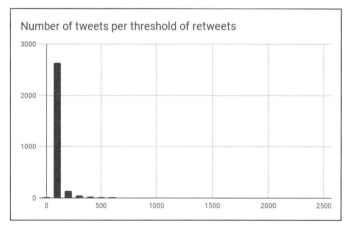

Figure 7-4: A chart showing the distribution of the number of tweets per threshold of retweets

We may also be interested in learning about the makeup of an entire data set, regardless of subdivisions like age brackets or retweet thresholds. In other words, we may just want to look at the *composition* of a data set, and we can use charts to understand how one part of a data set relates to the whole. In the example distribution chart in Figure 7-4, we see that the majority of tweets—more than 2,000—received between 1 and 100 retweets, which in this case shows us that the bots may have been somewhat effective in garnering engagement around tweets, but not remarkably so.

Bots are often used to amplify others' messages, which means they don't tweet as much original content. For that reason, it may be interesting to see what proportion of @sunneversets100's tweets were retweets. The pie chart in Figure 7-5 shows us that 99.4 percent of @sunneversets100 were retweets.

Figure 7-5: Pie charts and donut charts are great for showing proportions of categories within a whole.

Last but not least, you can use charts to show that data categories can have different relationships. For example, you can ask how one value relates to another and research whether the behavior of one value column *causes* the values of another to decrease or increase, or if the values of one column *relate* to how the values of another behave. Charts help us illustrate these relationships.

For instance, we might try to understand the relationship between the time of day when a tweet was sent and the number of retweets it received. In other words, are there times of the day when tweets performed particularly well in terms of retweet engagement? One good way to determine this is a *scatterplot*, where each data point is placed along an x-axis (the horizontal axis in a coordinate system) and a y-axis (the vertical axis).

Usually, researchers are interested in measuring how one dependent variable or data set that may change due to external factors, like the sale of umbrellas, is impacted by an independent variable or data set that cannot be controlled, like the occurrence of rain. In an experiment where researchers wanted to find out how much the occurrence of rain affects umbrella sales, we could use a scatterplot to see the relationship.

The convention is to plot the independent variable along the x-axis and the dependent variable along the y-axis. In this case, we could ask ourselves this: Did the time of day affect how many retweets a tweet received? Figure 7-6 shows a chart that plots these variables along the x- and y-axes.

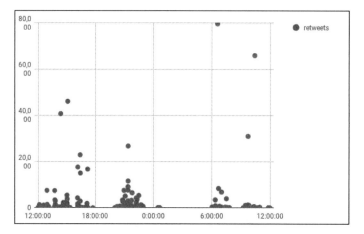

Figure 7-6: A scatterplot of all tweets that @sunneversets100 tweeted, plotted by the time of the tweet along the x-axis and by the number of retweets along the y-axis

Specifying a Time Period

One last aspect to keep in mind before making a chart is the *time period* that you want to use for your data set. The questions you ask of your data set will often require you to specify a particular point in time or a longer time frame. To plot this kind of chart, known as a *time series*, we'll have to aggregate our data into small chunks of time, such as by the timestamps of tweets or an even less granular time unit like a month or year.

In the previous chapter, for instance, we used pivot tables to tally the daily tweets for @sunneversets100 and @nostarch, thus creating a time series for our charts. Then we merged the two data sets based on the time frame they had in common. This allowed us to compare them side by side.

Now that you've seen some ways to help you choose the right visualization for your data, let's take a look at how to make a chart in Google Sheets.

Making a Chart

Whenever we set out to make a chart, we need to take several steps:

1. Formulate a question.
2. Do the data analysis that will help answer the question.
3. Choose the best chart format and tool to help answer your question.
4. Format and arrange the data in such a way that the selected charting tool understands it (in this case, that tool is Google Sheets).
5. Insert or select the data and then use the tool to create a chart.

Luckily, Google Sheets, like Excel, offers a helpful suite of charting tools that allow you to add quick graphics directly in your spreadsheets. To keep this exercise simple, we'll make a chart using our findings from the previous chapter. Let's walk through the steps just laid out.

The central question we tried to answer with our analysis was how the behavior of a bot compares to the behavior of a human. The analysis we did to answer this question resulted in a time series of a little less than three weeks. That takes care of steps 1 and 2.

Next comes choosing the best chart format for the analysis. We're trying to compare two data sets—the daily tweet activity of both a bot and a human—and we want to show this comparison over time. The flow chart from Figure 7-2 suggests using a column chart.

Now we format our data. As we discussed in the previous chapter, one central part of working with data—be it in Sheets or Python—is to clarify what kind of data each spreadsheet column contains. This will help our tools and programming languages interpret the data correctly.

In our column chart, we'll plot time values along the x-axis and numeric values (tweets from each account per day) along the y-axis. Thus, we should make sure that Sheets receives values for dates in one column and values for numbers in two other columns (the two columns representing the daily tweeting activities for our bot and human accounts), as shown in Figure 7-7.

	A	B	C
1	date	@sunneversets100	@nostarch
2	4/13/2017	421	6
3	4/14/2017	586	5
4	4/15/2017	191	1
5	4/16/2017	293	1
6	4/17/2017	12	5
7	4/18/2017	294	8
8	4/19/2017	0	10
9	4/20/2017	0	4
10	4/21/2017	0	2
11	4/22/2017	136	0
12	4/23/2017	330	0
13	4/24/2017	486	0
14	4/25/2017	47	2
15	4/26/2017	17	6
16	4/27/2017	0	10
17	4/28/2017	128	8
18	4/29/2017	26	0
19	4/30/2017	0	0
20	5/1/2017	1	2

Figure 7-7: A spreadsheet containing all the values needed for a chart plotting activity over time

Using what we learned in Chapter 6, we select the data in the column containing our dates and then format it by selecting **Format ▸ Number ▸ Date**. Then we select the columns containing tallies for each account's Twitter activity and format them as numbers by selecting **Format ▸ Number ▸ Number**.

For the next step, we need to select what kind of chart we want to use to plot our data. As before, make sure you select all the data you want to chart—in this case, the columns containing the formatted dates and Twitter activity levels—and then select **Insert ▸ Chart**.

This should insert a chart directly into our spreadsheet, as shown in Figure 7-8, and simultaneously open a window called the *Chart Editor*.

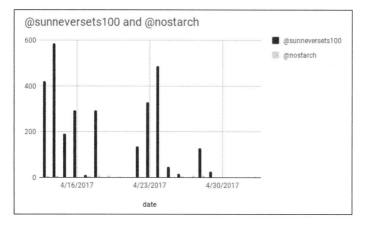

Figure 7-8: A chart showing roughly three weeks of Twitter activity for a bot and a human

The Chart Editor allows us to modify our chart and consists of two tabs: Data and Customize. From the Data tab, we can adjust or modify the content of our chart, like the range of cells we've selected to make the chart or which rows represent the chart headers. For this exercise, let's start by selecting **Column chart** under the **Chart type** drop-down menu.

From the Chart Editor's Customize tab, we can stylize our chart; for example, we can change the chart's title, set the minimum or maximum values of the axes, or select a different font for the chart text. Let's change the color that represents the bot data by selecting the menu item **Series**. This should expand a drop-down menu containing the two data series we plotted—the bot data and the human data. Each series is usually named after the column title. For this exercise, we could select @sunneversets100 and change the color of the columns using the color palette under the bucket icon.

Last but not least, we can move the chart onto its own sheet by clicking the three dots at the upper-right corner of the chart and selecting the **Move to own sheet...** option. This is helpful if there are nuances of your data set that are more visible on a larger screen.

While we can't explore every type of chart offered by Sheets, the principles laid out in this chapter should help clarify what steps you need to take before diving into data visualizations. As always, it's important to think about what you want to explore beforehand by asking questions about your data. If you follow the process set out in this chapter, you can more easily determine the right way to visualize your data for analysis.

Conditional Formatting

So far we've discussed how to format data as a chart so it's easier for our audience to interpret. While many people encounter charts and graphics at school, at work, or in the media, few may be aware of the alternative tools for formatting data within a spreadsheet. These tools allow you to visually analyze your data without needing to go through the process of creating a chart.

One particularly helpful feature in Sheets is called *conditional formatting*, a tool that colors cells in a spreadsheet based on a condition. It's a bit like being able to write if statements in your spreadsheet. For example, you could make a conditional format that says *if* the value in a cell meets a specific condition, *then* fill the cell with a specific color. You can picture conditional formatting as a robot going through your spreadsheet with a highlighter, changing the color of cells based on rules that you set.

Single-Color Formatting

To understand exactly how conditional formatting works, let's apply it to our Twitter data set. Let's say we want a quick way to tell whether a value is above our threshold for suspicious or highly suspicious tweeting activity. With conditional formatting, we can tell Sheets to use one color for any cell displaying a number equal or higher than 72 (and below 144) and another color for any cell displaying a number equal to or higher than 144.

In order to apply conditional formatting to our cells, first we need to select the cells to apply our rules to. Then we select **Format ▸ Conditional Formatting**, which opens a window in Sheets called Conditional Format Rules. This is where we'll specify the rules for our spreadsheet.

First let's see how we can apply *single-color formatting* to our spreadsheet, which means applying one color to a group of cells based on a condition. We'll start by coloring any cells that contain a number from 72 to 143 in yellow: these are days when the bot tweeted a suspicious amount of times. Select the **Add another rule** option in the window under the **Single Color** tab. Under **Format cells if...** select **Is between**. You should see two fields in which you can specify two values: a minimum and a maximum. To be colored yellow, a cell must contain a value within this range. For our Twitter example, enter **72** as the minimum and **143** as the maximum. Then, under **Formatting style**, select the color to highlight the cell. As mentioned, we're using yellow to indicate that the tweet activity is suspicious.

To add another formatting rule, select **Add another rule** in the single color tab. As we did before, select **Format cells if...**, but this time select **Is greater than or equal to** for the condition and set the value to **144**. Then, under **Formatting style**, choose a different color. In this case, I chose red.

Once you've set these two rules, your spreadsheet should color the cells that display values from 72 to 143 in yellow and values equal to or greater than 144 in red, as shown in Figure 7-9.

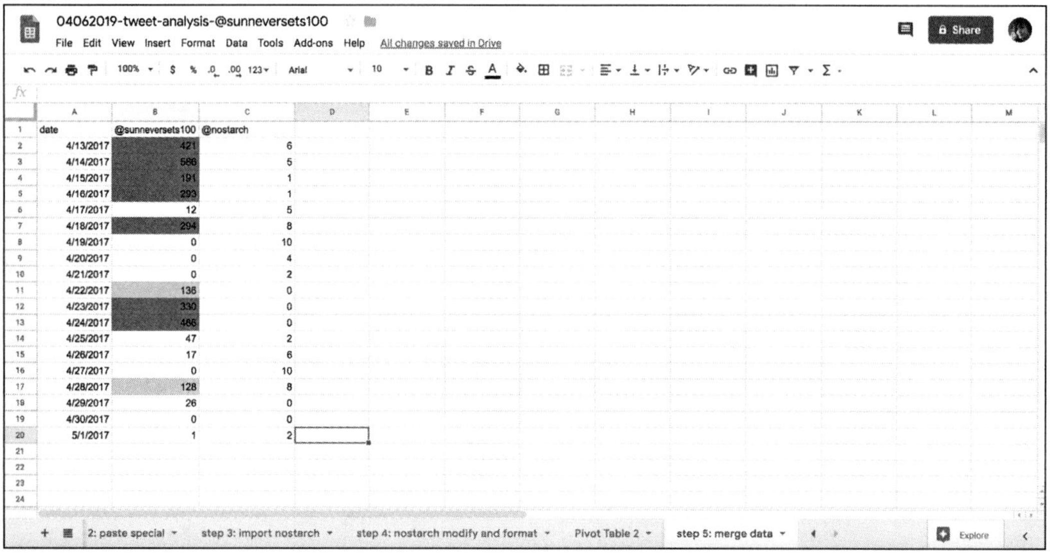

Figure 7-9: A spreadsheet that has been colored according to conditional formatting rules

Now you should be able to look at your spreadsheet and quickly detect suspicious behavior and highly suspicious behavior.

Not only can we use single-color formatting to set individual rules to color cells, but we can also format cells in a range of colors. We'll look at that next.

Color Scale Formatting

Instead of using individual rules to format our spreadsheet, we can use a *color scale*. If we choose this option, Sheets will look at all the cells we selected, find the lowest and the highest value in the data set, and then shade each cell according to a color scale. The cells containing values closer to the lowest value will be shaded in the color to the left side of the color scale. The closer a value is to the higher end of our data set, the closer it will be to the color on the right side of the color scale. This is an alternative way to look at the distribution of a data set if you're not ready to make a chart.

We open the menu for color scale formatting the same way we did for single-color formatting: highlight the data, select **Format ▸ Conditional Formatting**, and then select the **Color scale** tab in the Conditional Format Rules window. Your spreadsheet should now look something like Figure 7-10.

While this kind of formatting is not as precise as single-color formatting, it's an incredibly helpful tool for visualizing how the values of a data set compare to one another. Single-color formatting allows you to set specific thresholds. It's a little bit like picking out values from a category and asking whether or not they fit a specific criterion. In the previous example, that meant we were looking for dates where the bot displayed suspicious behavior. Our question required a true or false answer: on any given day, did the bot tweet 144 or more times? In contrast, the color scale serves more of an exploratory purpose. We don't quite know what our threshold is or how we want to qualify a value, but we want to understand the range and distribution of the values we have at hand.

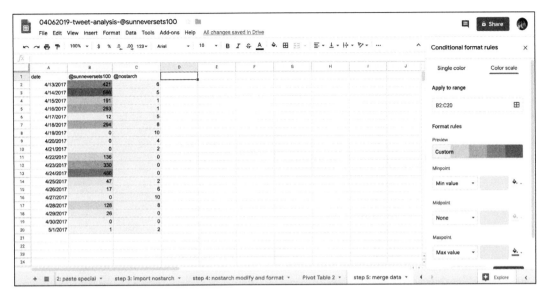

Figure 7-10: A spreadsheet formatted with a color scale

Summary

In this chapter, you learned about the different visual tools that Google Sheets offers. While we didn't have space to look at how every chart type works or how to modify the data for each one, you should now have a general sense of how Sheets visualizations work.

The easy-to-navigate buttons and menus of Google Sheets are a good way to familiarize yourself with data analysis through visuals. You'll find you can apply the same concepts you've learned from this chapter—casting the right data visualization for the right kind of analysis—when you start doing more code-driven analysis in the next chapters.

8

ADVANCED TOOLS FOR
DATA ANALYSIS

 In the previous chapter you learned that by using simple tools like Google Sheets you can analyze thousands of rows of data to understand a bot's activity. While Excel and Google Sheets can handle an impressive amount of data (more than 1 million rows and 16,000 columns for Excel and 400,000 cells for Google Sheets), these tools may not be suitable to run analyses on millions or billions of rows of complex data.

Every day, users create billions of posts, tweets, reactions, and other kinds of online data. Processing vast amounts of information like this is important for data sleuths who want to investigate human behavior on the web at a larger scale. In order to do that, you'll need to familiarize yourself with programmatic analysis tools that can handle large data files. Even if you don't end up using these tools on a regular basis, understanding each tool's capabilities is vital when deciding which one to use.

In this chapter, we'll practice reading in and exploring data using Python. During this process, you'll be introduced to several more programming-related tools and concepts. You'll learn how to set up a *virtual environment*, which is a contained, localized way of using libraries. After that, I'll show you how to navigate the web application *Jupyter Notebook*, an interface you can use to write and modify code, output results, and render text and charts. Finally, you'll install pandas, a Python library that enables you to do statistical analyses. As in the earlier chapters, you'll absorb all this new knowledge through a practical exercise—ingesting and exploring Reddit submissions data.

Using Jupyter Notebook

In the previous chapters, we used Python through a command line interface and scripts. This was a great way for us to get acquainted with the coding language in a quick and straightforward way.

But as we build our Python skills and start working on more-complex scripts, we should look into tools to make these kinds of projects more manageable, structured, and shareable. The more complicated and longer our scripts become, the harder it is to keep track of every single step of our analysis.

This is where learning how to use Jupyter Notebook can be helpful. Jupyter is an open source web application that runs locally on your computer and is rendered in a browser like Chrome. Notebooks allow us to run our scripts in chunks, a few lines at a time, making it easier for us to adjust parts of our code as we iterate and improve upon it. The Jupyter Notebook web app, which evolved out of the web app IPython Notebooks, was created to accommodate three programming languages—Julia, Python, and R (*Ju-Pyt-R*)—but has since evolved to support many other coding languages.

Jupyter Notebook is also used by many data scientists in a diverse range of fields, including people crunching numbers to improve website performance, sociologists studying demographic information, and journalists searching for trends and anomalies in data obtained through Freedom of Information Act requests. One huge benefit of this is that many of these data scientists and researchers put their notebooks—often featuring detailed and annotated analyses—online on code-sharing platforms like GitHub, making it easier for beginning learners like you to replicate their studies.

Setting Up a Virtual Environment

In order to use Jupyter Notebook, you'll need to take your coding skills to the next level by learning about three important concepts.

First, you'll need to be able to create and understand virtual environments. Virtual environments can be challenging to wrap your head around, so let's zoom out for a minute to examine their purpose.

As you've seen in the past few chapters, every time we've wanted to use coding libraries, we've had to install them by entering a command into a command line interface (CLI). Each library is installed in a default location on your computer, where it stays until it's uninstalled.

For Python developers who are just beginning to use libraries and may need only one or two for their work, this approach may be sufficient. But as you become a more sophisticated researcher, you may require more and more libraries to handle different tasks. For example, some tasks may require a library capable of recognizing text from PDF image files, while others may call for a library that can take screenshots of a website. As you improve your skills and tackle more diverse projects, you may need to install more and more libraries in this default location, which runs the risk of causing conflicts between them. This is where virtual environments can be helpful.

A virtual environment allows you to install libraries only within a specified environment. Think of it like a parallel universe created for each project where you are allowed to experiment without affecting your overall computer's environment. The virtual environment is like another computer inside of your computer. It enables you to take advantage of a coding library's power without having to worry about how it interacts with other parts of your machine.

Although you can use various third-party tools for making virtual environments, for this project we'll use Python 3's built-in virtual environment tool. First, though, we need to make a *python_scripts* project folder to store our Jupyter notebooks. Once you've done that, open your CLI and navigate to that folder. As we saw in Chapter 3, the command to get inside a folder through the CLI is cd (which stands for "change directory"), followed by the folder's path. If you stored your *python_scripts* folder in the *Documents* folder on a Mac, for instance, you would type this command into your CLI and hit ENTER:

---

cd Documents/python_scripts

For Windows, you would run this command:

---

cd Documents\python_script

Once you're inside your folder, you can make a virtual environment by running this command if you're a Mac user:

---

python3 -m venv myvenv

---

or this command for Windows users:

---

python -m venv myvenv

Let's break down this command. First we tell our CLI that we're using a command affiliated with python3 on Mac, or with python on PC. Then we use -m, a flag that tells Python 3 to call upon a module that is built into the programming language (*flags* allow you to access different functionalities that are installed onto your computer when you install Python). In this case we want to use the virtual environment module, venv. Last but not least, we give our virtual environment a name, which for simplicity's sake we'll call myvenv (you can call your environment anything you want, as long as the name has no spaces).

This command should create a folder inside your project folder with the name you gave it, which in this case is *myvenv*. This subfolder is where we'll put all the coding libraries we want to install.

Okay, you're almost ready to play in your virtual environment! Now that we've created this virtual environment, we start by *activating* it. Activation is like a light switch that turns your environment on and off using CLI commands.

If you're still in the folder that contains your *myvenv* subfolder, you can simply enter this command to activate, or "switch on," your environment (if not, navigate to the folder that contains your *myvenv* subfolder first). On Mac, this is the command:

```
source myvenv/bin/activate
```

On Windows, you would run this using the Command Prompt:

```
myvenv\Scripts\activate.bat
```

Let's break down this code. The word source is a built-in command that allows us to run any source code contained in a path we specify (the source command can also be swapped out with a period, so the line . myvenv/bin /activate will do the same thing). In this case the path is *myvenv/bin/activate*, which tells the computer to go to the *myvenv* folder, then the *bin* folder inside *myvenv*, and finally the *activate* folder inside *bin*. The *activate* folder contains a script that switches your environment "on."

Once you have run this code, your virtual environment should be activated! You can tell whether your environment is activated by looking at your command line: it should now start with the string (myvenv), parentheses included. To deactivate, or "switch off," your environment, simply enter the command **deactivate**, and the string (myvenv) should disappear!

Welcome to a new level of programming. Now that you've learned how to create and switch your virtual environment on and off, we can start setting up Jupyter Notebook.

Organizing the Notebook

First let's make sure we stay organized. While we're not required to adhere to a specific folder structure, by organizing our input data, notebooks, and output data early on, we can help prevent errors in our analysis later. It's also much easier to develop good habits early than to break bad ones later.

You need to create three separate folders that are stored outside of your *myvenv* folder but inside the overall project folder. First, you'll need to create a folder called *data* to store input data, which consists of files you have received, downloaded, or scraped from APIs or websites and want to explore. Then you need an *output* folder, which will contain any spreadsheets you want to export based on your analyses. We won't create spreadsheets in this book, but having an *output* folder is a great common practice for data analysts. The pandas library, which we will cover in "Working with Series and Data Frames" on page 143, offers a simple function called .to_csv() that allows for us to create *.csv* files from our analyses and that can easily be searched for on Google. Finally, we'll keep our Jupyter notebooks in one neat folder called *notebooks*.

You could create these folders, or directories, manually on your computer, but you can also create them programmatically using the mkdir command. To do this, navigate to your overall project folder in your CLI (if you're still in your *myvenv* folder, move up using cd ..) and enter these three lines:

```
mkdir data
mkdir output
mkdir notebooks
```

The command mkdir makes a directory with the name you specify. In this case, the three commands create the three folders just described.

Alternatively, you can use the mkdir command followed by all three folder names separated by a space, like so:

```
mkdir data output notebooks
```

Installing Jupyter and Creating Your First Notebook

Jupyter allows us to create *notebook documents* that can read different kinds of code, such as Python and Markdown, a language often used to format documentation. Because it is able to read various coding languages, a notebook can render the results of Python code alongside formatted text, making it easier for programmers to annotate their analyses.

What's even better is that we can download Jupyter Notebook from the web and install it on our computers like any other Python library: via pip. To install Jupyter Notebook, open your CLI and enter the following command:

```
pip install jupyter
```

Now you can launch it by running the following command from your project folder:

```
jupyter notebook
```

When you enter this command in your CLI, Jupyter Notebook will launch a local server, which is a server that runs only on your computer, and open a window in your default web browser, which, for the purposes of this book, should be Chrome.

You can see the Jupyter Notebook interface in Figure 8-1.

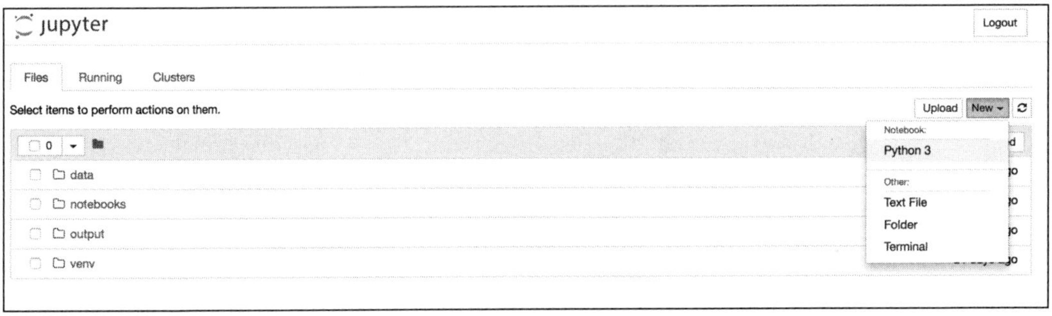

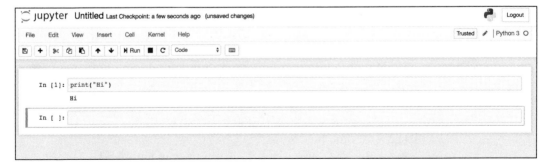

Figure 8-1: The Jupyter interface

This interface allows us to navigate into folders and create files in them. For this exercise, navigate into the *notebooks* folder and then, from the drop-down menu, select **New ▶ Python3**. This should create a new notebook inside the *notebooks* folder and open it in a new tab.

Jupyter notebooks look a lot like your average text document software, with editing tools and a full menu of options, except that they are, of course, tailored to the needs of a Python developer. What's particularly nifty about them is that they use *cells* to run different chunks of Python code one at a time. In other words, you can separate out your Python code into multiple cells and run them one by one.

Working with Cells

Let's give it a whirl. Your notebook creates a cell by default, which has the text In [ ]: and a text field where you can enter code. In that cell, enter this line of Python code:

```python
print("Hi")
```

Select the cell containing this code and press the **Run** button (or use the shortcut SHIFT-ENTER). This should execute the Python code that you just typed in the cell. In this case, the notebook should print the results of your code directly below the cell and create a second cell, as shown in Figure 8-2.

Figure 8-2: Two cells inside a Jupyter notebook

Congratulations! You have written your first notebook and run your first cell of Python!

There's one important thing to note here: now that Jupyter has run your cell, the square brackets to the left of the cell should no longer be empty. Since this is the first cell we ran in this notebook, they should contain the number 1.

What happens when we run the same cell with different code? Let's find out. Delete the code inside the first cell and enter the following code:

```
print("Hello!")
```

Now select the cell by clicking the area to the left of it (a blue bar should highlight the left side of whichever cell you're currently selecting). Then click the **Run** button again.

The cell should render the string Hello!, just as it did the string Hi before. But now the square brackets should contain the number 2. As you can see, Jupyter Notebook tracks not only the fact that you've run a cell but also the sequence in which you run it.

This kind of tracking is very important since the code in your notebook is separated into cells. Unlike a script, which runs top to bottom in one sitting, cells can be run out of order and one at a time. Tracking tells you exactly what code your notebook has already run and which code it still needs to run. This can help you avoid common Jupyter errors, like when code in one cell refers to a variable defined in a cell you haven't run yet.

Similar to text-editing software like Microsoft Word or TextEdit, Jupyter Notebook comes with a number of great tools in a visual interface. You can use the toolbar to do things like save your notebook (the floppy disk icon), cut cells (scissors icon), add cells (plus sign), and move cells up (up arrow) or down (down arrow).

Now you know the basics of how to run cells of Python code in Jupyter Notebook. But as you experiment more with code by rewriting, rerunning, deleting, or moving cells to improve your notebook, you might find you're storing a lot of "garbage" in the notebook's memory. For example, you might create variables you eventually decide to delete or store data that you later realize you won't use. This garbage can slow your notebook down. So how can you clear the memory of any Python code you've run in a notebook without destroying the lines of code you've written inside your cells?

There's a lovely trick for that: go to the menu and select **Kernel ▶ Restart**, which will clear all previously run code and any numbers within the square brackets next to the cells. If you run a cell again, it should render the results of your code and fill the square brackets with the number 1.

Last but not least, there's a great option for running multiple cells in a sequence. To illustrate it, let's first add another cell to our notebook. Click the plus sign (+) button, and then enter this code in the second cell:

```
print("Is it me you're looking for?")
```

While we're at it, why not add two more cells? One cell contains this code:

```
print("'Cause I wonder where you are")
```

and the other contains this line of code:

```
print("And I wonder what you do")
```

To run all four of these cells in sequence, select the first cell, which contains the line print("Hello!"). Then select the menu option **Cell ▶ Run All Below**. This should automatically run all the cells, starting with the one we selected and going all the way to the bottom. (Or, if one cell contains an error, our notebook will stop there!)

Notebooks can be used for a variety of tasks, and these rudimentary steps should get you started exploring Jupyter Notebook as a tool for data analysis. You can run almost any code you have written in a script as a notebook. You can even take the previous scripts you've written for this book, split the code up into cells, and run the code one chunk at a time.

Now that you've seen how to use the Jupyter Notebook interface, let's turn to exploring Reddit data with pandas.

What Is pandas?

Throughout this book, you've learned how to use various libraries to help you gather data. Now it's time to learn about a library that will help you analyze data.

Enter pandas.

Despite what you might guess, the pandas library has nothing to do with the adorable, bumbling bears native to Asia. The library actually got its name from the concept of *panel data*—a data set that spans measurements over time—and was constructed by its creator, Wes McKinney, to handle large, longitudinal data sets. It allows Python to ingest data from a variety of sources (including *.csv*, *.tsv*, *.json*, and even Excel files), create data sets from scratch, and merge data sets with ease.

To use pandas, as with Jupyter and other libraries, we first have to install it using pip. If you've followed all instructions thus far and have turned on your notebooks, you're also running a local server through your CLI that powers Jupyter Notebook. One way to tell if your local server is currently running Jupyter Notebook is to look for brackets containing the letter I, a timestamp, and the word NotebookApp, like this: [I 08:58:24.417 NotebookApp]. To install pandas without interrupting that local server, you can open a new window in your Terminal (leave the one running your server open!) or your Command Prompt, navigate to the same project folder, turn on your virtual environment again, and then install the new library.

Once you have followed those steps, you can execute this pip command to install pandas:

```
pip install pandas
```

After installing the library, you need to import it. The most conventional way to do so in a Jupyter notebook is by typing an `import` command into a cell and running it:

```
import pandas as pd
```

In this example `import` command, we've imported `pandas` and will be able to access its functions using the shorthand `pd`. In other words, when you use this command, instead of referring to the library as `pandas` throughout your code, you would call `pd`. So, for example, you would write `pd.Series([12,53,57])` instead of `pandas.Series([12,53,57])`. This `import` command is a convention used by many data analysts who work with `pandas` and helps keep code neat and easy to read.

Now let's start creating, reading, and manipulating some data structures!

Working with Series and Data Frames

One of the simplest data structures that we can load into `pandas` is a *series*, which is similar to a list or an array. To make a series in `pandas`, we can use the `Series()` function.

In a new cell below the one containing the `import pandas as pd` line, enter these two lines:

```
❶ numbers = [12, 53, 57]
❷ pd.Series(numbers)
```

The code stores the list of numbers [12, 53, 57] in the `numbers` variable ❶. In the next line, we call up the `pandas` library by its shorthand, `pd`, followed by a period and then the `Series()` function, to which we pass the argument `numbers` ❷. In other words, we're using the `Series()` function to make a data object of the type series, and placing the list of `numbers` into this series. This is the same way we accessed the functions within another library, Beautiful Soup, in Chapter 4: we first refer to the library via the shorthand that we assigned to it, and then we access the functions that it offers through their names.

Once we run that cell, the notebook should display the following text right under it:

```
0    12
1    53
2    57
dtype: int64
```

This is how `pandas` represents a simple data series, which can also be referred to as a *one-dimensional data set*. On the left side, there's a column that represents the index, or the position, of each data item. The index starts with 0, as is customary, and increments by 1 with each row. On the right side are the actual data values. At the end of the series you'll see the words `dtype` (data type) and `int64` (integer), separated by a colon.

Similar to dtype and `int64`, *strings are denoted by* `object` *and floats by* `float64`. *There are other data types, too, including* `datetime64`, *which stands for date and time values, but we won't need them for now.*

A series is perhaps the simplest kind of data set: it's one column of data where each row contains a value. But in pandas you are more likely to use a two-dimensional object that's able to handle multiple columns: a *data frame.* Think of a data frame as a spreadsheet that is read by Python instead of being opened in Excel or Google Sheets, and can hold a lot more data. Not unlike a spreadsheet, a data frame has an *index* (row labels) and *columns* (column labels).

To make a data frame, you can use pandas' built-in `DataFrame()` function. Let's give it a try. In a new cell, enter the following dictionary and line of code:

```
❶ numbers2 = {"one": [1.2, 2, 3, 4],
              "two": [4, 3, 2.5, 1]}
  pd.DataFrame(numbers2)
```

As before, we're creating a variable to store our data: `numbers2` ❶. Then we assign the variable `numbers2` a dictionary, where the key `"one"` is assigned the list of values `[1.2, 2, 3, 4]` and the key `"two"` is assigned the list of values `[4, 3, 2.5, 1]`. We're adding a line break between those two dictionary items within the braces for legibility, but it will not interfere with running your code.

You can see how Jupyter renders this code in Figure 8-3.

```
data = {"one" : [1.2, 2, 3, 4],
        "two" : [4, 3, 2.5, 1]}
```

```
pd.DataFrame(data)
```

	one	two
0	1.2	4.0
1	2.0	3.0
2	3.0	2.5
3	4.0	1.0

Figure 8-3: Two cells and a data frame rendered as a table

Like a series, this data frame features an index, which appears as a column on the leftmost side. The data frame also has two columns, named one and two, that contain our numerical data.

Reading and Exploring Large Data Files

Data sets come in all sizes and levels of detail—some are fairly straight-forward to understand while others can be quite convoluted, large, and unwieldy. Social media data can be especially difficult to manage: online users produce a large amount of data and content that, in turn, can produce many reactions, comments, and other responses.

This complexity can be compounded when we're dealing with raw data from a social media company, academics, or other data archivists. Often, researchers will collect more data than they need for individual analyses because it's easier to ask various questions of one large data set than to have to collect smaller data sets over and over again for projects that may change in objective and scope.

Due to API restrictions, it can be difficult for researchers, journalists, and other analysts to track media manipulation campaigns, trolling attacks, or other short-term online phenomena. To name one example, by the time Congress released the Twitter handles and names of Facebook pages that Russian operatives used to manipulate the 2016 US election, the accounts had been erased and were no longer traceable by researchers for examination.

As a countermeasure, various institutions and individuals have started harvesting and storing this social media data. The Internet Archive, for instance, does a monthly data pull and hosts millions of tweets on its servers that researchers may use for linguistic or other analyses. Academics have collected and archived Facebook information in an attempt to better understand phenomena like the spread of hatred against Muslims in Myanmar.

While these efforts are immensely helpful for doing empirical research, the data they produce can present challenges for data sleuths like us. Often we have to spend a considerable amount of time researching, exploring, and "getting to know" the data before we can run meaningful analyses on it.

Over the next few pages, you'll learn how to read and explore one such large data file. In this chapter and the coming ones, we'll look at Reddit data made available by Jason Baumgartner, a data archivist who believes it's vital to make social media data available to scholars and other kinds of researchers. This data contains all submissions between 2014 and 2017 made to *r/askscience*, a Reddit forum, or "subreddit," where people ask science-related questions. For the rest of this chapter, we'll get to know the data set's structure and size through pandas. You can download the data set here: *https://archive.org/details/askscience_submissions/*.

Once you've downloaded the data, you need to place it into the correct folder. In this case, that's the *data* folder you created earlier.

Then you need to go to the Jupyter notebook you created. The first cell, as is convention, should still contain the import pandas as pd command, since all import statements should run first. In a cell after that, load the *.csv* spreadsheet in the *data* folder as follows:

```
reddit_data = pd.read_csv("../data/askscience_submissions.csv")
```

The name `reddit_data` refers to the variable we create to store the Reddit data we're ingesting. Then, using the equal sign (=), we assign this variable a data frame that we create using the pandas function `read_csv()`. The `read_csv()` function requires as an argument the path to a data file (this is usually a *.csv* file, but `read_csv()` can also handle *.tsv* and *.txt* files as long as they contain data values that are separated by a comma, tab, or other consistent delimiter), and this argument needs to be a string. Since we're running the command inside a notebook, the path needs to reflect where the data file is located *in relation to* the notebook file. Using the two dots and forward slash allows us to navigate to a folder one level above our current folder (*notebooks*), which in this case is our project folder (*python_scripts*). Then we navigate into the *data* folder, which contains the *.csv* file named *askscience_subsmissions.csv* that you placed in the folder earlier.

NOTE *The data is over 300MB and may take several seconds to load. Loading it on my computer took a good 10 seconds.*

Once we run that cell, pandas will create a data frame that is stored inside the variable `reddit_data`.

Looking at the Data

Unlike programs like Excel or Sheets, which are constructed for users to manipulate data through visual interfaces, pandas will not actually render an entire data frame at once. You may have noticed that just now, pandas didn't render the data at all. This is because you assigned the output of `read_csv()` to a variable, storing rather than returning or printing it. If you run the function without assigning it, or run a cell with the `reddit_data` variable in it, you'll see a snippet of the data. While this truncation can be disorienting at first, it also saves a lot of computing power. Some software can crash or slow down when you open files containing a few hundred thousand rows, depending on their complexity. Thus, by not displaying the full data frame, pandas allows us to work more efficiently with much larger data sets.

This means that we need to find a way to read the different parts of our data set. Thanks to the pandas developers, we can do this very easily with a few handy functions.

To look at the first few rows of our data set, we can use a function called `head()`. This function takes an integer as its only argument, and defaults to 5 if you enter nothing. So if you want to see the first 10 rows of your data set, you could run a cell with this line:

```
reddit_data.head(10)
```

In this command, first we call upon the `reddit_data` variable that holds the data we ingested through the *.csv* file. Then, we call the `head()` function on the data in the variable. Jupyter Notebook should render the data frame as shown in Figure 8-4.

```
In [4]:  ask_science_data.head(10)
```

Out[4]:

	approved_at_utc	archived	author	author_cakeday	author_flair_css_class	author_flair_text	banned_at_utc	brand_safe	can_gild	can_mod_post
0	NaN	True	vertexoflife	NaN	NaN	NaN	NaN	NaN	NaN	NaN
1	NaN	True	[deleted]	NaN	NaN	NaN	NaN	NaN	NaN	NaN
2	NaN	True	SwoccerFields	NaN	NaN	NaN	NaN	NaN	NaN	NaN
3	NaN	True	[deleted]	NaN	NaN	NaN	NaN	NaN	NaN	NaN
4	NaN	True	[deleted]	NaN	NaN	NaN	NaN	NaN	NaN	NaN

Figure 8-4: Rendering the first 10 rows of the data frame

To see the last 10 rows of a data frame, you can use the tail() function, which follows the same structure:

```
reddit_data.tail(10)
```

Once you run your cell containing this code, you'll see the same rendering of your data frame as you did with the head() function, except for the last 10 rows of your data frame.

While you can't see the entire data set at once, that may not be all that important for now. Remember you're getting to know your data set right now. That means you want to know what *kind* of values each column contains and what the column names are. Seeing the first or last 10 rows of your data can certainly help with that.

You may have noticed, however, that you have to scroll sideways to reveal every single column of your data set. That can be a little unwieldy. Fortunately, there are some built-in tools that you can use to help summarize parts of your data set.

You can *transpose* your data set to see the column headers as rows and your data as columns. Transposing allows us to basically flip the data frame—it will look a bit like we just rotated the table 90 degrees counterclockwise. To do this, you append your call to the data set with a T like this:

```
reddit_data.T
```

To see all the column names as a list, you can use this line of code:

```
reddit_data.columns
```

To get a summary of all the data types that your data frame contains, use dtypes:

```
reddit_data.dtypes
```

Finally, you can use good old vanilla Python to find out the number of rows in your data frame. Remember the print() function we used back in Chapter 1 to display information in the interactive shell? We used it to find the length of a string or the number of items in a list using len(). We can also use these functions to see how large our data frame is:

```
print(len(reddit_data))
```

This code might look more complicated than it really is. First we use the len() function to measure the length of the data frame (that is, the number of rows it contains) by passing it the argument reddit_data, which is our data set. In other words, first we get the length of the reddit_data data frame. When used by itself, the len() function renders results only if no other statements follow it inside a cell, so it's good practice to place it inside a print() function to make sure the cell renders the result of what len() measured.

The number you should get is 618576 (or, more legibly to humans, 618,576). That represents the number of rows in our data frame.

If we run the same set of functions and pass reddit_data.columns as an argument to len(), we can get the number of columns in the data frame:

```
print(len(reddit_data.columns))
```

This line measures the length of the list of columns within the data frame. This particular data frame contains 65 different columns. So, if you multiply 65 columns of data by 618,576 rows, you find that we're dealing with *more than 40 million values*. Welcome to the big data leagues!

Viewing Specific Columns and Rows

Now we know how to get a feel for the structure of our data frames, meaning we know how to get a bird's-eye view of our data. But what if we want to take a closer look at specific parts of our data? That's where square brackets come in.

When tacked onto the variable that contains our data frame, square brackets can allow us to select, or *index*, different subsets of data. For instance, to view a specific column, you can specify the column's name inside the brackets as a string. In this line, we're selecting the column named title:

```
reddit_data["title"]
```

This lets us focus on just the column containing the values that are categorized as the title of each Reddit post. Fun fact: when run on its own, this line of code will render the column, but you can also use it to store a copy of a data column in a variable, like this:

```
all_titles = reddit_data["title"]
```

We can also view multiple columns with bracket notation, by assigning a list of them to another variable:

```
column_names  = ["author", "title", "ups"]
reddit_data[column_names]
```

First we create a variable called column_names to store a list of column names as strings. Keep in mind that each column name must be the exact string in the data set itself, capitalization included. Then we place this list inside the brackets to display just those columns.

There are also nifty ways to isolate individual rows. As we saw earlier in this chapter, each row has an index, which acts kind of like a label. By default, pandas assigns each row an integer as an index (we can assign each row custom indexes, too, but we won't do that in this exercise). We can use the iloc[] method to call on any given row by placing the row's index number inside the brackets (in programming lingo, this is referred to as *integer-location-based indexing*):

```
reddit_data.iloc[4]
```

If we run a cell with this line, we should see the fifth row of the data set (remember that programming often starts counting from 0).

Last but not least, we can combine these two methods. If, for instance, we want to call up the column named title and display only the value in the fifth row, we can do that like so:

```
reddit_data["title"].iloc[4]
```

These are just a few ways in which we can get to know our data set better. And this is no small feat, given that we're dealing with millions of values contained in what is essentially one large spreadsheet.

Now that you have all the basics down, you can start learning how to do calculations with the data.

Summary

You've now seen how to explore large data sets, which is an important first step for any data analysis. Only after we understand the nature of the data—its contents, formats, and structure—can we find the best strategies to analyze it for meaning.

In the next chapter, we'll continue working on this Jupyter notebook and discover ways of asking questions of our data set.

9

FINDING TRENDS
IN REDDIT DATA

Parts of social media data are structured in ways that enumerate human actions quantitatively, while other parts are very qualitative in nature. For example, we can measure the popularity of a Reddit post by counting its upvotes. This allows us to do simple aggregations like the average or median number of upvotes that posts have received during a specific period of time. Other parts of the same Reddit data, however, may be more difficult to summarize in quantitative ways. Comments, for instance, contain prose that can vary wildly in content and style.

Summarizing what people are talking about, and how they're talking about it, is much harder than calculating averages of engagement metrics like upvotes, but doing meaningful analyses of data from the social web requires us to navigate both kinds of information. Learning how to do this can be quite rewarding, though, because it lets us explore the behavior, thoughts, and reactions of real people (and the occasional and perhaps ever-more-prominent bot).

In this chapter, you'll learn how to navigate both qualitative and quantitative information. We'll explore how people are engaging with the topic of vaccinations in social media by analyzing the *r/askscience* data from Chapter 8 and ask targeted questions from our data set. First we'll try to better understand how to handle text-based information by searching this subreddit for submissions that feature the word stem *vaccin* (in words like *vaccinate* and *vaccination*). Then we'll compare the *engagement metrics*—the combined number of comments and upvotes—of the vaccine posts to those of non-vaccine posts.

Clarifying Our Research Objective

For this chapter, we'll use online conversations from the *r/askscience* subreddit, a popular forum for Reddit users to ask and answer questions related to science, to measure how vigorously vaccinations are discussed on the web.

While Reddit users are not representative of the entire US population, we can try to understand how controversial this topic is on this particular forum by looking at it relative to other topics on the platform. The key here, as in any other examination of the social web, is to acknowledge and understand the specificity of each data set we examine.

We'll begin by asking a very rudimentary question: do *r/askscience* Reddit submissions that include variations of the word *vaccination*, *vaccine*, or *vaccinate* elicit more activity than *r/askscience* subreddit submissions that don't?

Outlining a Method

Our analysis consists of the following steps:

1. **Filter and group our data into two data frames.** The first data frame will contain all submissions that use the words *vaccine*, *vaccinate*, or *vaccination*. The second data frame, which we'll compare to the first, will contain the submissions that don't mention those words.

2. **Run simple calculations on each data frame.** Summarizing our data by finding mean or median *engagement counts* (in this analysis, engagement counts are represented by the combined number of comments and upvotes), can help us better understand each subset of the *r/askscience* data received, and formulate an answer to our research question.

It's worth taking a second to clarify the terms used here. The *mean* is the result of taking all the values from a data set, adding them, and dividing their sum by the total number of values. The *median* is the number that appears halfway through the data set. To find it, first we need to sort all the values in the data set from smallest to largest. The number that is exactly midway between the smallest and the largest value is the median. If there's an even number of values, you'd take the mean of the two numbers in the middle. Both the mean and median are *measures of central tendency*, metrics that allow us to assess a data set by looking at some central point. When a data set contains a lot of values without many outliers, means are a great way to measure its central tendency. A data set with outliers, on the other hand, may be better measured through medians. In this chapter, we'll look at both measures for our analysis.

Narrowing the Data's Scope

Reddit data sets can be fairly large, even when you're looking only at a single subreddit. While it's important to start with as comprehensive a data set as possible, filtering the data based on your specific project gives you a better, less cluttered overview of it. Filtering also reduces the amount of time it takes to run each calculation.

This chapter also introduces the concepts of population and sample data. *Population data* describes a data set that contains the entirety of a specified group. In this case, this specified group comprises any submission posted between 2014 and 2017 in the *r/askscience* subreddit. *Sample data*, as the name suggests, is a subset or a sample of the data set. In this exercise, there will be two subsets: one consisting of submissions related to vaccinations (which we'll define in the coming pages) and one consisting of all other submissions. We'll run analyses on both of these subsets to compare them.

We'll use the virtual environment and Jupyter Notebook project set up in Chapter 8. The following exercises are intended to expand on that particular notebook, and you'll use the same variable names we established there.

Selecting Data from Specific Columns

To filter the data for our task, first we'll pare it down to include only the columns that contain information relevant for our analysis. Then we'll drop the rows that contain irrelevant samples, like null values.

Let's start by selecting the columns we need. We're particularly interested in two different kinds of data—the title of the submission, including the text that was submitted to *r/askscience*, and the reactions that the submissions garnered. As mentioned in the previous chapter, we can see all the column names as a list by running this line of code:

```
ask_science_data.columns
```

This should render a list of strings, each representing a column name:

```
Index(['approved_at_utc', 'archived', 'author', 'author_cakeday',
       'author_flair_css_class', 'author_flair_text', 'banned_at_utc',
       'brand_safe', 'can_gild', 'can_mod_post', 'contest_mode', 'created',
       'created_utc', 'crosspost_parent', 'crosspost_parent_list',
       'distinguished', 'domain', 'edited', 'from', 'from_id', 'from_kind',
       'gilded', 'hidden', 'hide_score', 'id', 'is_crosspostable',
       'is_reddit_media_domain', 'is_self', 'is_video', 'link_flair_css_class',
       'link_flair_text', 'locked', 'media', 'media_embed', 'name',
```

```
      'num_comments', 'over_18', 'parent_whitelist_status', 'permalink',
      'pinned', 'post_hint', 'preview', 'quarantine', 'retrieved_on', 'saved',
      'score', 'secure_media', 'secure_media_embed', 'selftext', 'spoiler',
      'stickied', 'subreddit', 'subreddit_id', 'subreddit_type',
      'suggested_sort', 'thumbnail', 'thumbnail_height', 'thumbnail_width',
      'title', 'ups', 'url', 'whitelist_status'],
    dtype='object')
```

There are 62 column names here. For the sake of this analysis, it makes sense for us to keep the columns containing the titles listed in the title column, the upvotes listed in the up column, and the number of comments on each submission listed in the num_comments column.

Just as we did in the previous chapter, we can now select specific columns in our data set using square brackets. Make sure you're still in the notebook from Chapter 8 *and* that you've run each cell. (Remember: if you've run it, the cell should have a number in the square brackets to its left.) Then, using the plus sign (+), add a cell under all the other cells and type the lines from Listing 9-1 into it:

```
columns = ["title", "ups", "num_comments"]
ask_science_reduced = ask_science_data[columns]
```

Listing 9-1: Selecting a few columns from a data set

We first create a variable called columns to which we assign a list of strings. The strings in our list ("title","ups","num_comments") represent the column headers for every column we want to include in our filtered data set. Make sure that the string of each column name *exactly* matches the string of the column header, down to the punctuation, capitalization, and spelling—minor mistakes can throw off the Python script.

In the next line, we create the variable ask_science_reduced, which stores a smaller data frame containing only the columns listed in the columns variable. Notice that instead of adding a single string inside the square brackets, as we did before, we now put the variable columns within them. Putting an entire list inside the brackets instead of one string allows us to select multiple columns.

Now that we've pared down our data to specific columns, let's drop rows of data containing values that aren't relevant to our analysis.

Handling Null Values

In a large, inconsistent data set, chances are that some rows or cells won't contain any information. These "empty" cells may hold either no values at all or a *placeholder*, an arbitrary string used by the institution or person who designed the data structure. If we're lucky, that placeholder will be described in a *data dictionary*, a document explaining the contents, structure, and format of a data set. Otherwise, we have to figure it out ourselves through research or, in the worst-case scenario, through sophisticated guesses based on the column names. (Fortunately, in this case we knew the person who collected the data and were able to field questions with him.)

In data parsing, we refer to these empty cells as *null values*. In Python, null values may be returned as None when we try to print them in our interactive shells or other Python interfaces. In pandas they may be referred to as *NaN values* (where NaN stands for "not a number"), and the rows of the data frame will display NaN as a placeholder for missing values.

Null values are particularly common in columns that gather information on actions that are optional for social media users. For instance, a column that collects links to videos posted to Facebook contains values only for posts where a user actually published a video. For any post that does not include videos, the data set will not have a value for that cell and may either use a placeholder, like the string "no video", or leave the cell empty, meaning it'll have a None value.

The issue is that placeholder, None, and NaN values can cause errors in analyses. When we apply functions or calculations, our script will run these calculations as instructed, until it gets to an empty cell. We'll cover two ways to handle null values, each with a slightly different purpose for data analysts: one drops these null values from the analysis altogether, while the other preserves the entirety of a data set and counts empty rows as zeros.

Dropping Null Values

We may choose to exclude entire rows of data if they contain null values for specific columns. The pandas library makes this easy for us with the dropna() function. Listing 9-2 shows the code that drops entire rows of data based on whether columns contain NaN values.

```
ask_science_dropped_rows = ask_science_reduced.dropna(
    subset=["ups", "num_comments"])
```

Listing 9-2: Dropping rows with NaN values in specific columns

With no specifications, this function tells pandas to drop whole rows from the data frame. But the dropna() function also comes with helpful parameters, like the subset parameter. In this example, we use subset to tell pandas to drop rows that contain NaN values in the ups and num_comments columns. (If we do not pass the dropna() function any arguments, pandas defaults to dropping rows that have *any* null values and will look for NaN values in every column of the data frame.)

Filling Null Values

To account for NaN values but preserve every row of the data frame, we can use the fillna() function to fill each empty cell with a string or a number instead of removing it. Listing 9-3 shows how to use the fillna() function to fill the empty cells in the num_comments column with the number 0:

```
ask_science_data["num_comments"] = ask_science_data["num_comments"].fillna(value=0)
```

Listing 9-3: Filling in the null values with 0

Within the parentheses of the `fillna()` function, we assign 0 to the `value` parameter. This code replaces the `num_comments` column with a modified version of itself that now contains zeros in lieu of `NaN` values.

Deciding whether to remove null values or fill them depends on your data set and how you want to answer your research question. For example, if we wanted to get the median number of comments for our entire data set, we might ask whether it's safe to assume that missing values simply mean that there were no comments on the submission. If we decide it is, we can fill those values with a 0 and calculate accordingly.

Depending on the number of rows that contain missing values or "empty cells," the median number of comments may shift significantly. However, because this data set *does* sometimes record the number of comments or upvotes as zeros and sometimes as null values, we can't automatically assume that rows that contain null values for those columns should be treated as zeros (if null values represented zeros, it may be reasonable to assume that the data set would not contain any actual zeros). Instead, maybe this is data that our archivist was unable to capture; maybe the posts were deleted before he could gather that information; or maybe those metrics were introduced for some of those years but not for others. Thus, for the sake of our exercise, we should work with the data we *do* have and drop the rows of data that do not contain a value for the `ups` or the `num_comments` columns, as we did in Listing 9-2.

Classifying the Data

The next step is to filter our data based on our specific research question about vaccinations. We need to classify what we consider a Reddit submission about vaccination.

This classification will be reductive. This is necessary when handling a large data set, because it's incredibly labor-intensive to read every single post and interpret each individually. And even if we could employ a large group of people to read each post and interpret it by hand—which is not uncommon in some prose-driven projects—it's difficult to make sure that everyone is using the same rubrics for their interpretation, which can make it difficult to categorize data in a standard, identifiable way.

In our example, we'll limit the sample to submissions that include the word *vaccinate* or *vaccination* in some shape or form. We'll look specifically for any title that includes *vaccin*. (In linguistics this is often referred to as a *stem*, the part of the word that is most common in various iterations and inflections of it.) This subset may not catch every post about vaccinations, but it can help us qualitatively understand the matter at hand.

We'll start by making a new column that classifies a row based on whether its submission title contains the string "vaccin". We'll fill this column with a *Boolean*—that is, binary—value, `True` or `False`. Listing 9-4 shows the code needed to create this column:

```
ask_science_dropped_rows["contains_vaccin"] = ask_science_dropped_rows["title"].str.
contains("vaccin")
```

Listing 9-4: Filtering a column based on whether it contains a certain string

On the left-hand side of the equal sign, we create a new column called contains_vaccin using square brackets. On the right side, we used a *chained* function: first we select the title column from our data using bracket notation, and then we use the str() function on that column to convert the values to strings so we can use contains() to determine whether column values contain *vaccin*.

The result of this chain is a Boolean value: if the title of the submission contains *vaccin* then it will return the value True; else it will return the value False. In the end, we should have a new column (contains_vaccin) with only True or False values.

Now that we have this extra column, let's filter our data! Run the code in Listing 9-5 inside a new cell of your notebook:

```
ask_science_data_vaccinations = ask_science_dropped_rows[ask_science_dropped_rows["contains
_vaccin"] == True]
```

Listing 9-5: Filtering data based on a conditional value

This should be familiar syntax. But notice that inside the brackets on the right-hand side, we used the condition ask_science_data_dropped_rows ["contains_vaccin"] == True instead of a column title. This tells pandas to check whether the value in the contains_vaccin column equals True. To filter our data to a subset that includes only rows that do *not* contain the stem *vaccin*, we can set our conditional to equal False:

```
ask_science_data_no_vaccinations = ask_science_dropped_rows[ask_science_dropped_rows["contains
_vaccin"] == False]
```

Now that we've filtered our data, let's query it for some interesting insights.

Summarizing the Data

To determine whether *r/askscience* Reddit submissions that include variations of the words *vaccination, vaccine,* or *vaccinate* get a bigger reaction than *r/askscience* submissions that don't, we'll look at the posts that received the most combined reactions, defined as the sum of the count of upvotes and comments.

NOTE   *There are a number of ways to answer this question, and it's important to recognize that fact. However, as mentioned before, in this book we're trying to tackle calculations and analyses from the most beginner-friendly stance, which means that we may use simple ways of doing mathematical calculations. They may not be the most elegant, but they introduce some of the most foundational pandas methods, which beginners can build on as they learn more about the library.*

Sorting the Data

First we'll create a column that combines the number of upvotes and the number of comments for each row. This is a very simple operation with pandas, as shown in Listing 9-6.

```
ask_science_data_vaccinations["combined_reactions"] = ask_science_data
_vaccinations["ups"] + ask_science_data_vaccinations["num_comments"]
ask_science_data_no_vaccinations["combined_reactions"] = ask_science_data_no
_vaccinations["ups"] + ask_science_data_no_vaccinations["num_comments"]
```

Listing 9-6: Combining several columns into one

Here, we create a column called combined_reactions in each data frame and assign it a value equal to the sum of the num_comments and ups columns. When you run this code, you may encounter a SettingWithCopyWarning, which is what its name suggests—a warning, rather than an error (though it looks a bit menacing, since it's displayed on a red background). The difference between an error and a warning is that the error stops your code from running, while a warning just nudges you to double-check that the code you're running is doing what you want. For this book, we know that the code shown here does what we want it to do: add the number of upvotes to the number of comments. If you're curious about what the developers who wrote this warning wanted you to investigate further, see *http://pandas.pydata.org/pandas-docs /stable/user_guide/indexing.html*.

NOTE   *When we read in the .csv file containing the data, we didn't specify which column contained which data type (an option pandas offers as a parameter). If you don't specify a column's data type, pandas automatically interprets the types within columns based on what it finds (and sometimes it doesn't assign a type to a column uniformly!). You can read more on data types in pandas under dtype at* https:// pandas.pydata.org/pandas-docs/stable/generated/pandas.read_csv.html.

Now that we have values for combined reactions in a column, let's sort the values using the sort_values() function, as shown in Listing 9-7.

```
ask_science_data_vaccinations.sort_values(by="combined_reactions", ascending=False)
ask_science_data_no_vaccinations.sort_values(by="combined_reactions", ascending=False)
```

Listing 9-7: Using sort_values() to sort the data frame

As its name suggests, sort_values() sorts your data frame. We've passed arguments to two parameters here: by, which tells pandas which column to sort by, and ascending, which tells pandas which order to sort in. In Listing 9-7, we passed False to ascending, meaning the data will be in order from largest to smallest.

Figure 9-1 shows some of the results of our sorted data frame for the ask_science_data_vaccinations column.

	title	ups	num_comments	contains_vaccin	combined_reactions
177230	I keep hearing about outbreaks of measles and ...	3621.0	662.0	True	4283.0
133287	Why are we afraid of making super bugs with an...	2377.0	548.0	True	2925.0
143663	Psychologically speaking, how can a person con...	1775.0	461.0	True	2236.0
82615	If unvaccinated people are causing outbreaks, ...	619.0	146.0	True	765.0
10563	How are combined vaccinations established? Who...	510.0	56.0	True	566.0
174803	Is the rise in Measles cases the result of the...	387.0	58.0	True	445.0
180101	Is Mercury all that bad for you? Why is it pre...	312.0	78.0	True	390.0
87383	Could you acquire a vaccination through a bloo...	304.0	55.0	True	359.0
412308	Why are vaccines mostly limited to providing i...	199.0	58.0	True	257.0
475068	How are infectious organisms "weakened" for li...	210.0	31.0	True	241.0

Figure 9-1: The Jupyter Notebook display of the partial data frame of the ask_science _data_vaccinations column sorted by the number of combined reactions

Figure 9-2 shows some of the results for the ask_science_data_no _vaccinations column.

	title	ups	num_comments	contains_vaccin	combined_reactions
477896	If we could drain the ocean, could we breath o...	18789.0	1018.0	False	19807.0
456459	If we detonated large enough of a nuclear bomb...	11690.0	1353.0	False	13043.0
461793	In terms of a percentage, how much oil is left...	9305.0	1624.0	False	10929.0
457979	How do you optimally place two or more Hot Poc...	9308.0	936.0	False	10244.0
457573	Carbon in all forests is 638 GtC. Annual carbo...	8856.0	834.0	False	9690.0
350040	Gravitational Wave Megathread	6778.0	2799.0	False	9577.0
455717	Why do flames take a clearly defined form, rat...	9109.0	344.0	False	9453.0
478215	If my voice sounds different to me than it doe...	8657.0	511.0	False	9168.0
471827	If fire is a reaction limited to planets with ...	8099.0	876.0	False	8975.0
465628	In this gif of white blood cells attacking a p...	8155.0	639.0	False	8794.0
474089	With today's discovery that hydrogen and anti-...	8227.0	467.0	False	8694.0
466870	Why are snowflakes flat?	7809.0	397.0	False	8206.0
475647	If you had a pinhole camera with an aperture t...	7680.0	427.0	False	8107.0
463366	How does radio stations transmit the name of t...	7198.0	738.0	False	7936.0
340964	Planet IX Megathread	5340.0	2495.0	False	7835.0

Figure 9-2: The Jupyter Notebook display of the partial data frame of the ask_science_ data_no_vaccinations column sorted by the number of combined reactions

As you can see, the top submission in the non-vaccination data frame got a lot more reactions than the top submission in the vaccination-related data frame. This is also true for the top 10 biggest submissions in both data sets. The number of combined reactions for the top 10 submissions is much higher for those that do not contain the stem *vaccin* than it is for those that contain *vaccin*. So, as measured in the total number of engagements for the top 10 submissions for each subset of the *r/askscience* data, we might conclude that vaccination-related submissions do not garner as much attention as other topics do.

But there's a problem here. We've only looked at the top 10 posts. Filtering and sorting our data sets can get us closer to a better understanding, but it shows us only a glimpse of the extreme values of a vast data set. In the next section, we'll look at some different methods for analyzing the data further.

Describing the Data

One common way to summarize data is by using the mean() function, shown in Listing 9-8.

```
ask_science_data_vaccinations["combined_reactions"].mean()
```

Listing 9-8: The mean() function

We use the mean() function here to find the average across all values in the column we selected (combined_reactions). When you run this code in a cell, you should get the following number:

```
13.723270440251572
```

Now run the same code for the ask_science_data_no_vaccinations data frame, swapping out the name of the data frames as shown here:

```
ask_science_data_no_vaccinations["combined_reactions"].mean()
```

This should return the following:

```
16.58500842788498
```

This number shows us that the average number of combined engagement metrics for submissions that don't contain *vaccin* is higher than the average number of engagements for those that do. In other words, our previous conclusion—that vaccination-related submissions solicit less engagement and, hence, may not garner as much attention from Reddit users as posts that don't—is also supported when we look at engagement averages across the entire data set, not just when observed for the top 10 posts.

Averages are just one way to summarize values. We can look at multiple metrics at once in pandas using the describe() function, shown in Listing 9-9.

```
ask_science_data_vaccinations["combined_reactions"].describe()
```

Listing 9-9: The describe() function

If we run the code in Listing 9-9 in one cell, it should return a roster of results:

```
count    1272.000000
mean       13.723270
std       162.056708
min         0.000000
25%         1.000000
```

```
50%         1.000000
75%         2.000000
max      4283.000000
Name: combined_reactions, dtype: float64
```

This summary includes the count, or total number of rows; the mean, or average; the std, the standard deviation; the min, the smallest number in that column; the 25th, 50th, and 75th percentiles (with the 50th being the median); and the max, the largest value in that column.

Let's run the same code in another cell for the ask_science_data_no _vaccinations data frame with the following code:

```
ask_science_data_no_vaccinations["combined_reactions"].describe()
```

If we run this code in another cell, we should get something like the following:

```
count    476988.000000
mean         16.585008
std         197.908268
min           0.000000
25%           1.000000
50%           1.000000
75%           2.000000
max       19807.000000
Name: combined_reactions, dtype: float64
```

This shows us that the median for both data frames is the same, which represents yet another way to measure the level of engagement of a post. However, here the mean is likely the best way for us to compare submissions, since the median for each data set, 1, doesn't allow us to make clear distinctions between the engagement of one data set over another.

Last but not least, it's important to give context to the various analyses we have just run when we present our findings. While it might be helpful to provide our audience with medians and means, it's also crucial to be transparent about everything we did to the data. Data analyses require context to be understood: we should not only present information about the scope of the data (which we learned about in Chapter 8), but also outline how we categorized the data (in this case by looking for the stem of the word *vaccination* or *vaccinate*) and any other helpful observations that can provide more context.

One of these observations may be to look into the distribution of our subsets. As noted earlier, both the mean and the median are designed to help us measure the central tendency of a data set, but they vary quite a bit in this case: the median is 1 upvote or comment for both subsets of our data, while the mean is between 13 and 16 for the vaccination-related post and all other posts. Usually this kind of discrepancy should prompt us to examine the distribution of our data set further (we briefly covered the concept of a data set's distribution in Chapter 7) and include some of the characteristics that may be unusual when we present our findings. For example, seeing that the median of both subsets of our data is 1, we can safely assume that at least half of the posts included in either subset garnered 1 or fewer upvotes or comments, a fact that may be worth noting.

Whatever we end up writing in a presentation, a paper, or an article, it is important to be descriptive of the data itself, the processes used, the results found, and any context that may be helpful for our audience to get a full grasp of our analysis.

Summary

In this chapter, you learned how to think through a research question using various steps like data processing, filtering, and analysis. We walked through the steps it takes to categorize and filter social media data based on the potential values in a column. We then saw how to run simple mathematical calculations on these filtered data sets.

It's important to understand that there's more than one way to tackle analyses like this. This can manifest itself technically: some data analysts may choose to use different functions to do the kinds of filtering and aggregation that we did in this chapter. In other cases, researchers may try to use different methodological approaches and think about different ways to categorize and summarize their data. For instance, a different developer may have used another way to classify what constitutes a post about vaccination and what doesn't—they may have filtered their data based on more than just one search term (which in our case was *vaccin*). There is no surefire way to answer a question with data, despite what some strongly opinionated online users may think, though it does help to experiment more with the data we have and to try different ways to answer the same research question, as we did in this chapter.

While in this chapter we summarized our data set using categorically driven subdivisions, in the next chapter, we'll be looking at how to summarize our data over different periods of time.

10

MEASURING THE TWITTER ACTIVITY OF POLITICAL ACTORS

In Chapter 9, we did our first data analysis with a large data set and saw how we could answer a research question based on a simple categorization. Although it produced good results, that sort of analysis is limited: it looked at the data at only one point in time. Analyzing data across time, on the other hand, allows us to look for trends and better understand the anomalies we encounter. By exploring the changes in data and isolating specific events, we can make meaningful connections between them.

In this chapter, we'll look at data as it changes over time. Specifically, we'll examine a data set Twitter published in 2018 that consists of tweets political actors based in Iran posted before, during, and after the 2016 US presidential election to influence public opinion in the US and elsewhere. The data dump is part of the platform's ongoing efforts to allow researchers to analyze media manipulation campaigns run by false and hired Twitter accounts. We want to look at tweets that used hashtags relating to Donald Trump and/or Hillary Clinton and determine how they behaved over time. Did they increase in the lead-up to the election? Did they drop right after the 2016 election or continue to grow?

Along the way, you'll learn how to filter data using a type of function called a *lambda*. You'll see how to format raw data and turn it into a time series or resample it. Last but not least, you'll learn about a new library to use alongside pandas, called matplotlib (*https://matplotlib.org/*). The matplotlib library will help us make sense of our data by visualizing it within the Jupyter Notebook environment, using simple graphics to illustrate data fluctuations. By the end of this project, you should have a strong grasp of pandas and the kinds of things you can do with it.

Getting Started

In 2017 and 2018, Twitter, Facebook, and Google were heavily criticized for allowing international agents to spread false or misleading content meant to influence public opinion in the US and abroad. This public scrutiny ultimately led to the publication of two major data bundles: one of Russian tweets that—according to Twitter, Congress, and various media reports— were used to manipulate the US media landscape, and another of Iranian tweets doing the same.

The Russian data set is much larger and could slow down our progress, as it would take a long time for it to load and process. So, as mentioned earlier, we'll focus on the other data set: the Iranian data. In particular, we'll be looking at the spreadsheet titled *iranian_tweets_csv_hashed.csv*, which you can download directly from Twitter (*https://storage.googleapis.com /twitter-election-integrity/hashed/iranian/iranian_tweets_csv_hashed.zip*) or from *https://archive.org/details/iranian_tweets_csv_hashed/*.

Our research question is straightforward: How many tweets related to Trump and Clinton were tweeted by Iranian actors over time? We'll define Trump- and Clinton-related tweets as tweets that use hashtags containing the string trump or clinton (ignoring case). As discussed in Chapter 9, this kind of categorization may miss some tweets related to the two presidential candidates, but we're only doing a simple version of this program for teaching purposes. In a real data analysis, we'd likely cast a wider net.

Now that we have a research question, let's get started on the project!

Setting Up Your Environment

As we did in the previous chapter, first we'll need to set up a new folder for our project. Then, within that folder, we'll need to create three subfolders: *data*, *notebooks*, and *output*. Once you've done that, place the downloaded Twitter data in the *data* folder.

Next, navigate to your project directory inside your CLI and enter python3 -m venv myvenv. This creates a virtual environment inside your project, which you can activate using the command source myvenv/bin/activate. Your virtual environment is activated if your CLI begins with (env) (revisit Chapter 8 if you need a refresher).

With the virtual environment activated, now we need to install all the libraries we'll be using. We want jupyter, pandas, and matplotlib, all of which we can install using pip as follows:

```
pip install jupyter
pip install pandas
pip install matplotlib
```

After installing all three libraries, enter **jupyter notebook** into your console and, once Jupyter starts, navigate into the *notebooks* folder and create a new notebook by selecting **New ▸ Python 3**. Lastly, let's rename the new notebook: click the title, which usually defaults to *Untitled*, and rename it *twitter_analysis*.

With all that done, you're ready to go!

Loading the Data into Your Notebook

First, let's ensure that we can use all the libraries we've just installed. To load pandas and matplotlib, we'll use the import statement. In the first cell of your notebook, type the following:

```
import pandas as pd
import matplotlib.pyplot as plt
```

In the first line, we're importing pandas and using pd as shorthand so we can simply refer to pd to access all of the library's functionalities. We'll do the same in the second line for matplotlib, except here we only need a subset of functions called pyplot, which we'll call plt as a shortcut. This means, instead of having to write out matplotlib.pyplot, we can simply use plt, which should help avoid cluttered code.

NOTE *The convention of using pd as shorthand appears in the documentation for the pandas library. Similarly, the plt shortcut is used in the matplotlib documentation.*

Click **Run** (or use SHIFT-ENTER) to run this cell, and you should be able to access both libraries in the cells that follow.

Next, we need to load in the data. Let's create a variable called tweets to hold the data we want to examine. Enter the following into the next cell and run it:

```
tweets = pd.read_csv("../data/iranian_tweets_csv_hashed.csv")
```

This line ingests the Twitter data in our *data* folder using the pandas function read_csv(), which takes a filepath to a *.csv* file and returns a data frame we can use. For a refresher on data frames, check out Chapter 8.

Now that our data is ingested, let's think about the next step we need to take. This data set includes tweets covering a wide array of topics, but we're interested only in tweets about Donald Trump and Hillary Clinton. This means we'll need to filter our data to only those tweets, just as we did in Chapter 9 when we filtered our *r/askscience* data to posts relating to vaccinations.

Once again, before we can narrow it down, we need to get to know our data a little better. Since we've already loaded it, we can begin exploring it using the head() function. Enter the following into a cell and run it:

```
tweets.head()
```

You should see the first five rows of data, as shown in Figure 10-1.

```
tweets.head()
```

	tweetid	userid	user_display_name	user_screen_name	user_reported_location	user_profile_description	user_profile_url	follower_count	follo
0	533622371429543936	299148448	Maria Luis	marialuis91	Nantes, France	journaliste indépendante/un vrai journaliste e...	NaN	8012	
1	527205814906654721	299148448	Maria Luis	marialuis91	Nantes, France	journaliste indépendante/un vrai journaliste e...	NaN	8012	
2	545166827350134784	299148448	Maria Luis	marialuis91	Nantes, France	journaliste indépendante/un vrai journaliste e...	NaN	8012	
3	538045437316321280	299148448	Maria Luis	marialuis91	Nantes, France	journaliste indépendante/un vrai journaliste e...	NaN	8012	
4	530053681668841472	299148448	Maria Luis	marialuis91	Nantes, France	journaliste indépendante/un vrai journaliste e...	NaN	8012	

5 rows × 31 columns

Figure 10-1: The loaded data frame

As you can see, this dump contains a large assortment of metadata related to the tweets. Every row represents one tweet and includes information about the tweet itself as well as the user who tweeted it. As you might remember from Chapter 8, to see all the column names as a list, you can use this line of code:

```
tweets.columns
```

Once you run that cell, you should see this list of columns:

```
Index(['tweetid', 'userid', 'user_display_name', 'user_screen_name',
       'user_reported_location', 'user_profile_description',
       'user_profile_url', 'follower_count', 'following_count',
       'account_creation_date', 'account_language', 'tweet_language',
       'tweet_text', 'tweet_time', 'tweet_client_name', 'in_reply_to_tweetid',
       'in_reply_to_userid', 'quoted_tweet_tweetid', 'is_retweet',
       'retweet_userid', 'retweet_tweetid', 'latitude', 'longitude',
       'quote_count', 'reply_count', 'like_count', 'retweet_count', 'hashtags',
       'urls', 'user_mentions', 'poll_choices'],
      dtype='object')
```

For our purposes, the most important columns are hashtags and tweet_time. The hashtags column displays all the hashtags used in each tweet as a list of words, separated by commas, between an opening and closing square bracket. Although they follow the pattern of a list, Python interprets them as one long string. Figure 10-2 shows that in the 359th row, for instance, the hashtags used are "Impeachment" and "MuellerMonday" and are stored as one long string '[Impeachment, MuellerMonday]'. Note that not every tweet uses hashtags and that our analysis will consider only those that do.

```
tweets.iloc[358]

tweetid                                    1026465539835785216
userid                     fa345559085c3eefd96303a1378c1a6164a036b0e24472...
user_display_name          fa345559085c3eefd96303a1378c1a6164a036b0e24472...
user_screen_name           fa345559085c3eefd96303a1378c1a6164a036b0e24472...
user_reported_location                                   Delaware, USA
user_profile_description   Progress is impossible without change, and tho...
user_profile_url                               https://t.co/i2omiuAU7S
follower_count                                                    1341
following_count                                                   1774
account_creation_date                                      2018-01-13
account_language                                                    en
tweet_language                                                      en
tweet_text                 #Impeachment: Last episode, arrestment of Trum...
tweet_time                                          2018-08-06 13:50
tweet_client_name                                   Twitter Web Client
in_reply_to_tweetid                                               NaN
in_reply_to_userid                                                NaN
quoted_tweet_tweetid                                      1.02495e+18
is_retweet                                                      False
retweet_userid                                                    NaN
retweet_tweetid                                                   NaN
latitude                                                          NaN
longitude                                                         NaN
quote_count                                                         0
reply_count                                                         0
like_count                                                          1
retweet_count                                                       0
hashtags                                 [Impeachment, MuellerMonday]
urls                       [https://twitter.com/i/status/1024946380857458...
user_mentions                                                     NaN
poll_choices                                                      NaN
includes_trump_or_clinton                                       False
Name: 358, dtype: object
```

Figure 10-2: The values stored in the 359th row of our tweets' DataFrame displayed using the `.iloc[]` method

The hashtags column, then, will allow us to identify tweets with hashtags that contain the strings trump or clinton. The tweet_time column contains a timestamp of when the tweet was sent. We'll use the tweet_time column after we've filtered our data to calculate a monthly tally of Trump- and Clinton-related tweets.

To filter our data, we'll repeat some of the same steps from our previous analysis of vaccination-related data. There, we created a new column and filled it with True or False by selecting another column and using the contains() function to see whether it contained the string vaccin. For this project, we'll also create a True or False column, but instead of using the contains() function, we'll be using a new pandas feature that's much more powerful: lambda functions.

Lambdas

A lambda function is a small, nameless function we can apply to every value in a column. Instead of being confined to the functions that pandas developers have already written, like contains(), we can use custom lambdas to modify our data however we want.

Let's take a look at the structure of a lambda function. Say we want to add 1 to a number and return the new number. A regular Python function for this might look like the following:

```
def add_one(x):
    return x + 1
```

Here we've used the def keyword to create a function and name it add_one(), defined x as the only parameter, and written our main line of code on an indented new line after a colon. Now let's look at the lambda equivalent of the same function:

```
lambda x: x + 1
```

Unlike indented Python functions, lambdas are mostly written as compact one-liners and used inside of an apply() function. Instead of using def to write and name a new function, we're using the word lambda followed by the parameter x (note that we don't need to use the parentheses). Then we specify what we want to do to x—in this case, add 1. Notice that there's no name for this function, which is why some people call lambdas *anonymous* functions.

To apply this lambda function to a column, we pass the function itself as an argument, as shown in Listing 10-1.

```
dataframe["column_name"].apply(lambda x: x + 1)
```

Listing 10-1: Passing a lambda function to apply()

In this example, we select the column with the name column_name from a hypothetical data frame called dataframe and apply the lambda x + 1 to it. (Note that for this to work, the values in column_name would need to be numbers, not strings.) This line of code would return a series of results that we'd get from adding 1 to the value of each row in the column_name column. In other words, it would display each value in the column_name column with 1 added to it.

In cases where you need to apply more-complex operations to a column, you can also pass traditional Python functions to apply(). For example, if we wanted to rewrite Listing 10-1 using the add_one() function we defined earlier, we'd simply pass the name into the apply() function, like so:

```
dataframe["column_name"].apply(add_one)
```

Lambdas can be a very helpful and efficient way for us to modify entire columns. They are ideal for one-off tasks, since they are unnamed (anonymous) and are easy and quick to write.

All right, enough about lambdas! Let's get back to our analysis.

Filtering the Data Set

We want a data frame that contains only tweets relating to the 2016 presidential candidates. As mentioned before, we're going to use a simple heuristic for this: include only tweets whose hashtags include the strings trump, clinton, or both. While this may not catch every tweet about Donald Trump or Hillary Clinton, it's a clear-cut and easily understandable way to look at the activities of these misinformation agents.

First, we need to create a column that contains the Boolean values True or False, indicating whether a given tweet contains the string trump or clinton. We can use the code in Listing 10-2 to do this.

```
tweets["includes_trump_or_clinton"] = tweets["hashtags"].apply(lambda x:
"clinton" in str(x).lower() or "trump" in str(x).lower())
```

Listing 10-2: Creating a new True or False column from our tweets data set

This code is pretty dense, so let's break it down into parts. On the left side of the equal sign, we create a new column, includes_trump_or_clinton, that will store the results of our lambda function. Then, on the right side, we select the hashtags column and apply the following lambda function:

```
lambda x: "trump" in str(x).lower() or "clinton" in str(x).lower()
```

The first thing we do in the lambda function is check whether the string "trump" is within the longer string of hashtags using the line "trump" in str(x).lower(). This line takes the value passed in the hashtags column, x, uses the str() function to turn x into a string, uses the lower() function to make every letter in the string lowercase, and finally checks whether the string trump is in that lowercase string. If it is, then the function will return True; if it isn't, it will return False. Using the str() function is a great way for us to turn any value we have to work with, even empty lists and NaN values, into strings that we can query; without str(), null values could cause errors in our code. It also lets us skip the step of filtering out null values, as we did in our analysis in Chapter 9.

On the other side of the or in our lambda function, we use the same code but for clinton. Thus, if the hashtag contains either the string trump or clinton (ignoring case), then the row will be filled with True; otherwise, it will be filled with False.

Once we have our True or False column, we need to filter our tweets down to only those with True values in includes_trump_or_clinton. We can do that with the code in Listing 10-3.

```
tweets_subset = tweets[tweets["includes_trump_or_clinton"] == True]
```

Listing 10-3: Filtering the tweets down to only those that include trump or clinton

This creates a new variable called `tweets_subset` that'll store the reduced data frame containing only tweets that used Trump- or Clinton-related hashtags. Then we use the brackets to select the subset of `tweets` based on a condition—in this case, whether the value `tweets["includes_trump_or_clinton"]` is `True`.

Through these lines of code, we have now narrowed down our data set to the body of tweets that we're interested in observing. We can use the code `len(tweets_subset)` in a separate cell to find out the number of rows in our `tweets_subset`, which should be 15,264. Now it's time to see how the number of tweets containing Trump- or Clinton-related hashtags has changed over time.

Formatting the Data as datetimes

With our data set filtered, we want to count the number of tweets containing Trump- or Clinton-related hashtags within a certain time period—a count that is often referred to as a *time series*. To accomplish this, we'll format the data columns as timestamps and use `pandas` functions to create tallies based on these timestamps.

As we saw during our adventures with Google Sheets in Chapter 6, it's important that we specify to our code the kind of data we're dealing with. Although Sheets and `pandas` can autodetect data types like integers, floats, and strings, they can make mistakes, so it's better to be specific rather than leave it to chance. One way of doing that is by selecting the column that contains the timestamps for each tweet and telling Python to interpret them as a `datetime` data type.

First, though, we need to find out how `pandas` is currently interpreting our data columns. To do this, we'll use the `dtypes` attribute, which, as you saw in Chapter 8, allows us to look at some characteristic of our data (in this case, the data types each column contains):

```
tweets_subset.dtypes
```

If we run this line in a cell, our Jupyter notebook should display a list of the columns in our data frame alongside their data type:

```
tweetid                      int64
userid                       object
user_display_name            object
user_screen_name             object
user_reported_location       object
user_profile_description     object
user_profile_url             object
```

```
follower_count              int64
following_count             int64
account_creation_date       object
account_language            object
tweet_language              object
tweet_text                  object
tweet_time                  object
tweet_client_name           object
in_reply_to_tweetid         float64
in_reply_to_userid          object
quoted_tweet_tweetid        float64
is_retweet                  bool
retweet_userid              object
retweet_tweetid             float64
latitude                    float64
longitude                   float64
quote_count                 float64
reply_count                 float64
like_count                  float64
retweet_count               float64
hashtags                    object
urls                        object
user_mentions               object
poll_choices                object
dtype: object
```

As you can see here, there are two columns that contain time-related data: account_creation_date and tweet_time. We're interested in understanding the tweets, not the accounts, so we'll focus on tweet_time. Currently, pandas interprets the tweet_time column as an object data type, which in pandas most commonly means a string. But pandas has a data type specifically made for timestamps: datetime64[ns].

To format this data as datetime64[ns], we can use the pandas function astype(), which will replace the tweet_time column with a data column that contains the same data but interpreted as a datetime object. Listing 10-4 shows us how.

```
tweets_subset["tweet_time"] = tweets_subset["tweet_time"].
astype("datetime64[ns]")
```

Listing 10-4: Formatting the data type of the tweet_time column using the asytype() function

As before, we select the "tweet_time" column by putting it in square brackets, and then we replace it by applying the .astype() function to it. In other words, this converts the selected column (tweet_time) into the data type we specify inside the parentheses ("datetime64[ns]").

To check whether our conversion worked, we can simply run dtypes on the tweets_subset variable again in a separate cell:

```
tweets_subset.dtypes
```

Below the cell containing this code, we should now see that the tweet_time column contains datetime64[ns] values.

```
--snip--
account_language            object
tweet_language              object
tweet_text                  object
tweet_time                  datetime64[ns]
tweet_client_name           object
in_reply_to_tweetid         float64
in_reply_to_userid          object
--snip--
```

Now that the tweet_time data is in the right data type, we can use it to start tallying up the values in includes_trump_or_clinton.

Resampling the Data

Remember that we're hoping to find a count of the number of tweets containing Trump- or Clinton-related hashtags per time period. To do this, we'll use a process called *resampling*, in which we aggregate data over specific time intervals; here, this could mean counting the number of tweets per day, per week, or per month. In our analysis, we'll use a monthly tally, though if we wanted a more granular analysis, we might resample by week or even day.

The first step in resampling our data is to set tweet_time as an index (remember an index acts like a row label). This will allow us to select and locate entries based on their tweet_time value, and later apply different kinds of mathematical operations to it.

To set the tweet_time column as an index, we can use the set_index() function. We apply set_index() to tweet_time by passing tweet_time as its argument. The set_index() function will return a newly indexed data frame, which we'll store in a variable called tweets_over_time (Listing 10-5).

```
tweets_over_time = tweets_subset.set_index("tweet_time")
```

Listing 10-5: Setting a new index and storing the resulting data frame

To see what a newly indexed data frame looks like, run the tweets_over _time.head() function, which should return something like Figure 10-3.

```
tweets_over_time = tweets_subset.set_index('tweet_time')
tweets_over_time.head()
```

tweet_time	tweetid	userid	user_display_name
2018-02-16 16:55:00	964543820389109760	1394743334	RealProgressiveFront
2017-03-18 06:21:00	842984240140763140	e13ac4c5a61faca60ae766c342791c3f6ed8a72d7ad7e5...	e13ac4c5a61faca60ae766c342791c3f6ed8a72d7ad7e5...	e13ac4c5a61faca60ae76
2018-01-11 10:27:00	951400129356951552	f2a00a04e99197ee4e5fdfac4597bcc048695f6e588ae4...	f2a00a04e99197ee4e5fdfac4597bcc048695f6e588ae4...	f2a00a04e99197ee4e5f
2017-12-27 20:09:00	946110924645109760	3683769196	Alwaght en Español
2018-01-20 07:30:00	954617032972087296	853233898398121984	RiseAgainstTheRight

5 rows × 31 columns

Figure 10-3: A data frame that has taken on the `tweet_time` column as an index

There's a subtle but important visual change here: the values in the `tweet_time` column have replaced the integer-based index numbers on the left side of our data and are now displayed in bold. This means that we've replaced the number-based indexes with timestamps in the `tweet_time` column.

With our new index, we can group and aggregate our data over time using the `resample()` function, as in Listing 10-6.

```
tweet_tally = tweets_over_time.resample("M").count()
```

Listing 10-6: Grouping and aggregating data in a data frame using `resample()`

We can specify the frequency at which we want to aggregate our data over time—every day, every week, or every month—inside the `resample()` function's parentheses. In this case, because we're interested in how these tweets may have been used to influence the 2016 US presidential election, we want a monthly tally, so we pass in the string `"M"` (short for *month*). Last but not least, we need to specify how we want to aggregate our data over time. Since we want a monthly count of tweets, we'll use the `count()` function.

Once we run this cell, we can run `tweet_tally.head()` in a new cell to look at our data. We should see a data frame containing a count of all the values in each column per month, as shown in Figure 10-4.

```
tweet_tally = tweets_over_time.resample('M').count()
tweet_tally.head(20)
```

tweet_time	tweetid	userid	user_display_name	user_screen_name	user_reported_location	user_profile_description	user_profile_url	follower_count	following_co
2013-08-31	1	1	1	1	1	1	1	1	
2013-09-30	0	0	0	0	0	0	0	0	
2013-10-31	0	0	0	0	0	0	0	0	
2013-11-30	2	2	2	2	2	2	2	2	
2013-12-31	0	0	0	0	0	0	0	0	
2014-01-31	0	0	0	0	0	0	0	0	
2014-02-28	1	1	1	1	1	1	1	1	
2014-03-31	1	1	1	1	1	1	1	1	
2014-04-30	1	1	1	1	1	1	1	1	
2014-05-31	0	0	0	0	0	0	0	0	
2014-06-30	2	2	2	2	2	2	2	2	
2014-07-31	0	0	0	0	0	0	0	0	
2014-08-31	5	5	5	5	5	5	5	5	
2014-09-30	1	1	1	1	1	1	1	1	
2014-10-31	2	2	2	2	2	2	2	2	
2014-11-30	1	1	1	1	1	1	1	1	
2014-12-31	0	0	0	0	0	0	0	0	
2015-01-31	3	3	3	3	0	3	0	3	
2015-02-28	7	7	7	7	4	7	4	7	
2015-03-31	5	5	5	5	5	5	5	5	

20 rows × 31 columns

Figure 10-4: A resampled data frame containing the monthly counts for each column value. Note the variance in counts for the data in the row indexed as 2015-01-31.

As you can see, pandas has counted the number of values contained in every column for each month and stored that result as the new column value. Every row now represents one month, beginning with the date in tweet_time.

That result is not ideal. We now have a lot of values strewn across some 30 columns, and in addition to that, the counts in each column for a given month can vary, too. Take the row labeled 2015-01-31 in Figure 10-4, for instance. For that month, we counted zero values in the user_profile_url column even though the count in the tweet_id column is 3. That means that the Iranian agents posted three tweets with hashtags containing the strings trump or clinton during that month, but none of them contained a user profile URL.

Based on this observation, we should be careful about what we rely on to best determine the total number of tweets per month—we should be careful about which values we count. If we counted the number of values in the user_profile_url column, we would only catch the tweets that featured user profile URLs; we wouldn't be catching the tweets that didn't feature those URLs, and we would be undercounting the number of overall tweets that are in our data frame.

So before we even resample our data set, we should look at a data column that contains a value for every single row and count those values. This is a critically important step: there are values that may seem like they occur in every row when we render the data using the head() or tail() function, but we can't be sure of that simply by looking at one relatively small part of a massive data set. It helps to think about what column most reliably represents a distinct entity that cannot be omitted in the data collection (for example, a tweet may not always contain a tag, but it must have a unique identifier or ID). In the data set that is stored in the tweets_over_time variable back in Listing 10-5, there is a value in every row of the tweetid column.

Because we need only the total number of tweets per month, we can use only the tweetid column, which we'll store in the variable monthly_tweet_count as follows:

```
monthly_tweet_count = tweet_tally["tweetid"]
```

Now, if we inspect our monthly_tweet_count using the head() function, we get a much cleaner monthly tally of our data frame:

```
tweet_time
2013-08-31    1
2013-09-30    0
2013-10-31    0
2013-11-30    2
2013-12-31    0
Freq: M, Name: tweetid, dtype: int64
```

Our code has now created a data frame that allows us to better understand our data over time, but this row-by-row preview is still limited. We want to see the major trends across the entire data set.

Plotting the Data

To get a fuller picture of our data, we'll use matplotlib, the library that we installed and imported earlier in this chapter. The matplotlib library allows us to plot and visualize pandas data frames—perfect for this project, as time series are often much clearer when visualized.

At the beginning of this project, we imported the matplotlib library's pyplot functions as plt. To access these functions, we type **plt** followed by the function we want to use, as follows:

```
plt.plot(monthly_tweet_count)
```

In this case, we use the plot() function, with our data frame monthly_tweet _count as its argument, to plot the dates of our data frame on the x-axis and the number of tweets per month on the y-axis, as shown in Figure 10-5.

NOTE   *There are many ways to customize plots in* matplotlib; *to learn more about them, go to* https://matplotlib.org/.

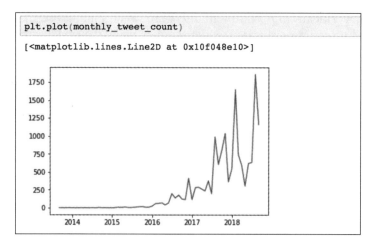

```
plt.plot(monthly_tweet_count)
```

```
[<matplotlib.lines.Line2D at 0x10f048e10>]
```

Figure 10-5: A chart created by matplotlib inside Jupyter Notebook

Ta-da! Now we have a graph that shows the number of tweets that used Trump- or Clinton-related hashtags. As we might've expected, they increased drastically toward the end of 2016, showing us that these false agents became very active in the lead-up to, and aftermath of, the 2016 US presidential election—though there seems to be a lot of variability in their activities several months after the election took place. While we won't be able to do all the research necessary to explain this activity, researchers at the Digital Forensics Research Lab have published a deeper analysis of the Iranian accounts at *https://web.archive.org/web/20190504181644/*.

Summary

This project has demonstrated the power of doing data analysis in Python. With a few lines of code, we were able to open a massive data set, filter it based on its contents, summarize it into monthly counts, and visualize it for better understanding. Along the way, you learned about lambda functions and resampling data based on datetime objects.

This chapter concludes the practical exercises for the book. In the next, and final, chapter, we'll discuss how you can take these introductory lessons further on your own to become an active and self-sufficient Python learner.

11

WHERE TO GO FROM HERE

Over the past 10 chapters, you've learned a plethora of new tools to help you investigate the social web. You've gotten an overview of the social media ecosystem and built a solid technical foundation you can use to collect data and analyze it. In this final chapter, you'll learn about a few resources that can help you deepen that knowledge, strengthen your coding abilities, and become a better data scientist.

Coding Styles

As with prose, everyone has their own style of writing code. In this book, for example, we wrote code intended to convey concepts and help you navigate Python and the libraries we needed. This meant that our code, while functional, was also verbose: we broke down our analyses into steps and spelled out each one, like using variables to store data frames at different points in time or creating new columns to filter our data. That kind of code is great because it can help you (and other collaborators) understand every stage of the process. But as you start writing longer and more complex scripts or Jupyter notebooks, you may want to use more compact syntax than what you've seen here.

Likewise, as you move on to more complicated analyses and start to use more and more libraries, you'll have to learn how to read a wide variety of coding styles. We briefly touched on the idea of writing reusable code when we rewrote our Wikipedia scraping script in Chapter 5. But there's much more to writing clean, smart, and effective code. Coding is a much more collaborative process than media representations of isolated, antisocial coders would have you believe. Library authors, for example, benefit from the feedback of hundreds (sometimes thousands) of other coders who used their libraries and encountered issues. Coders are always using the work of others to enhance their own programs—and the first step to using someone else's code is being able to understand it!

To that end, what follows are a few helpful resources on writing clean code with Python and pandas, as well as producing reproducible data analysis in Jupyter Notebook. While by no means a comprehensive guide, they're a good starting point:

- The general Python style guide (*https://docs.python-guide.org/writing /style/*) and a style guide for data scientists (*http://columbia-applied-data -science.github.io/pages/lowclass-python-style-guide.html*)
- *Think Python*, 2nd Edition, a book by Allen B. Downey (O'Reilly, 2015), available for free under the Creative Commons license on the author's site (*https://greenteapress.com/wp/think-python-2e/*)
- "A Beginner's Guide to Optimizing Pandas Code for Speed," an article by Sofia Heisler (*https://engineering.upside.com/a-beginners-guide-to -optimizing-pandas-code-for-speed-c09ef2c6a4d6/*)
- "What We've Learned About Sharing Our Data Analysis," an article by Jeremy Singer-Vine (*https://source.opennews.org/articles/what-weve -learned-about-sharing-our-data-analysis/*)

The libraries and tools we've used in this book have stood the test of time among Python users, but new libraries pop up all the time and may do certain things better than what is already available. It's the nature of an open source programming language to evolve with the needs of its users. As you continue your journey, look for blogs and forums maintained by people in your industry to stay informed about the latest trends in Python. As someone who learned Python on the fly, I can personally attest to the value of seeking out resources about Python and specific libraries like pandas.

Statistical Analysis

Throughout this book, we've used some basic concepts from the field of statistical analysis. But concepts like mean and median analysis, and aggregating and resampling raw social data, represent only a sliver of the sorts of statistical analyses you can run on the data sets available from the social web.

Here are a few resources that'll help you develop your statistical analysis skills:

- *Statistics Done Wrong*, a book by Alex Reinhart (No Starch Press, 2015) that covers some of the major missteps in statistical analyses and how to learn from them (*https://nostarch.com/statsdonewrong/*)
- *Naked Statistics*, a book by Charles Wheelan (W. W. Norton, 2014) that provides a great introduction to statistics with relatable—and often amusing—examples (*https://books.wwnorton.com/books/Naked-Statistics/*)
- "Tidy Data," an academic paper by Hadley Wickham that lays out helpful approaches to "tidying" data, or restructuring it for more efficient data analyses (*https://www.jstatsoft.org/article/view/v059i10*)

Other Kinds of Analyses

Finally, there are some more-advanced kinds of analysis, particularly suited to social web data, that have resulted in some fantastic research over the past few years.

One example is *natural language processing (NLP)*, the process of turning text into data for analysis. Many NLP methods are available through Python libraries, including the Natural Language Toolkit, or NLTK (*https://www.nltk.org/*), and spaCy (*https://spacy.io/*). These libraries allow us to break text down into smaller parts—like words, word stems, sentences, or phrases—for further analysis. You might count the occurrences of specific words in a given data set, for instance, and study their relationship to other key phrases to understand how people discuss specific topics on the social web, where speech evolves within specific communities and around every news event. What words are affiliated with a specific news phenomenon? How does this vocabulary differ from group to group? Does each community use different language to discuss the same thing? More and more groups are forming online—based on identity categories, shared politics, and other cultural factors—that eventually form a common vocabulary, cadence, and ideology. NLP can help us better understand how the members of these groups come together and form a new information universe with its own language.

Another exploding field is *machine learning*, a subsection of artificial intelligence that's been deployed in everything from the Google search bar's autocomplete text to insurance estimates. In research, machine learning can also be a powerful tool to "classify" the social web. Put simply, machine learning works by feeding a bunch of data into a program and having it find patterns from that data. For instance, if we fed some of the data from Chapter 10 about false agents on Twitter to a machine learning algorithm, we could then feed it new data and see if it could classify those accounts as false agents based on patterns in the first data set. While this isn't a surefire way to detect false political actors, it may help narrow down a larger pool of tweets and Twitter accounts for further scrutiny.

Here are some suggested resources on NLP and machine learning:

- *Natural Language Processing with Python*, a wonderful online primer for NLP by Steven Bird, Ewan Klein, and Edward Loper that clearly explains some of the most important concepts for learners while also teaching technical skills (*https://www.nltk.org/book/*)
- "spaCy 101: Everything You Need to Know," a helpful introductory tutorial to spaCy, a Python library that allows for linguistic analyses (*https://spacy.io/usage/spacy-101*)
- "An Introduction to Machine Learning with scikit-learn," which offers helpful tutorials on the scikit-learn library for people who are just getting started with machine learning (*https://scikit-learn.org/stable /tutorial/basic/tutorial.html*)

Conclusion

There's only so much you can learn in the course of 10 chapters. As with any skill, there's room for us to grow and hone our skills, adapting them to the specific fields we work in. What I aimed to do in this book was provide you with a solid foundation on which to build future analyses of the social media ecosystem. Above all, I hope that I've sparked in you the kind of curiosity it takes to interrogate the social media world and better understand human behavior online. We've only been able to observe social media's impact for a short time. Hopefully, this book has equipped you to examine its influence for years to come.

INDEX

Reinhart, Alex, 179
rendering, 4
requests library, 47, 49
resampling data, 172–175
research questions, 37–41
resources on writing code and data analysis, 178–180
robots exclusion protocol, 80–81
Rocha, Roberto, 80

S

scatterplots, 127–128
scikit-learn library, 180
scraping data. *See* web scraping
scripts, 28–29, 44–46
search parameter, 29
series, 143–144
servers, 4, 82
set_index() function, 172
Silverman, Craig, 38
Singer-Vine, Jeremy, 38, 178
single-color formatting, 131–132
sleep() function, 96
sort_values() function, 158
sorting and filtering data, 114–117, 158–160
spaCy, 179–180
spiders, 80–81
spreadsheets, 49–50, 72–74
start tags, 5
statistical analysis, 179
Statistics Done Wrong (Reinhart), 179
stems, 156
string concatenation operator (+), 17
strings, 16, 17
style attribute, 7–8
style sheets, 9
summarizing data, 157–162
summary data, 102
syntax highlighting, 43

T

tags, 5
tail() function, 147
templates, 57–61
Terminal, 14
terms of service, 82
Think Python, 2nd Edition (Downey), 178
third-party libraries, 46
time periods, 128

time series, 128, 170–172
timestamps, 23
transposing data, 147–148
troubleshooting, xxii–xxiv
Twitter, 163–176
types, 16

U

unicode, 60
unminified code, 87
Unminify, 87
unordered lists, 90
URL-based API calls, 29, 48–49
URLs (uniform resource locators), 4
user-agent, 81

V

values, 19–20, 34
variables, 17–19, 49–50, 57–58, 88–92
virtual environments, 135–138
visualizations, 123
    charts, 124–130
    conditional formatting, 131–133
=vlookup() formula, 117–118
void elements, 5

W

Web Inspector, 10–11
web robots, 80–81
web scraping
    best practices, 80, 94–98
    Facebook, 64–70
    robots exclusion protocol, 80–81
    template, 92–94
    terms of service, 82
    variables, 88–92
    Wikipedia, 83–87
websites, HTML and, 4–6
Wheelan, Charles, 179
Wickham, Hadley, 179
Wikipedia, 83–87
Windows, xxi
writeheader() function, 74
writer() function, 50
writerow() function, 50

Y

YouTube, 31–41